1933
WARNINGS FROM HISTORY

1933
WARNINGS FROM HISTORY

Edited by Paul Flewers

MERLIN PRESS

This collection first published in 2021 by
The Merlin Press
Central Books Building
Freshwater Road
London RM8 1RX

www.merlinpress.co.uk

ISBN. 978-0-85036-765-2

Peter and Irma Petroff, *The Secret of Hitler's Victory*, was first published in 1934 by The Hogarth Press

Introduction © Paul Flewers, 2021

Translations of *Schleicher, Hitler or Revolution* and *A Group of Revolutionary Syndicalists* © A.W. Zurbrugg, 2021

Cataloguing in Publication Data is available from the British Library

Printed in the UK by Imprint Digital, Exeter

Contents

Glossary	6
Chronology	8
Introduction	18
Peter and Irma Petroff: The Secret of Hitler's Victory	
I: The World Stands Before a Riddle	41
II: The Weimar Republic and its Pillars	43
III: The Internal Decay of the German Labour Movement	57
IV: The Crisis	69
V: Under the Brown Yoke	87
Hippolyte Etchebehere: The Tragedy of the German Proletariat	115
Appendix: Letters to an Argentine Comrade	150
Daniel Guérin: Schleicher, Hitler or Revolution?	166
Paul Strehl: Politicians Put Skids Under Strike of Berlin Transport Workers	175
A Group of Revolutionary Syndicalists, To Organised Workers	179
Index	183

Glossary

Allgemeiner Deutsche Gewerkschaftsbund (ADGB) – General German Trade-Union Federation: main German trade-union federation, associated with SPD

Antifaschistische Aktion – Anti-Fascist Action: paramilitary organisation formed by KPD

Communist International, Comintern: international federation of Communist parties

Deutsche Zentrumspartei or Zentrum – German Centre Party: Roman Catholic party

Deutsche Demokratische Partei (DDP) – German Democratic Party: main liberal party

Deutsche Volkspartei (DVP) – German People's Party: main conservative party

Deutschnationale Volkspartei (DNVP) – German Nationalist People's Party: hard-right, monarchist party

Eiserne Front – Iron Front: paramilitary organisation formed by SPD and ADGB

Freikorps – Unofficial right-wing paramilitary forces

Kommunistische Partei Deutschlands (KPD) – Communist Party of Germany: German section of the Communist International

Kommunistische Partei Deutschlands (Opposition) (KPD(O)) – Communist Party of Germany (Opposition): faction expelled from KPD

Nationalsozialistische Betriebszellenorganisation (NSBO) – National Socialist Factory Cell Organisation: Nazi labour organisation

Nationalsozialistische Deutsche Arbeiterpartei (NSDAP) – National Socialist German Workers Party, commonly Nazi Party

Reichsbanner Schwarz-Rot-Gold – Flag of the Reich, Black-Red-Gold: paramilitary organisation formed by SPD

Reichstag – German federal parliament

Reichswehr – Regular German army

Revolutionäre Gewerkschafts Opposition (RGO) – Revolutionary Union Opposition: trade-union organisation formed by KPD

Rotfrontkämpferbund (RFB) – Alliance of Red Front-Fighters: paramilitary organisation formed by KPD

Schutzstaffel (SS) – Protection Squad: élite NSDAP paramilitary organisation

Schwarze Reichswehr – Black Reichswehr: unofficial wing of Reichswehr

Sozialdemokratische Partei Deutschlands (SPD) – Social-Democratic Party of Germany: main socialist party

Sozialistische Arbeiterpartei Deutschlands (SAPD) – Socialist Workers Party of Germany: split from SPD

Stahlhelm, Bund der Frontsoldaten – The Steel Helmet, League of Frontline Soldiers: right-wing paramilitary organisation

Sturmabteilung (SA) – Storm Battalion: NSDAP paramilitary organisation

Unabhängige Sozialdemokratische Partei Deutschlands (USPD) – Independent Social-Democratic Party of Germany: left-wing split from the SPD

Chronology

1918

November

Widespread unrest in armed forces and working class; workers', soldiers' and sailors' councils formed.

Armistice: defeat of Central Powers.

Abdication of Kaiser Wilhelm II.

Establishment in Berlin of Council of People's Deputies, provisional government under Social-Democratic Party (SPD) and Independent Social-Democratic Party (USPD) leadership.

SPD leader Friedrich Ebert becomes Chancellor; forms alliance with armed forces head Wilhelm Groener.

Military chiefs call for volunteers, leading to formation of Freikorps paramilitary forces.

People's State of Bavaria established with Kurt Eisner (USPD) as Premier.

Adolf Hitler returns to Munich.

December

National Congress of Councils held with large SPD majority.

Stahlhelm (Steel Helmet) right-wing paramilitary organisation formed.

USPD resigns from government after SPD leader Gustav Noske orders troops to repress insurgent sailors.

Communist Party of Germany (KPD) formed.

1919

January

Noske put in charge of Freikorps, which are deployed alongside regular forces against insurgent workers in Berlin.

Freikorps assassinate KPD leaders Karl Liebknecht and Rosa Luxemburg.

Army reconstituted as Reichswehr.

National Assembly (parliament) elections: SPD obtains 37.9 per cent of vote and 165 seats.

Proto-fascist German Workers Party (DAP) formed in Munich.

February

National Assembly opens, Ebert elected Reich President.

Strike wave across Ruhr and central Germany.

Eisner assassinated in Munich by right-wing extremist.

April

Bavarian Soviet Republic established.

May

Bavarian Soviet Republic overthrown by right-wing forces; Bavaria becomes centre for far-right activism.

July

Constitution of the German Reich ('Weimar Constitution') approved by National Assembly, Germany proclaimed as parliamentary federal republic.

August

Hitler starts work as political instructor for Reichswehr.

September

Hitler attends DAP meeting, then joins party.

1920

February

DAP rebranded as National Socialist German Workers Party (NSDAP).

March

Kapp Putsch against the Weimar Republic; Reichswehr maintains friendly neutrality towards putschists; massive workers' general strike leads to its collapse.

May

National Assembly replaced by Reichstag as German federal parliament.

June

Reichstag elections: SPD obtains 21.9 per cent of vote and 103 seats; USPD obtains 17.6 per cent of vote and 83 seats; KPD obtains 2.1 per cent of vote and four seats.

October

USPD left votes to join KPD.

December

Merger of USPD left and KPD.

NSDAP launches *Völkischer Beobachter* as party paper.

1921

January

Paris Conference demands from Germany 226 billion gold marks in war reparations, later reduced to 132 billion gold marks.

KPD membership peaks at 450,000.

March

KPD launches 'March Action' adventurist bid for power, leads to repression of KPD and substantial decline in membership.

June

Inflation of mark begins upon first reparations payment.

July

Hitler becomes NSDAP Chairman and demands full control of party.

October

Sturmabteilung (SA — Storm Battalion) established as NSDAP paramilitary organisation.

1922

June

Foreign Minister Walther Rathenau assassinated by right-wing extremists.

October

Mussolini forms Fascist government in Italy.

1923

January

French and Belgian troops occupy Ruhr, sparking off wave of nationalist fervour; Wilhelm Cuno's government calls for passive resistance.

Widespread rumours in Bavaria of imminent NSDAP coup.

February

Start of hyperinflation of mark.

March

KPD champions nationalist line on Ruhr occupation.

Freikorps reactivated.

May

Freikorps member Leo Schlageter executed by French for sabotage, becomes nationalist hero.

Proletarian Hundreds (workers' defence squads) banned by SPD government in Prussia.

June

Karl Radek delivers eulogy to Schlageter at Communist International Executive Committee meeting.

July

Hyperinflation of mark intensifies.

August

Strike wave against Cuno government; SPD leaders oppose call for official general strike.

Cuno replaced as Chancellor by Gustav Stresemann, whose cabinet includes four SPD ministers.

September

Stresemann calls off passive resistance.

KPD membership stands at 294,000.

October

KPD joins SPD governments in Saxony and Thuringia.

Reichswehr bans Proletarian Hundreds and takes over police in Saxony and Thuringia; then enters Saxony and Thuringia, deposes governments.

KPD calls for and then calls off insurrection; Hamburg KPD stages unsuccessful uprising.

November

NSDAP attempts seizure of power in Munich, suppressed by state forces.

NSDAP banned but continues under other names.

Hyperinflation of mark reaches its peak; Stresemann introduces Rentenmark to stabilise the economy.

KPD declared illegal and press banned.

1924

February

Reichsbanner Schwarz-Rot-Gold paramilitary organisation established by SPD, Centre Party and German Democratic Party; becomes largely SPD subsidiary.

March

Hitler convicted of treason and jailed; starts short comfortable sentence during which he writes *Mein Kampf*.

April

Ban lifted on KPD; membership declines to 121,000, starts patchy revival.

May

Reichstag elections: SPD obtains 20.5 per cent of vote and 100 seats; KPD obtains 12.6 per cent of vote and 62 seats; NSDAP (as National Socialist Freedom Movement) obtains 6.5 per cent of vote and 32 seats.

July

Rotfrontkämpferbund (RFB — Alliance of Red Front-Fighters) established as KPD-affiliated paramilitary organisation.

August

Signing of Dawes Plan; leads to regularisation of reparation payments, evacuation of Ruhr and US-led stabilisation of economy.

December

Hitler released from prison.

Reichstag elections: SPD obtains 26.0 per cent of vote and 131 seats; KPD obtains 9.0 per cent of vote and 45 seats; NSDAP (as NSFM) obtains 3.0 per cent of vote and 14 seats.

1925

February

Ban lifted on NSDAP, party relaunched with Hitler firmly as Führer.

November

Schutzstaffel (SS – Protection Squad) established as élite NSDAP paramilitary organisation.

1926

April

Presidential election: monarchist military hero Paul von Hindenburg elected in second round; SPD supports Centre Party candidate Wilhelm Marx; Ernst Thälmann (KPD) obtains 6.4 per cent of vote.

July

Hitler Youth formed, combining various Nazi youth groups.

1928

May

Reichstag elections: SPD obtains 29.8 per cent of vote and 153 seats; KPD obtains 10.6 per cent of vote and 54 seats; NSDAP obtains 2.6 per cent of vote and 12 seats.

June

SPD leader Hermann Müller becomes Chancellor and head of coalition government.

July

Sixth Comintern Congress opens, confirms ultra-left 'Third Period' policies for Communist parties.

Nationalsozialistische Betriebszellenorganisation (NSBO — National Socialist Factory Cell Organisation) set up as Nazi labour organisation.

December

Communist Party of Germany (Opposition) formed by expelled KPD members.

Stalinist faction in full control of KPD.

1929

May

KPD's Berlin May Day demonstration attacked by SPD-controlled police, 40 killed; RFB banned.

Comintern journal considers social-democracy to be 'social-fascism'.

October

Wall Street Crash, onset of world economic crisis, massive impact upon German economy with slump in production and mass unemployment.

December

Revolutionäre Gewerkschafts Opposition (RGO – Revolutionary Union Opposition) formed by KPD.

1930

January

Ratification of Young Plan to regularise reparation payments.

March

Centre Party leader Heinrich Brüning becomes Chancellor and head of coalition government, ruling mainly by parliamentary decrees; SPD not represented in government, but gives it support; Brüning's deflationary economic programme causes great hardship.

August

KPD promotes German nationalism in Programme for the National and Social Liberation of the German People.

September

Reichstag elections: SPD obtains 24.5 per cent of vote and 143 seats; NSDAP obtains 18.3 per cent of vote and 107 seats; KPD obtains 13.1 per cent of vote and 77 seats.

December

KPD membership stands at 176,000; continues to rise through economic crisis.

1931

March

Eleventh Plenum of Comintern Executive opens, continues Third Period line against 'social fascism'.

July

Darmstädter and Dresdner Banks fail; intensification of economic crisis; Brüning continues with deflationary programme.

KPD declares support for Nazi-inspired referendum against SPD Prussian government.

October

Hard-right Harzburg Front formed by NSDAP and German National People's Party (DNVP), Stahlhelm, big businessmen and big agrarians.

Socialist Workers Party (SAP) formed by expelled SPD members.

December

Eiserne Front (Iron Front) paramilitary organisation formed by SPD and ADGB union federation.

SA membership rises to 260,000.

1932

January

Hitler addresses 650 businessmen at Düsseldorf Industry Club.

March

KPD membership rises to 287,000.

April

Presidential election: Hindenburg elected in second round with SPD support; Hitler obtains 36.8 per cent of vote; Thälmann obtains 10.2 per cent of vote.

SA membership rises to nearly 400,000; SA and SS banned in Reich.

NSDAP gain in state elections: Württemberg: 26.4 per cent; Bavaria 32.5

per cent; Prussia: 36.3 per cent of vote; Anhalt: 40.9 per cent; and 31.2 per cent in Hamburg city election.

May

Antifaschistische Aktion (Anti-Fascist Action) formed by KPD.

NSDAP obtains 48.4 per cent of vote in Oldenburg state election.

June

Franz von Papen becomes Chancellor and head of non-party government, the 'Cabinet of Barons'.

Reich ban on SA and SS lifted; upsurge in political violence.

NSDAP obtains 44.0 per cent of vote in Hessen and 49.0 per cent in Mecklenburg-Schwerin state elections.

July

SPD state government in Prussia removed in constitutional coup.

Reichstag elections: NSDAP obtains 37.3 per cent of vote and 230 seats; SPD obtains 21.6 per cent of vote and 133 seats; KPD obtains 14.3 per cent of vote and 89 seats.

August

Twelfth Plenum of Comintern Executive opens, continues Third Period line against 'social fascism'.

October

Unemployment, including 'hidden' jobless and short-term working, estimated at 8.75 million.

November

Berlin transport strike: ADGB refuses to support strike; KPD and NSDAP activists engage in joint activity.

Reichstag elections: NSDAP obtains 33.1 per cent of vote and 196 seats; SPD obtains 20.4 per cent of vote and 121 seats; KPD obtains 16.9 per cent of vote and 100 seats.

December

Kurt von Schleicher becomes Chancellor and head of non-party government; makes unsuccessful bid to split 'left' Nazi Gregor Strasser from Hitler.

1933

January

Hitler appointed Chancellor and heads government in which NSDAP has minority of members.

February

Sustained violence by SA against SPD and KPD members and premises.

Reichstag fire, leading to state of emergency with mass suspension of democratic rights and intensified SA terror.

March

Final Reichstag elections, held under conditions of Nazi terror: NSDAP obtains 43.9 per cent of vote and 288 seats; SPD obtains 18.3 per cent of vote and 120 seats; KPD obtains 12.3 per cent of vote and 81 seats.

Enabling Act passed in Reichstag with DNVP and Centre Party support, establishes NSDAP dictatorship.

Dachau concentration camp opened for political opponents of regime.

KPD officially outlawed; KPD Reichstag deputies arrested or in hiding.

April

Dismissal of public employees who are Jewish or politically hostile.

May

NSDAP 'National Day of Labour' proclaimed on 1 May.

All trade unions outlawed and assets confiscated.

Assets of SPD seized.

June

SPD officially outlawed; DNVP dissolved.

July

Centre Party dissolved.

One-party state formally declared.

Introduction

The coming to power of Adolf Hitler's National Socialist movement in Germany in 1933 was one of the biggest political disasters in human history. Eighty-eight years after the event, the Third Reich still exerts a macabre fascination upon the imagination of the general public. There is, however, one aspect of the Nazi regime which remains very much under-represented within the endless array of popular and scholarly books, films and television programmes on the subject, and that is the Nazis' destruction of Germany's powerful labour movement. Let us cite from one of the very few substantial accounts of this event:

> On the eve of Hitler's victory, the Social-Democratic Party published no fewer than 196 daily newspapers, eighteen weeklies and one monthly theoretical journal. The German trade-union federation, allied with but officially independent of the SPD, also published numerous journals for its various affiliated unions. And with a membership of approximately five million workers, they commanded an entire parallel apparatus alongside that of the Social-Democrats. Then there was the German Communist Party, whose membership at the end of 1932 was, at about 350,000, one-third of the SPD's. The Communist Party, apart from publishing nearly a score of daily papers, produced several weeklies and its own theoretical journal. And it too had its own trade-union organisation, the Red Trade-Union Opposition, which at its peak claimed about 320,000 workers. So, allowing for the inevitable overlapping of membership in these organisations, we still have a compact and centrally-directed proletarian army of some six million troops, who at election times with clockwork regularity gathered around themselves a further six to seven million voters. Indeed, in the last free parliamentary elections of 12 November 1932, the combined Communist–Social-Democratic vote exceeded by nearly 1.5 million that of the Nazis. Yet the Nazis won![1]

This book presents two vivid eye-witness accounts by left-wing activists, the first by Peter and Irma Petroff, the second by Hippolyte Etchebehere, and other texts. Together they document the death throes of the Weimar Republic, the period during which the Nazis made their way into power, and the first few months of the Nazis' dictatorship. These accounts emphasise how the short-sighted behaviour of the organisations of the German labour movement inadvertently made Hitler's victory that much easier, thereby facilitating their own destruction at the hands of the Nazi rabble.

★ ★ ★

To grasp the underlying reasons for the disaster of 1933, it is necessary to return to the German Revolution of 1918–19 and the ensuing years of the Weimar Republic. The revolutionary upheavals that shook Germany at the end of the First World War were indeed profound, but it is not merely the case that they did not result in the birth of a socialist republic as radical left-wingers desired, but the society which did emerge from the fall of the German Empire was severely deficient in respect of its actually being the modern democratic republic which it claimed to be. The price to be paid for this by the German labour movement was horrendous: the creation of a far more authoritarian regime than the pre-1918 Empire had ever been, and in conditions of much deeper crisis. Whereas the German Empire had harassed and repressed the organisations of the working class, Hitler utterly eradicated them.

In 1919 the leaders of the Social-Democratic Party of Germany (SPD), the largest socialist party in the world, believed that their demands had been satisfied by the departure of the Kaiser, the formation of a parliamentary republic based on universal suffrage, and the enactment of a series of social reforms. Yet despite the abdication of the Kaiser and the proclamation of the Republic, much of the old imperial state remained intact and, faced with economic problems and repeated waves of working-class militancy, the SPD's leaders attempted to stabilise their position by way of an alliance with their hereditary enemies in the *Reichswehr*, the highly caste-conscious army, and the state bureaucracy, both of which were congenitally hostile to the very idea of a democratic republic. An American liberal journalist later wrote that with the parliamentary majority that the Social-Democratic and liberal parties enjoyed at the start of the Weimar republic:

> The Republicans could have done anything they wished! They could have abolished the old institutions and created new ones of their own, they could have filled the key positions with faithful followers and eliminated

the hostile and doubtful, they could have gone far towards socialising and democratising business and possession. Yet they did none of these. ... *The Weimar Republic offered little or nothing which could not conceivably have been reached under a modified Imperial Monarchy.*[2]

It would be wrong, as some people on the left do, to accuse the Social-Democratic leaders of betraying a socialist revolution, as they never wanted one in the first place, but it is certainly valid to accuse them of betraying their actual desire for a democratic republic, a betrayal which was to cost them and their party members and voters very dearly indeed.

The SPD's leaders' alliance with the *Reichswehr* was symbolised by the secret telephone link between the Social-Democratic President of the Republic Friedrich Ebert[3] and the second-in-command of the German armed forces, Wilhelm Groener,[4] and by the latter's agreement to support the Republic on condition of his being given a free hand to suppress working-class militancy. It was not merely the official state forces who were involved in this suppression. Alongside the army and the heavily armed police were the *Freikorps*, fiercely anti-working-class freelance military formations, proto-fascist in many instances, which were brought in by the Social-Democratic Defence Minister Gustav Noske,[5] the self-styled 'bloodhound', to put down the many outbreaks of working-class activity during this period, and which were responsible for the murder of Karl Liebknecht and Rosa Luxemburg, the leaders of the German Communist Party (KPD), in January 1919. Many members of the *Freikorps* were subsequently incorporated into the 'Black Reichswehr', unofficial armed forces which were secretly organised in order to evade the limits imposed by the Versailles Treaty. Finally, there were informal organisations such as the *Stahlhelm*, which was ostensibly an ex-servicemen's organisation but in practice an extreme right-wing paramilitary formation which by the end of the 1920s had a membership of half a million men. Many members of these semi-official and informal groups subsequently made their way into the Nazi movement.

The old imperial judiciary remained intact and showed its political bias in many of its decisions,[6] and such powers were left in the hands of the President under Clause 48 of the constitution that he could act as emperor in all but name, with the ability to dismiss the *Reichstag* almost at will and to govern by emergency decree through Chancellors whom he could select.

The military and state bureaucracy therefore only accepted the Republic on sufferance. There was a serious attempt at seizing power by right-wing forces, the Kapp Putsch, on 12 March 1920, only a year after the Republic had agreed its constitution, and which was only beaten off after the government had fled to Stuttgart and the trade unions' call for a general strike had been immediately taken up not merely by the vast majority of manual workers but by white-collar workers and civil servants in an unprecedented nationwide work stoppage.[7]

The Weimar Republic was plagued by governmental instability, and there were no less than thirteen separate administrations in office between 1919 and 1930, when emergency rule was imposed, of which only six enjoyed majority support in the *Reichstag*. Proportional representation shackled the Social-Democrats permanently to liberal and confessional parties and made short-lived coalitions out of all their governments, which were paralysed in the face of the slightest upset. Even the federal character of the state had a reactionary effect, for it prevented the left-wing parties in Prussia, which covered two-thirds of the country, from exerting their relative weight in Germany as a whole.

Finally, there was the key matter of the weakening of the working class itself, whose political allegiance throughout the life of the Republic remained permanently split: initially amongst the SPD, the Independent Social-Democratic Party[8] and the KPD, and after 1920 between the SPD and KPD, roughly in the proportion of two-thirds to one-third.

Although the German Revolution is often regarded as a single incident limited to the winter of 1918–19, or as a number of disparate episodes, it was a process involving several peaks of activity, and could only be regarded as coming to an end in 1923 with the abortive 'German October'. The KPD's attempts at seizing power in 1921 and 1923 did not at all coincide with the highest point of the radicalisation of the masses, which was the general strike against the Kapp Putsch. This massive upsurge of workers' power saw Carl Legien, the right-wing leader of the *Allgemeiner Deutschen Gewerkschaftsbund* (ADGB), the Social-Democratic trade-union federation, vainly approach the leaders of the workers' parties asking what programme they had for power.[9] The SPD leaders failed to take advantage of the situation to reinforce the position of their party within the Republic and to purge the state machinery of anti-republican elements, whilst the KPD leaders at first refused even to involve their party in the strike, on the grounds that it had been called by reformist trade-union leaders.

The KPD earned itself the reputation of the singer cited by Trotsky who sang funeral songs at weddings and wedding songs at funerals and was soundly thrashed at both of them. And at each failed attempt Moscow scapegoated the existing leadership and replaced it, usually with an inferior one, until the party ended up with Ernst Thälmann as General Secretary, whose response to the threat of Hitler the day before he came to power was reputed to be: 'Let's go to Lichtenberg to play skittles.'[10] At each stage of the degeneration of its leadership, the party's political level and understanding of the national and international situation sank lower and lower, and at various times it dabbled dangerously with German nationalism.[11]

Even during the comparative stability of the 'Stresemann Era',[12] the Weimar Republic showed its essential character as a temporary stalemate, existing by grace of the mutual exhaustion of both left and right. During the early years, whenever the economy plunged into crisis, the basic instability of its political superstructure produced the same pattern – a failed left-wing attempt at power followed by a similar right-wing one. Within a few years of the revolutionary upheavals of 1918–19 and the Kapp Putsch of 1920, the Ruhr crisis, with the French occupation of Germany's foremost industrial area and a resulting wave of officially-approved nationalist resistance, produced the KPD's abortive 'German October' with the bungled Hamburg uprising,[13] followed by the Hitler's Beer Hall Putsch,[14] which was a sinister portent of the future in the appearance of the National Socialist German Workers Party (NSDAP) in national politics for the first time. This was an indication that the German right was beginning to realise that the coming of the Weimar Republic had inaugurated an era of mass politics, and that the army and aristocratic and paramilitary groups were simply not sufficiently widely based to root out the support enjoyed by the working-class parties. Hitler understood that paramilitary activity in and of itself was insufficient and that it had to have clear political objectives and thus had to be subject to direction by a far-right political party, and the Nazis' own militia, the *Sturmabteilung*, or SA, was to add a new explosive dimension to German politics: a violent politically-oriented mass movement.

In the meantime, the central government's funding for the general strike against the French occupation of the Ruhr, supported by both left and right without distinction, was ruining the country's currency in wild scenes of hyperinflation, wiping out the value of pensions, salaries and savings, and permanently alienating that section of the middle class that relied on state salaries and pensions, and those who had put their savings into government securities. These classes provided the constant campaigning cadre that kept alive Hitler's movement until the opportunity came for it to appeal to wider layers of the population with its potent populist brew of the vengeful nationalism of a defeated great power, a virulent strand of anti-Semitism which blamed 'the Jews' for all that it found unpalatable in the Republic, a violent anti-Communism in which 'Marxism' meant anything from mild social reform to cultural experimentation as well as actual workers' revolution, and a fraudulent anti-capitalism which obscured the real class divisions in society and would leave the commanding heights of the economy in the hands of millionaire tycoons.

Even during the relatively prosperous mid-1920s, the axis of politics continued to shift to the right. The first warning of this was the election in 1925 of Field Marshal Hindenburg,[15] providing the spectacle of a President of a parliamentary republic who believed in neither parliaments nor republics. The second was the depression in agriculture, which led to the decay of the centre ground in politics and the splintering of the liberal and democratic parties. This gave Hitler the opportunity to break out of his petty-bourgeois ghetto in the Catholic south and into national mass politics for the first time. It was broadly felt in liberal and Social-Democratic circles that the victory of fascism was possible in less-developed countries lacking a strong working class, but not in an advanced industrial country such as Germany with its powerful labour organisations. As late as 1927 Karl Kautsky, the noted Social-Democratic theorist, was expressing this view. 'To be politically effective, the Fascists must appear in large numbers', he wrote, which meant that in Germany 'they will have to be almost one million strong', but that 'in an industrialised country, it is impossible to get hold of such a large number of scoundrels in the prime of life for capitalistic purposes.'[16] It is true that the German workers remained loyal to their parties,[17] and at this point were quite impervious to the appeals of even Goebbels' demagogy, but large sections of society remained outside their ranks. Hitler began to pick up support, first from the Protestant peasantry of the north German plain, then from the debris of the parties in the middle of the political spectrum, and then from the conservative and nationalist parties themselves.[18] But his most spectacular success was surely among the dust of society, those marginal groups who traditionally neither vote nor take any other part in politics, goaded into desperation by the misery of the slump which hit Germany with a vengeance in 1929.

The fragile stalemate of Weimar politics could not survive the impact of the Wall Street Crash of 24 October 1929. The American bankers called in their short-term loans on which the relative prosperity of the latter years of the 1920s had been based, and by the winter of 1931 official figures claimed that six million were unemployed. The NSDAP vote, which in 1928 stood at only 810,000, or 2.6 per cent of the electorate, with only twelve seats in parliament, now climbed to over six million in September 1930 and to more than thirteen million by July 1932, and the Nazis started to make limited but nonetheless worrying inroads into the working class. At the same time Hitler began for the first time to pick up substantial funding from heavy industry, starting with Kirdorf's coal, Thyssen's steel, IG Farben's chemicals and

Cuno's Hamburg–America line. And along with money came respectability, as it always does. Hitler's gangsters were no longer simply the brown-booted thugs of the beer hall brawls, when in the Harzburg Front[19] of October 1931 they allied with the traditional party of the conservative nationalist right, the DNVP, the German Nationalist People's Party.

With seismic shocks taking place below them, parliamentary politics, based as they were upon alliances between the different parties produced by the system of proportional representation, came apart almost immediately. When Hermann Müller's[20] Grand Coalition left office in March 1930, this meant not only the end of the Social-Democrats in government but the end of any government based upon a majority in the *Reichstag*, and indeed the end of parliamentary politics in their ultimate sense, for, after all, the SPD had been the only consistent defender of the Republic. For the right now saw the opportunity to use the crisis to finish off political democracy and by degrees to bring in an authoritarian system of the imperial type. For the next two years three administrations succeeded one other, those of the 'Hunger Chancellor' Heinrich Brüning (1930–32),[21] Franz von Papen[22] (May–December 1932) and Kurt von Schleicher[23] (December 1932–January 1933), each governing by Presidential decree, and each further to the right than the previous one. Each of these Chancellors had a smaller basis in parliament and in the country as a whole than his predecessor. Brüning could at least rely upon the support of his own Centre Party,[24] with the reluctant backing – the infamous 'toleration' – of the SPD, whereas von Papen's only support in the chamber was the forty or so Nationalist MPs, and Schleicher's power rested upon the army alone. By then it was obvious that an authoritarian regime which would utterly annihilate both political democracy and the working-class institutions could only base itself upon the sole mass right-wing force, the Nazis. This was a step that the political establishment had been reluctant so far to take, as they feared a repetition of the general strike that had brought down the Kapp Putsch, accompanied by civil war. Such fears had at first appearance some substance, as the KPD had its own militia, the Red Front Fighters League, which had a membership of over 100,000, and the Iron Front, an alliance formed mainly of sporting and paramilitary organisations associated with the SPD and the ADGB, claimed a membership of around one million. It was first necessary for the ruling class to test the cohesion of the working-class institutions and the will to fight of the working-class parties. This was to be done by a combination of government and police executive action from above and Nazi provocation from below. The focus of politics shifted from cabinet plots and *Reichstag* manoeuvres into the streets.

On 17 July 1932, a heavy police guard was provided to protect the Nazis marching through the district of Red Altona, adjoining Hamburg, in which the Communists enjoyed mass support, with the result of nineteen killed and 285 wounded. Von Papen used this to claim that the Braun–Severing[25] Social-Democratic government of Prussia was incapable of maintaining order, and he quite unconstitutionally dissolved it, sending in a commissioner and removing its police chief, who had two-thirds of Germany's police under his direction. The Social-Democratic ministers made no attempt to mobilise resistance to this coup. Fewer than a dozen soldiers were required to remove them physically from their offices, and they did no more than issue a formal protest, claiming that they were yielding to *force majeure*. This dismissal of the government in what was by far the largest of Germany's states helped to reduce the SPD's influence within the country as a whole and caused much dismay and consternation amongst the party's members and supporters.

Far from encouraging a unified working-class response, the economic crisis that commenced in 1929 was accompanied by the worsening of the disunity of the German working class and a further intensification of the hostility between its two main political parties that had existed from the early years of the Weimar Republic. Although the Social-Democrats were not represented in Brüning's cabinet, their toleration of his deflationary policies of strict austerity, which precluded any state-subsidised attempts at economic revival, cut state spending and thus increased unemployment in the state sector, and savagely reduced unemployment benefits, completely undermined any commitment they might have had to defend working-class interests. The SPD leaders' desire to maintain the Republic in the face of the Nazi threat led them to back Hindenburg as the lesser evil to Hitler in the 1932 Presidential election. A certain degree of disillusionment in the SPD was reflected in its general election voting figures, which declined from 8.6 million in September 1930 to 7.2 million in November 1932. Unemployment also impacted upon those fortunate still to have a job: workers' wages fell and their working and living conditions deteriorated as the precariousness of employment both discouraged many workers from taking action in their defence and encouraged the reformist union leaders to concede to the demands of the employers as the economic crisis dragged on. Membership of the trade unions declined massively during the slump; the ADGB's membership, which had stood at over eight million in 1920, had fallen to 3.5 million in 1932. Divisions grew between the employed and unemployed and were often reflected in and exacerbated through political affiliations, with the SPD retaining the support of the former and the KPD gaining support amongst the latter.

The Communists excoriated the Social-Democrats for their inability to defend the working class, and the KPD grew during the years of crisis, more than tripling its size from 117,000 in 1929 to 360,000 in 1932, and increasing its vote from 4.6 million in September 1930 to 5.9 million in November 1932. But the party's presence in the working class was slender as a high proportion of the party's recruits were unemployed and membership turnover was massive, its own trade-union federation, formed in late 1929, amounted to no more than 350,000 members, and after more than a decade of unending factional strife, instability and expulsions the political level of the party's leadership and membership alike was lamentably low, with class-conscious workers amongst the rank-and-file being sidelined by desperados with nothing to lose and who saw hope only in a violent overthrow of society. The Communists' hostility towards the Social-Democrats was based upon a wide variety of factors, some historical, others contemporary, some valid, others brought about by their own sectarianism or by way of instructions from Moscow. Communists were reluctant to forgive the Social-Democrats for the deaths of Liebknecht and Luxemburg in 1919, and the killing a decade later of forty demonstrators by police under the control of Zörgiebel,[26] the Berlin municipality's Social-Democratic police commissioner, when the KPD defied an official ban upon their May Day march in 1929, did much to maintain that hostility.[27] The Comintern's ultra-left 'Third Period' policies, starting in 1928, tapped into a vein of ultra-leftism that had long been present in German left-wing politics and exacerbated the Communists' existing hostility to the SPD. This encouraged them to concentrate their attacks primarily upon the Social-Democrats, and they denounced them as 'Social Fascists' who posed the biggest threat to the working class, perhaps worse even than that posed by the Nazis.[28]

The Social-Democrats considered that the Communists' adventurism and violent tactics were scaring the middle classes and driving them into the hands on the Nazis, who, despite their far greater predilection for street violence, made a great appeal to the middle classes for 'law and order' against 'red thuggery'. Hostility ran deep on their side too, and it was not unknown for Social-Democratic union officials to inform employers of Communist activists in their workplaces, thus enabling the bosses to victimise them.

Some of the KPD's tactics could only further confuse and divide the working class. Its policy of 'National Bolshevism' during 1930–32, when it tried to outdo the Nazis in nationalist demagogy, could only redound to the benefit of its enemies, for whom virulent nationalism was a central feature of their politics. And whilst the KPD's Red Front Fighters regularly engaged in desperate street-battles with the Nazis' SA, there were also occasions when the KPD even worked with the Nazis against the Social-Democrats. A year before von Papen had dismissed the Braun–Severing government, the Communists had prepared the way for it by taking over as their own a Nazi referendum calling for its dismissal, which they baptised 'the Red Referendum', and only two months before von Papen actually sent in his soldiers they moved a motion of no confidence in the Prussian *Landtag* (state parliament), which the Nazis were only too glad to support. The Berlin transport-workers' strike of November 1932, in which Communist militants and Nazi storm-troopers linked arms on picket lines in an alliance against the city's Social-Democratic administration, completed the internal disintegration of the working-class movement.

Small groups of dissident Communists and Socialists called urgently for the unity of the working class in the face of the employers' offensive and the Nazi onslaught, but their entreaties were ignored by the leaders of the big battalions of the Communist and Social-Democratic Parties, who refused to join forces and blamed each other for that lack of cooperation even as the Nazi menace grew ever more threatening and the position of the working class became increasingly parlous.

The final test of the combativity of the working-class parties occurred with the Nazis' march in front of Karl Liebknecht House, the KPD's national headquarters, on 22 January 1933. This represented more than a mere provocation by the Nazis against the KPD, as the French radical Simone Weil noted. She had been staying in Germany, and her observations were published in the journal of a French teachers' union. She felt that the events of that day demonstrated 'the powerlessness of the Communist Party'. The KPD saw the Nazis' demonstration purely as a provocation, aimed at provoking a violent response and thereby getting the party banned, and so it refused to confront them, even though by Nazi standards it was not a massive show of strength and could have been successfully repelled. The KPD's assessment, she wrote, was 'entirely false':

> It was not a question of a curtain raiser to the banning of the Communist Party, it would have been pointless to stage such a show for that purpose. What was involved was a sort of dress rehearsal for the Fascists, intended to test the strength of the Berlin proletariat's resistance, and, when put to the test, that strength was found to be nil.[29]

When the numerically and organisationally powerful but politically deeply divided labour movement failed to respond to the Nazis' demonstration, the German ruling class was finally convinced that there would be no working-class struggle against the Nazis. This was the final proof they required that there would be no strikes, uprisings or civil war were the Nazis to assume power, and that it was therefore safe to allow Hitler into office.

As far as the German right was concerned, by then it was none too soon. By the autumn of 1932, the unemployment figures began to drop, and with them Hitler's support. The Nazis lost two million votes in the elections of November 1932, costing them thirty-four seats in the *Reichstag*. Cracks began to appear within the NSDAP with the Strasser split in December.[30] The fear of big business, that letting Hitler into power would provoke a militant working-class response, was now giving way to the opposite fear: that his movement might vanish as rapidly as it arose, making it impossible to use its mass base to crush the working-class organisations. Von Papen and Hitler met on 4 January 1933 to sort out the terms of their alliance and the allocation of the seats in their government, and to secure the finance necessary for the elections. Within a month Hindenburg had sent for Hitler and appointed him Chancellor.

With the appointment of Göring, on 30 January 1933, as Minister of the Interior for Prussia, thus putting him in control of two-thirds of the police of Germany, and of fellow Nazi Wilhelm Frick as Interior Minister for the Reich, and the recruitment of vast numbers of the SA and *Stahlhelm* into the police force, a reign of terror was imposed upon the organisations of the German labour movement. Germany lived in an atmosphere of civil war, but with only one side doing the fighting. The detachments of the Socialist and Communist defence organisations waited in vain for the signal from their party headquarters to march against the Nazis, for together the working-class militias, backed by a general strike, could have driven the Nazis off the streets. But that call never came. The 'Decree for the Protection of the People and the Reich' signed by Hindenburg the day after the *Reichstag* fire on 27 February suspended civil liberties, and the general election held on 5 March gave a majority in the *Reichstag* to the Nazis and their Nationalist allies, once the outlawed Communist deputies were prevented from taking their seats.[31] When the Centre Party added its votes to those of the government on 23 March, Hitler received the two-thirds required for his absolute powers under the Enabling Act, the Social-Democrats alone casting their votes against. The nightmare of National-Socialist Germany was underway.

★ ★ ★

Peter and Irma Petroff's book *The Secret of Hitler's Victory* was published by Leonard and Virginia Woolf at the Hogarth Press, 52 Tavistock Square,

London WC, in 1934. The scanning and annotation of the text in this collection was carried out by Paul Flewers. Permission has been granted by their grand-daughter Fiona Miller and by Penguin Books to republish this book.

For many people interested in the history of socialism, Peter Petroff is just a name in a small number of books, the subject of a few academic articles, the author of articles in long-gone and barely-remembered publications. Peter Petroff's wife Irma is even less known. Yet both Irma and Peter Petroff were lifelong socialists, active in three countries, Britain, Germany and Russia, at crucial periods in the history of those countries.

Peter Petroff was born into a Jewish family in Ukraine in 1884 and joined the Russian Social-Democratic Workers Party in 1901. He sided with the Menshevik wing in the party's split in 1903 and participated in the 1905 Revolution. He arrived in Britain in 1907, and, alongside many of his fellow Russian émigrés, took a very active part in the activities of the left-wing movement in Britain. He was a familiar figure at the conferences of the Social-Democratic Federation and the British Socialist Party (BSP), at which he strongly criticised the right-wingers around Henry Hyndman, and was a regular contributor to the British socialist press on a wide range of topics. He opposed the First World War from the outset, and, moving from London to Glasgow in 1915, he worked with John Maclean and other socialists in and around the Clyde Workers' Committee in mobilising the Scottish working class against the government's wartime policies, for which he was jailed on several occasions.

Petroff met Irmentrante Gellrich at a socialist Sunday School in Hampstead in 1911. Irma, as she was known, was born in Obernigk (now Oborniki Śląskie) in Silesia in 1891, and was at this point a member of the Radical Democratic Association, but was soon to join the German Social-Democratic Party and to support the left wing in the party around Karl Liebknecht. Irma and Peter rapidly entered into a close relationship, one which endured until Peter's death in 1947. Irma was also active in the BSP, and was interned as an enemy alien in 1916.

The Petroffs left Britain in 1918 and travelled to the new Soviet republic, where they immediately became active in a remarkably wide range of official posts and activities in many parts of the country. Peter gained a reputation with Lenin as a kind of 'Comrade Fix-It': he was able to intervene in difficult situations with sufficient good sense, detachment and subtlety to resolve matters in a way that was both beneficial to the new regime and acceptable to those in dispute with it. Irma was heavily involved in propaganda work amongst the German prisoners-of-war on Soviet territory. The Petroffs soon became quite critical of some of the practices of the Bolshevik regime; they were both believers in working-class power and were dismayed at the way in which the party-state apparatus was starting to raise itself above the working class. Nevertheless, the Petroffs stayed on good terms with Lenin, not merely because he valued their work, but almost certainly because their criticisms of the running of the Soviet republic did not constitute any form of political opposition to the Bolsheviks or impact upon their dealing with the difficulties which they were detailed to solve.

Disillusioned with the course of events in the Soviet republic, the Petroffs leapt at the chance of working abroad for the regime, and they moved to Germany in 1921, where they found work in the Soviet Embassy. Irma was employed as an administrative worker, Peter as an economist, and he edited an economics magazine and wrote two books on the Soviet economy. However, the political malaise that had dismayed them in the Soviet republic was replicated within the Soviet diplomatic corps, and geographical distance failed to stem the Petroffs' disillusionment with Soviet affairs. In 1925, they resigned from the Soviet Communist Party and left the employ of the Soviet embassy. The Petroffs remained in Germany for another eight years, leading a somewhat precarious existence. In June 1932, with their clear understanding of the threat posed by Hitler's National Socialists, they made an application to emigrate to Britain. This proved unsuccessful, and, after Hitler's coming to power in early 1933, the Petroffs and their two young children lived at first in clandestinity in Germany, then left for Belgium in May, and finally reached Paris in June. After much prevarication on the part of the British authorities and much assistance from various British labour movement figures, the Petroffs arrived in Britain in December 1933. They rapidly became active once more in the British labour movement, an involvement that lasted until Peter's death in 1947 and Irma's in 1968.

Whilst there were plenty of books and newspaper and magazine articles published in Britain which described the appalling events following Hitler's coming to power in 1933, *The Secret of Hitler's Victory* was unusual as it brought to the fore the political ineptitude of the organisations of the German labour movement, the Social-Democratic Party and their associated trade-union leaders and the Communist Party, in the face of the terrible threat that the Nazis posed, and firmly condemned them for their responsibility in allowing this disaster to occur.[32]

The Communist Party of Great Britain's *Daily Worker* ran a review of the book, by an unnamed 'German comrade', in its issue for 29 August 1934. It was unremittingly hostile, and unsurprisingly remained silent in respect of the Petroffs' revealing comments upon the subordination of German Communist policy to Soviet diplomatic requirements and the German

Communist Party's repeated adaptation to German nationalism, most notoriously in 1931 when the party joined with the Nazis in a referendum aimed at ousting the Social-Democratic government in Prussia. On the other hand, the Independent Labour Party's *New Leader* gave the book an enthusiastic review in its issue for 21 September 1934, endorsing its sharp criticism of the paralysis shown by the Social-Democrats and trade-union leaders in the face of the Nazi menace.[33]

★ ★ ★

The essay by Hippolyte Etchebehere first appeared as two articles in the magazine *Masses*, which was published in Paris by the 'Amis du Monde' group, in 1933 under the pseudonym of Juan Rustico. The entire material, was reprinted as booklet no. 111 in the 'B' series of the *Spartacus* monthly *cahiers* in Paris in 1981, with the supplementary letters at the end also appearing in 'Allemagne 1933: Documents sur la tragédie du prolétariat allemand', which makes up no. 35 of the *Cahiers du CERMTRI* issued in December 1984. Our translation was made by Al Richardson and corrected against the original by Harry Ratner, and first appeared in *Revolutionary History*, Volume 5, no. 1 (1993).

Etchebehere's widow Mika provided a vivid biographical introduction, 'Hippolyte Etchebehere, Called Juan Rustico', for the *Spartacus* edition of this work, and we publish it below.

★ ★ ★

Hippolyte Etchebehere was thirty-six years old when he was killed in combat at Atienza (near Guadalajara) on 16 August 1936, at the very beginning of the Spanish Civil War. He was advancing, leading a detachment that he had trained in grenade throwing, trying to approach a fortified emplacement which had to be taken whatever the cost, when a machine gun bullet killed him.

Out of the thirty-six years that Hippolyte Etchebehere had notched up the day he fell at Atienza, seventeen of them were totally devoted to the revolutionary struggle that he had chosen one day in January 1919, when, from the balcony of his house, he saw the police dragging white-bearded Jews taken from the Buenos Aires ghetto behind their horses, tied to their saddles. Jews were called Russians in those days in Argentina. To be a Russian was to be a Bolshevik, a revolutionary, responsible for the struggle that at that time was being carried on by the workers of one of the largest factories in the country in a strike which made the bourgeoisie tremble by its extent and firmness.

During the 'tragic week' of January that remains like a bloody milestone in the history of Argentine repression, Hippolyte Etchebehere came to the revolution as others come to religion, forever, up to his final heartbeat, filled with lucid and reasoned hatred, ever vigilant, sharp at every turn, as taut as a bowstring ever ready to shoot at this absurd, murderous and rapacious social system.

His first steps as a militant were made in the anarchist movement. During the days that followed the 'tragic week' he feverishly wrote a pamphlet entitled *Listen to the Truth* and went out into the streets of the city to distribute it to the policemen. A few hours later he was in prison, accused of an offence against state security. Because he belonged to a highly regarded family, and because he was a university student, he was not sent to the sinister Ushuaia concentration camp in Tierra del Fuego at the extreme south of Argentina. When he regained his freedom, he left his family home in order to avoid creating difficulties among his own people, and along with a group of students he organised the university 'Insurrexit' group, a small revolutionary formation that was so ardent and so combative that in its two years of existence it placed its mark on an entire generation, not only in Argentina, but in the whole of South America.

Marxism and the Russian Revolution led him into the ranks of the Communist Party, where he was soon noticed for the breadth of his knowledge and his qualities as a political speaker, to such an extent that the Central Committee tried to recruit him to it by all possible means.

When the struggle against Trotsky began in the Communist Party of the Soviet Union, Etchebehere, who was a fervent admirer of the leader of the Red Army, rallied to his cause. So great was his reputation as a revolutionary, and so exemplary was his conduct as a militant, that when they expelled him from the party in 1925, the Central Committee, as was the habit in those days, did not dare smear him with accusations of being a 'paid agent provocateur of the police', or other insults of that type, but restricted itself only to his Trotskyism, his factional activity and his 'anti-Bolshevism'. His fragile health, threatened by tuberculosis and undermined by the years of privations and enormous activity, required a period of rest from which he profited to deepen his Marxist and military studies; in his notebooks I found a series of sketches illustrating guerrilla formations, the description of an airborne machine gun, and a plan for the rapid training of officers ...

Then came our years in Patagonia, the strongest temptation of our lives, a foolish desire to settle down on firm ground, battered by the winds of the Atlantic coast and softened by the pastures of the Andes pre-Cordillera and Cordillera. These regions were still lands of adventure offering a quick fortune at the end of three or four years' work, and an expansive material life, without the constraints of the city, and among people who seemed to have come straight out of Jack London's books. It was, as I say, a temptation, and a very strong one, but the vows taken in our early youth forbade us to do it. With the money we had earned during a season of hard work, we left for Europe in search of the struggle that we believed to be more imminent in the countries with solid working-class organisations.

We landed in Spain two months after the inauguration of the Republic.[34] We marched in tumultuous demonstrations in the streets of Madrid demanding the separation of church and state,[35] learning day after day that the republican Assault Guards[36] already knew how to use the truncheon with as much violence as the old Civil Guards. We left for Paris three months later.

Settled into tiny lodgings in the rue Claude Bernard, and free of material preoccupations, we were to spend our most unclouded days in the library of St Geneviève, reading books there which we judged to be indispensable to our training as revolutionary militants. We discovered our first French comrades in the 'Amis de Monde' group.

In October 1932, convinced that we were to find fertile terrain in Germany for the decisive struggle, we arrived in Berlin. With the intention of perfecting our knowledge of the language and of making contact with the German workers, we enrolled in the Marxist school of the German Communist Party (KPD), which was at the same time a school with courses for adults, and which was the school where we learned to understand the paralysing, pernicious policy of the Communist International, faithfully applied by the leaders of the German Communist Party. There was no revolutionary struggle in Germany. In the two articles that appeared in the journal *Masses* published by René Lefeuvre in Paris and which are reproduced in this booklet, Rustico describes the events we witnessed during the days which preceded Hitler's coming to power.

On our return to Paris, we again waited, but not with folded arms. Along with Kurt Landau, the magnificent Austrian revolutionary militant assassinated by the Stalinists in 1937 in Barcelona,[37] we began the slow work of renewing our contacts with the so-called 'Wedding' Communist oppositional group that Landau had led in Berlin.[38]

When the revolt of the Asturian miners broke out in Spain in October

1934,[39] we updated our passports to go there. The bloody repression of this exemplary movement, so close to the Paris Commune in its motives and its development, shook us. Rustico wrote some magnificent pages on the Asturian struggle which unfortunately disappeared in Barcelona when the Stalinists pillaged the offices of the POUM during the 1937 May Days.[40]

One of the founders along with Comrade Landau and some French militants of the magazine *Que Faire*,[41] Etchebehere continued to live solely for his revolutionary mission, despite his poor health. When a medical checkup revealed that he had tubercular tissue in both lungs, he had to accept a stay in a sanatorium, the only effective means of treating it at the time; at the same time it provided him with a rest from his work. For six months in the sanatorium he extended his literary studies: all Flaubert, all Stendhal, the French and Spanish classics, and all that had appeared on Nazism, and he filled his notebooks with notes.

When he left the sanatorium in much better health, the doctors advised a change of climate. Madrid was chosen, not only on account of its sun and its dry climate, but also because workers' struggles were intensifying day by day in Spain. He arrived there in May 1936. I was to join him two months later, on 12 July to be exact, having already decided to spend a dream walking holiday across the land of Asturias. We had not finished exchanging news of our doings during our separation when the uprising of the Fascist generals broke like a clap of thunder which erased the past and gave birth to new hope.

For the whole afternoon of that same 18 July[42] we sought for weapons and activity, going from one UGT trade-union office to another CNT[43] one, among young people who were still children and men who were already old, our heads buzzing with rumours and speeches, with songs and slogans, submerged in the sea which was mounting in great waves from all the districts of Madrid towards the Puerta del Sol. The next night we finally joined the fight among the comrades of the POUM, the political organisation that was the closest to our oppositional group.

Our column, 120 militiamen strong, went off to war under the title of 'The Motorised Column of the POUM', justified by our three lorries and as many cars. Its commander, or the 'responsible comrade', as they called it then, was Hippolyte Etchebehere. The battle only lasted for twenty-six days; for him, the most radiant, the richest in hope, and the happiest days of his life.

He died on 16 August 1936, arms in hand, when the revolution was still beautiful …

★ ★ ★

Finally, we have three brief articles from syndicalist papers: the first by Daniel Guérin, in the Paris *La Révolution Prolétarienne*, 10 October 1932, translated from the French by A W Zurbrugg; the second by Paul Strehl, a member of the Industrial Workers of the World in Germany, in the Chicago *Industrial Worker*, 3 January 1933; and the third by 'a group of revolutionary syndicalists' in the Geneva *Le Réveil*, 1 May 1933, also translated from the French by A W Zurbrugg. Guérin's eye-witness account of Germany in mid-1932 describes the political divisions within the German working class, Strehl looks at the Berlin transport strike of November 1932, whilst the syndicalist authors survey the collapse of the German labour movement after Hitler came to power. All three of these articles emphasise how the bureaucratic nature of the German labour organisations served to stifle the activity and creativity of the working class, and eventually paralysed it in the face of the Nazi onslaught.

NOTES

1. Robert Black, *Fascism in Germany*, Volume 1 (Steyne, London, 1975), p. 1 – available online: https://www.marxists.org/subject/fascism/blick/index.htm.
2. Edgar Ansel Mowrer, *Germany Puts the Clock Back* (Penguin, Harmondsworth, 1937), pp. 83–84, emphasis in original text.
3. Friedrich Ebert (1871–1925) was a saddler. He joined the SPD in 1889 and stood on the right wing of the party. He became its General Secretary in 1905, and Chairman in 1913. He was elected to the *Reichstag* as a deputy in 1912. He led the first postwar German government, being Chancellor from November 1918 to February 1919, and he deployed both the regular army and the *Freikorps* against militant workers. He became the first President of the Weimar Republic in February 1919, and held the post until his death.
4. Karl Eduard Wilhelm Groener (1867–1939) was a senior career army officer. During the revolutionary period he forged a secret deal with the Social-Democrat Chancellor Friedrich Ebert (see note 3) by which the armed forces would suppress left-wing uprisings in exchange for their supporting the new Republic. He was variously Minister of Defence, Transport and the Interior under the Weimar Republic, and retired after being attacked by the Nazis in the *Reichstag* in 1931.
5. Gustav Noske (1868–1946) was a manual worker. He joined the SPD in 1884, and was the *Reichstag* deputy for Chemnitz during 1906–18. He stood on the right wing of the SPD, and advocated a colonial policy for Germany. At the end of the First World War, he went to Kiel to calm the sailors' radical revolt, and managed to restore the authority of the officers. He returned to Berlin to oversee military governance. In 1919, he became Minister of Defence, ordered the *Freikorps* to crush the Spartakist rebellion, but resigned in March 1920 after the Kapp Putsch when party colleagues accused him of failing to deal sufficiently sternly with the putsch organisers. During 1920–33, he served

as Upper President of Hanover. He was arrested in July 1944 in connection with the failed assassination attempt upon Hitler.

6. Between 1919 and 1923 there were 22 killings committed by left-wingers; 18 of those convicted were sentenced to 15 years in prison, and 10 were executed: during the same period there were 354 right-wing political murders; 326 of those involved were found not guilty, and the other 28 received prison sentences averaging four months.

7. Named after its leader Dr Wolfgang Kapp (1858–1922), a Prussian civil servant. He conspired with the *Freikorps* and part of the army to overthrow the Republic and institute a military dictatorship. Despite the fact that the *Freikorps* played a leading role in the putsch, within days of its collapse Noske called upon them to suppress working-class militancy in the Ruhr.

8. The Independent Social-Democratic Party (USPD) was formed in April 1917 by SPD members who had been expelled because of their opposition to Germany's involvement in the First World War. Whilst it never overtook the SPD in membership size or electoral gains, it became a mass party of between 750,000 and a million members standing to the left of the SPD, enjoying considerable support in various areas of Germany and within the workers' councils that emerged at the end of the war. The party congress at Halle in October 1920 saw a majority of delegates vote to fuse with the KPD, and the party split, with approximately one-third of the members joining the KPD, one-third remaining in the USPD, and one-third dropping out of membership. Much of the rump USPD returned to the SPD over the following years. A small remnant continued as the USPD until 1931, when it joined the newly-formed *Sozialistische Arbeiterpartei Deutschlands* (SAPD – Socialist Workers Party of Germany), see note 46, p. 110.

9. Carl Legien (1861–1920) was a woodworker. He joined the SPD in 1885, and headed the General Commission of the German Trade Unions from 1891 to 1919, and the ADGB upon its formation in 1919. He was a *Reichstag* deputy during 1893–98 and 1903–20. He stood on the right wing of the SPD, and he played a leading role in mobilising the organisations of the German labour movement behind the Kaiser's government in the First World War. When the Kapp Putsch took place he called a general strike, and approached the leaders of the SPD, USPD and KPD with the proposal for a government of workers' parties. According to Arthur Rosenberg, the proposal fell because of the refusal of Däumig, the leader of the USPD left wing, to take part in a government that included the discredited right-wing leaders of the SPD: Arthur Rosenberg, *History of the German Republic* (Methuen, London, 1936), p. 139.

10. Ernst Torgler, letter of 30 January 1942, cited in Robert Black, *Fascism in Germany*, Volume 2 (Steyne, London, 1975), p. 913 – available online: https://www.marxists.org/subject/fascism/blick/index.htm. Ernst Thälmann (1886–1944), a manual worker, joined the SPD in 1903 and the USPD in 1917 and sided with the faction that joined the KPD in 1920. He became KPD Chairman in 1925. He stood as the KPD's presidential candidate in 1925 and 1932, and as a loyal Stalinist headed the KPD from 1925 until its collapse in 1933. Arrested in March 1933, he was finally executed in Buchenwald concentration camp in 1944.

11. This was sponsored by some Soviet leaders, such as Karl Radek with his infamous 'Schlageter speech' that praised a *Freikorps* member who had been killed in the Ruhr by the French in 1923: 'Leo Schlageter: The Wanderer into the Void', *Labour Monthly*, Volume 5, No. 3, September 1923, pp. 152ff.

12. After the elaboration of the Dawes Plan, which involved giving short-term American loans to Germany, for a brief period (1924–29) German industry (but not agriculture) enjoyed relative prosperity. It is generally called after Gustav Stresemann (1878–1929) who was Chancellor at the beginning of the period and later foreign minister for most of the rest of it.

13. On 23 October 1923, the KPD sent out orders for a nationwide uprising. At the last minute these were countermanded, but the message failed to get through to the party branch in Hamburg, which rose on its own and was suppressed after heavy street fighting. It remains to this day a matter of conjecture as to whether the KPD could have successfully seized power during 1923: that the KPD leadership failed to take advantage of a revolutionary situation and thus let slip an exceptionally advantageous opportunity to seize power is an enduring belief of the Trotskyist movement. August Thalheimer, one of the top KPD leaders at that juncture, later concluded that a revolutionary situation did not exist and any attempt at seizing power would have failed: August Thalheimer, '1923: A Missed Opportunity? The Legend of the German October and the Real History of 1923', *Revolutionary History*, Volume 8, No. 4, 2004, pp. 90–124.

14. On 8 November 1923 Hitler took control of a meeting held in the *Hofbrauhaus* in Munich and tried to take over the city in a putsch, preparatory to a march to overthrow the government in Berlin. This was easily dispersed by the local police, and, although Hitler was found guilty of treason, his sentence was brief and he had a comfortable time in prison.

15. Paul Ludwig Hans Anton von Beneckendorff und von Hindenburg (1847–1934) was a senior career army officer and a staunch monarchist. Brought back from retirement in 1914, he was appointed Chief of the General Staff in 1916, retired in 1919, but was persuaded to stand in the presidential election in 1925, which he won on the second round. He stood again in 1932, and again won on the second round, beating Hitler with support from the Social-Democrats. Personally very hostile to Hitler, he was badgered by his advisors into appointing him Chancellor in January 1933.

16. Karl Kautsky, *The Materialist Conception of History* (Yale University Press, New Haven, 1988), p. 394.

17. The combined voting figures in general elections for the two major working-class parties were quite consistent. In the elections held in May 1924, the SPD received 20.5 per cent of the vote; in December 1924: 26.0 per cent; May 1928: 29.8 per cent; September 1930: 24.5 per cent; July 1932: 21.6 per cent; November 1932: 20.4 per cent. The corresponding figures for the KPD are 12.6, 9.0, 10.6, 13.1, 14.6 and 16.9 per cent.

18. The vote for the main conservative and liberal parties, the *Deutsche Volkspartei* (DVP, German People's Party) and the *Deutsche Demokratische Partei* (DDP, German Democratic Party) declined from 13.9 and 8.3 per cent respectively in the 1920 general election to 4.5 and 3.8 per cent in the 1930 general election. Their decline continued, with the DVP obtaining 1.2 and 1.9 per cent in the general elections held in July and November 1932, and the *Deutsche Staatspartei* (German State Party, as the DDP had become) obtaining 1.0 per cent in each of these elections. The vote of the hard-right *Deutschnationale Volkspartei* (DNVP, German Nationalist People's Party) peaked at 20.5 per cent in the December 1924 general election, dropped to 7.0 per cent in 1930, and only slightly revived to 8.3 per cent in November 1932. Taking into consideration that all these parties moved rightwards in the last years of the Weimar Republic, and that

the electoral support for the left-wing parties and the Catholic Centre stayed relatively constant, the drop in support for the DVP, the DDP/DSP and the DNVP shows that a sizeable chunk of the German middle class moved rapidly rightwards into the orbit of the Nazis, whose vote stood at 2.6 per cent in 1928, 18.3 per cent in 1930, and 37.4 and 33.1 per cent in July and November 1932.

19. On 11 October 1931 leading industrialists, bankers, landowners, military personnel, monarchists, nationalists and Nazis met at Bad Harzburg. They approved a resolution combining extreme hostility towards the working class, a call for 'a strong national state', and 'the restoration of German military grandeur'.

20. Hermann Müller (1876–1931) was born into a middle-class family, and joined the SPD in 1893. At first he stood on the party's left, but moved to the party 'centre'. He became a leading party official and was a *Reichstag* deputy during 1916–18. He was Reich Foreign Minister in 1919–20, during which time he signed the Versailles Treaty. He was twice Chancellor, leading coalition governments during March–June 1920 and June 1928–March 1930.

21. Heinrich Brüning (1885–1970) was the leader of the Centre Party (see note 24) and a staunch monarchist. He was appointed Chancellor on 28 March 1930, and for the next two years ruled by Presidential decree backed by Hindenburg. He stated in his memoirs that one of his major goals as Chancellor was to restore the monarchy; however, it seems that he did not produce a detailed plan to effect this: Richard Evans, *The Coming of the Third Reich* (Penguin, New York, 2005) pp. 250–51.

22. Franz Joseph Hermann Michael Maria von Papen zu Köningen (1879–1969) was a military-trained diplomat. He became a leader of the right wing of the Centre Party (see note 24), and was a member of the Prussian parliament during 1921–32. He was appointed Chancellor on 1 June 1932, ruling by Presidential decree with the backing of Hindenburg, and resigned on 17 November. He was appointed Vice-Chancellor under Hitler, but subsequently resigned and was appointed German ambassador to Austria and then Turkey.

23. Kurt von Schleicher (1882–1934) was a career army officer. He was Groener's assistant during the revolutionary period, and also helped organise the *Freikorps*. In the early 1920s, he played an important role in establishing secret Soviet-German military cooperation, and also was in close contact with the unofficial 'Black Reichswehr' that was set up to evade the Versailles Treaty's restrictions on Germany's armed forces. He was the primary liaison figure between the military leadership and the political world. He became Minister of Defence in June 1932 and was Chancellor from December 1932 to January 1933, when he was replaced by Hitler. His attempt to build a broad base for his government, by bringing in big business, the army, the trade unions and the Strasser wing of the Nazis, failed miserably. He was killed during the Night of the Long Knives in June 1934.

24. The *Deutsche Zentrumspartei* or *Zentrum* (German Centre Party) was founded in 1870 to defend the social and political position of the Roman Catholic Church within Germany, and was the traditional party of the liberal Catholics of the Rhineland, as opposed to the more conservative regionalist Bavarian Peoples' Party of the south. It participated in every government coalition from 1919 to 1932, and provided four Chancellors: Konstantin Fehrenbach (1920–21), Joseph Wirth (1921–22), Wilhelm Marx (1923–25, 1926–28) and Heinrich Brüning (1930–32). After Hitler's victory the party attempted to establish a *modus vivendi* with the Nazi government and although it

supported the Enabling Act that gave the Nazis overwhelming power, this proved in vain and it dissolved itself in July 1933.

25. Otto Braun (1872–1955) was apprenticed as a lithographer and joined the SPD in 1888. He became a leading member of the party in Prussia, specialising in agricultural matters. He was Prime Minister of Prussia for much of the Weimar period. He was also the SPD's candidate in the Reich presidential election in 1925; he came second, but withdrew to allow a straight contest between the Centre Party's Wilhelm Marx and Hindenburg. Wilhelm Severing (1875–1952) was apprenticed as a lithographer and at first was a radical trade-union activist. He gravitated to the extreme right wing of the SPD, and was the Reich Minister of the Interior during 1928–30, and the Minister of the Interior of Prussia during 1919–26 and from 1930 until his removal from this post by von Papen on 20 July 1932.

26. Karl Zörgiebel (1878–1961) was a cooper and trade-union activist. He joined the SPD in 1901. He was a *Reichstag* deputy during 1920–24. In 1926 he became the Social-Democratic police commissioner for the municipality of Berlin, and his ban on the Communist Party's May Day march in 1929 resulted in a police confrontation and 40 deaths in barricade fighting.

27. Zörgiebel became a hate-figure in Communist circles, and as Hitler was coming to power there were even cases of school playgrounds ringing with the unedifying slogan of 'Drive out the little Zörgiebels' as young Communists launched attacks against the children of Social-Democrats.

28. The hostility towards Social-Democracy of the Third Period was more intense in Germany than elsewhere, and this reflected not merely domestic politics but also the needs of Soviet foreign policy. One study explains why: 'At the worker-base of the KPD, and even up to quite high levels of its central as well as local leadership, the strident leftism of the "Third Period" was taken as good Communist coin, as a genuine attempt to break Social Democracy as the essential prerequisite for the proletarian revolution. True, Stalin did seek to destroy the institutions and mass influence of German reformism – but not in order to clear the road for socialist revolution. His aim was the formation of an ultra-nationalist government in Berlin, dominated by the pro-Eastern *Reichswehr* generals, a regime bent on an aggressive anti-French course in foreign policy, and eager to collaborate with Moscow in providing Stalin with desperately-needed economic and technical assistance for his First Five-Year Plan. Even the rise of National Socialism did not divert Stalin from his chosen German policy. Indeed, all the available evidence indicates that Stalin saw in the Nazis not an enemy that sought the destruction of both German Communism and the USSR, but a potential, if unreliable, ally in the struggle against the "social fascists", whom the KPD vied with the Nazis in denouncing as agents of French and Anglo-American imperialism.' – Black, *Fascism in Germany*, Volume 2, p. 755.

29. Simone Weil, *Formative Writings 1929–1941* (University of Massachusetts Press, Amherst, 1987), p. 135.

30. Gregor Strasser (1892–1934) was a *Freikorps* leader who joined the NSDAP in 1922 and rapidly became a leading member, doing much to enable the party to emerge from its Bavarian base to become a nationally-based organisation. He was a *Reichstag* deputy during 1924–32. He and his brother Otto (1897–1974) led the 'left' wing of the Nazi Party, which emphasised the 'socialist' aspects of the party's programme and thereby had an uneasy relationship with Hitler. He entered into discussions with von Schleicher

about bringing his wing of the Nazis into a coalition government, thus isolating Hitler. The attempt failed, and, although Strasser then withdrew from political activity and gave up his *Reichstag* seat, Hitler repaid him by ordering his murder during the 'Night of the Long Knives'.

31. Even during this last general election, held under conditions of Nazi terror, the workers' parties still commanded the support of nearly one-third of the electorate: the SPD won 18.3 per cent of the vote, the KPD 12.3 per cent.
32. The Petroffs' conclusion, with its breezy prognosis of the early fall of the Nazi regime, will be disconcerting to today's readers, familiar as they are with the history of the Third Reich. Here, the authors were following a consoling trend that was common in left-wing and liberal circles during the 1930s, that, for all its boasting, the Nazi regime would be incapable of dealing successfully with the challenges that it would face and that it would thus be vulnerable to a revived opposition.
33. Details on Peter and Irma Petroff have been provided by Scott Reeve, who is writing a biography of Peter Petroff.
34. That would be June 1931. The Republic was proclaimed on 14 April.
35. Article III of the proposed constitution proclaimed that the new Republic had no religion. On 7 May the Archbishop of Toledo condemned the attack on the privileged position of the church, and six convents in Madrid were destroyed in the disturbances that followed.
36. The Assault Guards (*Asaltos*) were created by the Spanish Republic 'to maintain order'.
37. On Kurt Landau (1903–1937), see Hans Schafranek's article 'Kurt Landau' in *The Spanish Civil War: The View from the Left* (*Revolutionary History*, Volume 4, Nos 1/2, Winter 1991–92), pp. 54–72.
38. In May 1930, ten delegates of the Wedding (north Berlin) section of the KPD signed a declaration solidarising themselves with the Left Opposition. When these delegates and their supporters were expelled, they formed part of the Berlin organisation of the Trotskyists led by Landau.
39. In October 1934, the miners of Asturias in northern Spain rose against the growing influence of the reactionary Catholic CEDA party within the centre-right government of Lerroux. They ran Asturias as a council republic for a fortnight, but were isolated by the failure of the movement in the rest of Spain, and were finally crushed by Franco's army.
40. The Barcelona May Days was a spontaneous uprising of the Catalan working class in response to a counter-revolutionary coup instigated by the PSUC, the Spanish Stalinists. As a result, the Workers Party of Marxist Unification (POUM) was suppressed and its offices sacked.
41. The *Que Faire* group was founded at the end of 1934, and included among its leaders André Morel, called Ferrat, who had been editor of *L'Humanité*, the paper of the French Communist Party (PCF), Georges Kagan, otherwise known as Pierre Lenoir, who had also filled important posts in the PCF, and some former members of the Left Opposition such as Pietro Torielli (Pierre Rimbert) and Kurt Landau, who edited its journal.
42. The uprising of the Spanish generals against the Republic began on 18 July 1936, followed by a working-class counter-insurrection.
43. The CNT, organised by the Anarchists, and the UGT, dominated by the Socialists, were the two main Spanish trade-union federations. Along with such political parties as the POUM, they organised armed militias to fight the uprising of the generals.

The Secret of Hitler's Victory

Peter and Irma Petroff

Publisher's Note

Peter Petroff is a Russian: his wife, Irma Petroff, a German. They have lived through the Red revolution in Russia and the Brown revolution in Germany. Both are now exiles from their own countries. For his part in the Russian revolution of 1905, Peter Petroff was imprisoned, but after serving two years, he escaped and fled to England, where he lived until 1917 as an active worker in the British labour movement. During the war he was interned in this country. After the October Revolution of 1917, he returned to Russia, was appointed Chairman of the Foreign Relations Committee of the Soviets, and acted as Under-Secretary for Foreign Affairs in the Soviet government during M Chicherin's absence at Brest-Litovsk. In the next few years he held various offices, but in 1925 he and his wife resigned from the Russian Communist Party. They have lived for many years in Germany, working with the Socialists. Irma Petroff, before the war a lecturer and organiser for the Social-Democratic Party, was at one time head of the Education Department of the German Volga Republic. She is joint author with her husband of two books: *The Economic Regeneration of the Soviets* and *The Economic Development of the Soviet Union*.[1] When the Nazis seized power, the Petroffs' house was raided, their library and manuscripts were destroyed, and they and their children had to live underground. Finally, they managed to escape across the Belgian frontier ... In this book, they set out to answer the question that has perplexed so many onlookers in other countries: How did it come about that the apparently mighty forces of the German Left fell in one night, and without resistance, before the Nazi attack?

I. The World Stands Before a Riddle

In the short period of the Nazi rule in Germany a great deal has been written on the effects of this 'Brown pest'. Much has been said about the beastly terror, the ghastly torturing of scores of defenceless prisoners, about the concentration camps, where tens of thousands of innocent people are languishing, the persecution and humiliation of the Jewish part of the German people, the disgraceful robbing or destruction of institutions created in the past by the hard toil and sacrifices of the working class. Yet only a small portion of the vile crimes and atrocities committed by the Nazi regime have found reflection in the press.

No serious attempt has as yet been made, however, to answer the question how, in a great industrial country with a working class of high cultural standing, it was possible for a Hitler to destroy, within a few weeks, all the rights and liberties of the people and to gain unlimited power almost without any attempt at resistance. Yet this question is of vital importance.

How was it possible that such a strong and complex working-class movement, built up in decades of struggle, a movement absorbing all spheres of life of the workers, could collapse without resistance?

Were there not five million trade unionists, a million organised Social-Democrats, ready to meet the fascist onslaught? Had not the Socialist leaders at their disposal the *Reichsbanner*,[2] a strong military organisation counting over a million men, built up as a protective force against fascism? Had they not with them hundreds of thousands of men and women organised in labour, sport and cultural associations (amongst whom the Freethinkers' Union alone had more than 600,000 members), and also the youth organisations? Were not all these bodies, with their strong, influential press, their own clubrooms and meeting-places, their tremendous apparatus of paid organisers and secretaries, their numerous unpaid officials, in a position to mobilise their members rapidly?

Did not leading men of all these organisations hold important offices in the Reich, the states and the municipalities, which would have enabled them, as commissioners of police, mayors and magistrates, to use forces of the state on their side, or at all events to neutralise them? Was not a large part of the Prussian police organised in the *Reichsbanner*? Further, had not the Communist Party hundreds of thousands of militant members and millions of enthusiastic supporters? It is true their military organisation, the Red Front Association, was proscribed; but it existed illegally. And their auxiliary organisations – their youth, cultural and sport organisations, 'Red Help', 'Anti-Fascists', etc – were hardly less extensive than those of the Social-Democrats. Here again, there was a very strong and influential press, an army of organisers and secretaries, numerous unpaid officials, a fighting spirit, an almost militarised organisation adapted to rapid mobilisation.

Yet with all this such a complete breakdown, such a humiliating surrender! Never in the world's history has there been, after so much flag-waving and drumbeating, such a crushing defeat, such a complete collapse. The world stands before a riddle ... This phenomenon cannot be explained by the treachery or cowardice of certain leaders, nor by 'tactical' or even 'strategic' mistakes. What has happened here has been a complete collapse of well-organised and trained masses in face of an enemy of whom every individual of these masses had to expect personally the severest possible persecution, a phenomenon that stands in flagrant contradiction to all the notions of mass psychology!

Nevertheless, no one who has followed with open eyes – not through party spectacles – the developments in Germany during these last years could fail to see the approaching disaster. Of course nobody could have believed that the catastrophe would arrive so suddenly and under such disgraceful circumstances; but the elements of the approaching disaster were becoming more and more apparent. Not like a thunderbolt from the hands of a god, unexpected and inexplicable, did the catastrophe come. Striking into our consciousness like lightning, it nevertheless was the final result of a long and complicated process.

The unbiased analysis of the innate laws of these developments, with complete impartiality to all parties, groups or creeds, is the object of this work. It is not an easy task. And this, not only because the Hitler bandits have seized, together with the rest of our library, the material gathered during a number of years – newspaper cuttings, pamphlets and leaflets. The difficulty is enhanced by the fact that at present thousands of responsible and active men and women of all sections of the German labour movement are suffering in the hell of the concentration camps, have been tortured or done to death. A clear understanding of the causes of failure in the past may assist in finding the way out of disaster in the future. A movement that does not learn the lessons of its defeats is doomed.

II. The Weimar Republic and its Pillars

The breakdown of the Kaiser regime in 1918 suddenly put the power of the state into the hands of the German Social-Democracy, into hands that were not then prepared to take it by force.

Only with hesitation the new governing party settled down to the new situation. They did not use the newly-gained power in order to carry the revolution farther. The masses were eager to move forward – the Social-Democratic Party forced them back; and it had at times to rely on the support of reactionary forces, so that the Independent Social-Democratic Party withdrew from co-responsibility. In those days originated that bitter antagonism, that rift in the working-class movement, which later on led to the split also in the Independent Social-Democratic Party, and which so far has defied all attempts at reconciliation.

Thus the ruling party had got itself into an ambiguous position; the feeling of timid uncertainty never left them; they could not act with the resolution of the victor who clears away all that he finds unsound, so that he may rebuild on a new, stronger foundation. Instead, they tried to patch and shore up wherever possible. Reluctantly, under pressure from the mass, they had established the Republic; timidly they tried to set it to work. To them, danger appeared to be coming chiefly from the left.

The members of the Junker caste, who had always been the support of the darkest reaction in the darkest corners of Prussia, suffered by not so much as the loss of a hair of their heads. On the contrary, they liquidated their old debts by the aid of the inflation which followed, while keeping their old power. The Republic showed itself just as willing to shower gifts on the Junkers as the monarchy. The Junkers found for their dull, arrogant, monarchist sons open doors in the new *Reichswehr* and in the diplomatic service of the Republic, as in the days of the Kaiser. And their old party, the monarchist reactionary German Conservative Party, after cleverly renaming itself the German Nationalist People's Party,[3] could continue its struggle against the people, progress and liberty unmolested.

The magnates of capital, through the rapid growth of combinations and trusts, gained a monopolist position in the internal market, to the detriment of the consumers. This opened the way for them to increase the high war gains by no less high inflation gains in peacetime. Through the inflation, the state had given them a vehicle to shift the little savings of the millions into their own huge pockets, and thus hasten the proletarianisation of the middle classes, a tendency innate in the capitalist system. Their political party, the National Liberal Party, now renamed the German People's Party,[4] had tremendous influence. In coalition with this party, the Social-Democratic Party had perforce to carry on a big money policy – in its entire economic and financial policy, it was held in the net of the money lords. For this has always been the rule. In a highly developed capitalist country, every party coming into power, even if it is socialistic, must (if it does not change the system) carry on more or less avowedly the policy of the dominating capitalist class. So it was at that time in Germany; so it is today in Sweden; so it would be tomorrow in France. It is only necessary to call to mind the part old Stinnes[5] was allowed to play during the inflation, the power wielded by Thyssen,[6] Vögler,[7] and the rest in the state, the subsidies paid by the Reich to the capitalists of the Ruhr district, and to the banks.

The Civil Code, and the old Kaiserist Penal Code, were left in force in the Republic. Even the petrified judiciary remained fixed to the bench, because this curious 'revolution' respected their fixity of tenure. Instead of sweeping away the entire judicial and penal system, and rebuilding it in accordance with the changed ideas of the people, merely a few useful though trifling reforms were introduced; the prisons were humanised, and frequent amnesties were granted. The fact that during the period of the Weimar Republic sentences for similar offences were heavy as lead on offenders of the left and light as a feather on those of the right – a fact which caused much bitterness and discontent among the people – was regarded by consecutive Socialist and republican governments with complacency.

In internal administration also, they refrained from radical revolutionary changes. They supported the collapsing parts of the old structure with some no-longer-avoidable little reforms. They contented themselves with filling positions which became vacant, or were newly created, with their own partisans, or at any rate with republicans. However, these newly-manufactured republican civil servants failed to infuse a new spirit; most of them became victims of the stifling atmosphere. The popularly hated Civil Service, which under the Kaiser had been evolved into a caste ('true German and *pensionsberechtigt*'[8] was a byword before the war), and always trimmed its sails to suit the wind, was not reduced, but received new accretions. It realised the situation, changed its language and soon became 'true republican and *pensionsberechtigt*' (just as today it is 'true Nazi and *pensionsberechtigt*').

Even the Church, which in Germany had always been a formidable stronghold of reaction, received new revenues and new rights. Only those who had formally renounced it were liberated from its grip.

This development found symptomatic expression also in a variety of smaller things. No 'Vendôme Column'[9] was destroyed; the names of streets and institutes were left undisturbed. During the fourteen years of the Weimar Republic the many Socialist and democratic town councils could not find the courage to rename all those Kaiser Wilhelm Squares, Kaiserin Augusta Victoria Streets and Hohenzollern Avenues, of which there were dozens and hundreds in all towns of the Reich and all parts of Berlin. The exceptionally ugly Puppen-Allee (Dolls' Alley, in the local vernacular), an avenue in the Tiergarten flanked on both sides with Hohenzollern monuments – this testimony to the Kaiser's lack of taste was carefully preserved by the Republic. Even the birthday of the Republic, 9 November, they did not dare to proclaim a public holiday. In its place, 11 August, the date of the Constitution of Weimar, which satisfied nobody, was celebrated.

Instead of confiscating the properties of the imperial and lesser royal families, they were left in possession of all their property and huge sums were paid to them and their friends and concubines from the taxation of the people. Thus they were provided with the means to finance counter-revolution. In addition to that, the generals coming from the Junker caste enjoyed large pensions, even those who had risen against the Republic in the Kapp Putsch,[10] or who had taken an active part in monarchist gangs like the *Orgesch* or the Ehrhard Brigade.[11]

Even in the newly-formed army, the *Reichswehr*, these elements were accepted, and soon they had it under their control. When the *Reichswehr* was formed, the Socialists were in a dilemma. Just released from the war, they had little inclination to don again the grey coats which they had just discarded with a sigh of relief, and to surrender themselves to the hated militarism for another twelve years – the term of service prescribed by the Versailles Treaty. (They could not then know that the new German militarism would regard the military part of that treaty merely as a scrap of paper!) Should the Socialists advocate the workers to join the *Reichswehr*? Such a procedure promised little success and much loss of prestige, besides bringing the advocate himself who did not wish to join into an unpleasant position. On the other hand, there was a danger that the *Reichswehr* would attract exclusively reactionary, or at any rate unenlightened, elements, and thus in the hands of reactionary officers become a dangerous weapon against the working class and even against the Republic itself. This problem was well recognised and much discussed in Socialist circles, but no solution was found. Thus the inevitable happened: the *Reichswehr* became a reactionary force which, in the hands of reactionary officers, soon created a policy of its own and grew into a factor of first-class importance in the political life of the country.

The twelve-year term was as much a fiction as the strength of 100,000 men. With the military budget swelling under various ridiculous heads (military courts, for instance), the number of legal and illegal *Reichswehr* soldiers grew. Though the term of military service was twelve years, the men seemed never to get older. To prevent the lifting of the veil from these dangerous secrets, which were always respected by the Social-Democrats, who professed to be pacifists, the inevitable Gessler[12] remained permanently Minister of War, no matter how often governments changed. Finally, the government did not control the army, but the army the government. Gessler left the War Office only when the counter-revolution had become strong enough to put a general in his place. First, General Seeckt,[13] next General Groener,[14] and then General Schleicher.[15]

The complete breakdown of German militarism and the Kaiser regime left the German Social-Democracy as the only active force in the state, and so compelled them to take the liquidation of the war into their own hands. The lamentable short-sightedness of the Allied politicians and militarists increased the difficulties of this task, and compelled them finally to attach their signatures to that inglorious document, the Treaty of Versailles. At the moment, all sections of German public opinion were grateful to the Social-Democrats for this deed. However, the situation soon changed. When the natural consequences of this treaty brought about in Germany a nationalist reaction, the opponents turned the tables upon them and pointed their fingers at them, saying: 'It is you who have signed this disgraceful Treaty of Versailles!'

The Social-Democratic Party, by jumping into the breach, had allowed the war criminals to shift the responsibility for the mad policy of the Kaiser on to their own shoulders. Their further policy made it possible, even when there was no necessity, to strengthen in the eyes of the masses the appearance of responsibility. This happened in the case of the Dawes Plan and, again, of the Young Plan.[16] In both cases the reactionary parties and the classes they represented were anxious to get these schemes adopted by the *Reichstag*, though trying to screen themselves from responsibility. Instead of leaving these people to answer for it, the Social-Democrats rushed forward to take the burden – perhaps a very generous, but a very stupid, policy, which was used against them by their unscrupulous opponents, both from right and left, with much success.

In another respect, the Versailles Treaty had dangerous results for the internal policy of the German Republic. The clauses referring to disarmament were on the one hand so drastic, and on the other hand so full of loop-holes, that militarist minds were simply invited to evade them. As the Republic had not, at the very outset, deprived the Junkers and the militarists of their power, but, on the contrary, had left to them a free hand in the military sphere, the latter soon embarked upon a course of secret rearmament. Consecutive governments, including many Socialist ministers, consciously closed their eyes to these developments, but thereby put themselves increasingly into the hands of the militarists, who clearly understood their opportunities. As to the Communists, they were muzzled by Moscow, because the Soviet government in matters of technical and industrial assistance had established a strange mutual relationship with the *Reichswehr*. Thus, the regulations of the Versailles Treaty, designed to destroy German militarism, actually helped to endow it with new life.

If Social-Democracy in 1918 had, in its fear of the revolutionary masses, failed to go down to bedrock and effect sweeping changes, the Kapp Putsch in 1920 and the murder of Rathenau[17] in 1922, with the popular movement arising out of it, provided it with an opportunity to make up for its omission. But as the priest of law and order it was fearful of mass action, and tried to replace it by the institution of the *Staatsgerichtshof* (a special court with the democratic drunkard Niedner[18] as chief judge) and by the promulgation of the infamous Defence of the Republic Act.

The Weimar Constitution gave expression to the democratic and social ideas on which the Republic was built up. It proclaimed that all power emanates from the people; it created at last the franchise system, fought for for decades: adult suffrage and secret ballot, equal and direct vote, in the Reich, the states and the municipalities. It proclaimed liberty of opinion and conscience and made some attempts at establishing a right to work or maintenance of the citizen. Nevertheless, it contained the germ of counter-revolution.

The Weimar Constitution endowed the President with far-reaching powers. He was in control of the armed forces of the country. He had the right to dissolve the *Reichstag* and govern the country till the next election, by Article 48 of the Constitution, which permitted him to suspend important parts of the Constitution. The part played by this article in preparing the ground for the fascist counter-revolution is well known.

The President who was endowed with such enormous powers was not elected by Parliament, which could have exercised a certain control over him, but by a direct vote of the people. While a member of parliament represented only sixty thousand electors, Hindenburg[19] in 1932 received nineteen million votes. That gave the President a preponderance over the *Reichstag*. The authors of the Weimar Constitution learned nothing from history.

The direct vote of the people had already put the power of the state into the hands of an adventurer once before.

When, in France, the saviour of bourgeois society, Cavignac[20] (the French Noske),[21] had piled up in the streets of Paris thousands of proletarian corpses; when the achievements of 1848 had been destroyed step by step, the little Napoleon, elected by the direct vote of the people, was able, in 1851, to put an end to the republic by a *coup d'état*.

In Germany, when the modest achievements of the so-called revolution of 1918 had been sufficiently reduced, and when the enormous power given to the President by this Constitution fell into the lap of an old monarchist general, the way was open for counter-revolution. The way was even already mapped out for him by the Social-Democratic President, Ebert,[22] when he made the *Reichswehr* march into Saxony and Thuringia to turn out the red governments he disliked; and down this precipitous path Hindenburg now slid, when on 20 July 1932, also with the assistance of the *Reichswehr*, he turned out the Prussian government, putting in its place as Commissar of the Reich the hero of wartime fame, von Papen.[23] Though there was one difference — while Ebert required two divisions for the job, the Field-Marshal von Hindenburg accomplished it with one lieutenant and four men.

★ ★ ★

The birth hour of the Republic, which was the death hour of the World War, brought to the masses of the people in Germany a rapid and considerable improvement of their position. The men returned from the war, the blockade was raised, and long-vanished foods and goods reappeared in the market — the 'turnip period'[24] had come to an end. The change-over of industry to peace production immediately provided work for many hands; an industrial boom began. It is true that in the following years of increasing inflation the German workers became the coolies of the whole world, but at least they had not to suffer from nerve-racking unemployment. The eight-hour day had become a reality, although it was not incorporated in an Act of Parliament, but only in the demobilisation orders. The *Betriebsrätegesetz* (Works Committee Act) strengthened the power of the working class; the trade unions experienced a tremendous influx of membership and became a power in the state. The workers, hitherto always politically oppressed in Germany, had gained much in self-confidence; the women had risen from second-rate human beings to citizens; the abolition of conscription had liberated youth from a much-detested servility.

Social legislation developed in every direction. Social institutions established in the towns became a model for the whole world. Here, many thousands of Socialist men and women found a field of activity where they could engage in extensive social work. From the cradle to the grave the German citizen was under the social care of the state. The maternity and infant welfare service directed its attention to the first appearance of the future citizen. Crèches, infant schools, day nurseries, school feeding, school clinics, school doctors and nurses, holiday homes, served the up-growing proletarian child. The *Jugendämter* (Municipal 'Youth Service'), which were unequalled in the whole world, cared also for youth after school age — youth clubs, hostels, sports and playgrounds, occupational advice, sexual advice, classes of all kinds, were only a few of their many beneficent activities. The communal health service with its preventive measures against tuberculosis, health insurance covering numerous institutions, the insurance against accident, disablement and old age, and especially the insurance against unemployment and crisis, the municipal house-building schemes — all this is an indelible page in the history of the Weimar Republic – and, this must be admitted, also in the history of German Social-Democracy, on whose shoulders the whole structure rested.

Of no less importance than its triumphs in the social field were its attainments in the cultural field. It would be no exaggeration to say that the influence of German Social-Democracy has within the last thirty years, culturally, completely reshaped the German proletariat – the dance-hall girl had become a hiking girl. The reader of printed trash had grown into a literary epicure. The large masses of the German proletariat stood, as regards their interest in natural science, economics, history and high-class fiction, shoulders high above the proletarian masses of other countries. However, it must be said that apart from the twelve to fifteen millions of proletarians under the influence of Communist and Socialist organisations there were also in Germany many millions of indifferent lower-middle-class people, peasants and loafers, and it is to them that Hitler now owes his strength.

Nevertheless, in the cultural field the Weimar Republic failed in many respects, and could not but fail. German political Catholicism since the days of Bismarck's *Kulturkampf*[25] had created a powerful political instrument, the Centre Party,[26] which, after having been always the most faithful ally of the reactionary Junkers, now with flying banners came over to the republican ranks, at least in all those states where the monarch had been a Protestant. In Bavaria, where the throne had been occupied by the Catholic Wittelsbach,[27] the position was somewhat different. The Bavarian part of the Centre Party split up and established itself as a separate organisation under the name Bavarian People's Party. In the Reich, however, in Prussia, and in most of the other states, the now republican Centre Party with its many working-class adherents became the second pillar of the Weimar Republic. Its acute politicians, who always knew how to suck honey out of all blossoms, utilised the situation to their best advantage. By their alliance with the atheist masses of Social-Democracy they succeeded in increasing the power of the Catholic Church to an extent which they could never have attained under the avowedly Christian monarchy. Out of consideration for the 'Republican' Centre Party, the Social-Democratic Party did not fully realise any of the demands of its own programme in the educational field – it segregated neither the state nor the school from the church, it did not even remove the blasphemy clause from the penal code. The attacks of the Communists, who called this Republic a *Pfaffenrepublik* (a priests' republic) were to a great extent justified. This unholy alliance weighing down the Social-Democrats has to be borne in mind; otherwise their whole policy appears incomprehensible.

In spite of all this, the revolution brought about great changes in the school system. The eight years' primary school lost its dull, oppressive, barrack-like character. The slogan 'school reform' became very popular. Through the parents' councils and parents' meetings, the parents were interested and their collaboration was sought for. Large meetings of workers were discussing educational problems. The uniformity of the entire school system, the admission of capable proletarian children to secondary schools, which hitherto had been an almost exclusive privilege of the well-to-do, the introduction of new methods of teaching – all this was adopted in principle although never completely realised. Modern methods, improved textbooks, shaping the lessons of the children to suit the current interests and environment, cultivating the community spirit – all that was certainly great gain. With new teachers a new spirit was introduced into primary education. However, the old teachers also were retained, but only a small part of them adapted themselves. The parents were granted the right to withdraw their children from religious instruction; though where such children were in a small minority they were often subjected to persecution by reactionary teachers. In industrial, towns, largely atheist, 'the two pillars' came to an agreement behind the scenes in a kindly mutual accommodation – secular schools were provided for the sake of the children of Social-Democrats (though opposed by the Communists, who feared losing the chance of influencing the bulk of the children). In return, the Social-Democrats permitted, besides the ordinary Christian school, the provision of Catholic schools. The new methods of the secular schools, in the spirit of mutual aid, built up on the child's world, permeated the entire primary-school system. The secular system comprised only a small part of the children (in Berlin there were about fifty such schools), but these schools became the means of an enormous educational elevation in the circles affected by them.

The secondary schools and universities were entirely neglected by the Social-Democrats, who almost alone were responsible for all progress in primary education. In this field they were content with a few isolated nurseries for higher culture with a proletarian colour, like the Berlin Karl Marx College – this college being, it is true, the apex achievement for the world. Otherwise, the whole field of secondary education was left to the reactionaries. Small wonder, therefore, that the secondary schools and the universities became the breeding-ground for nationalist ruffianism. But the youth coming from those modern schools, together with those affected by the proletarian children's movement – the Social-Democratic 'Red Falcons' and the Communist 'Pioneers' – and, along with the rest of the young generation, influenced by the Socialist and Communist youth movement, have during the short period of the Weimar Republic built up a peculiar proletarian culture such as has not yet been attained in any other country. The students, however, and the pupils of the ordinary high schools still remained under the influence of the old petrified professors and teachers. Many proletarian parents consequently declined, on principle, to give their children secondary education for fear they might be lost to the working class.

★ ★ ★

In the economic history of the German Republic, three consecutive phases can be discerned – inflation, concentration, rationalisation.

The big war-profiteers like Stinnes, Thyssen, Otto Wolff,[28] *et hoc genus omne*,[29] who had known how to distil minted gold out of millions of corpses, now transformed themselves into revolution and inflation profiteers, or were overtaken by newcomers.

If the war had meant for these a source of new capital, the revolution and its child the Weimar Republic had provided new chances. It is true that the Republic at the outset aimed at getting rid of large fortunes, but its good intentions proved, especially in its economic policy, to be again the stones paving the way to Hell. In its unparalleled self-denial, this 'social state' actually bred types like Stinnes and Flick,[30] who hated the Republic and used this hatred as a moral justification for tax-defaulting, robbery of the state, and financing counter-revolutionary plots. Yet the state continued to feed them with credits which they used to further inflation, and which they 'repaid' in valueless paper marks.

This time of whirlwind-raging proletarianisation of the middle class, which diverted huge slices of the property of the people into the gaping jaws of industrial sharks, gave birth to that type of capitalist which indiscriminately bought up concerns and enterprises of all descriptions – the type which in the minds of their contemporaries is indissolubly bound up with the name of Stinnes. Stinnes was not the creator of mighty concerns systematically built up and internally connected. At random he bought anything: steelworks, newspapers, hotels, ships, coalmines, textile mills, foodstuffs – and politicians. Though these blown-up trusts and concerns soon burst like soap bubbles, many ruined small and medium businessmen strewed the path, and these, together with the unemployed officers and the impoverished intellectuals, formed the shock battalions of the coming counter-revolution.

When again – at the expense of the working class – the mark was stabilised, the inflation profiteers gave way to deflation profiteers; or became such. A period of comparatively coherent concentration followed, combining industrial enterprises of a definite interconnection into powerful trusts: the epoch of monopoly capitalism dawned.

Everywhere, steam power was superseded by the victorious advance of electricity, which brought about equivalent production with a much smaller number of hands. Now, in the trustified industry, an enormous mechanisation and rationalisation set in. The influx of foreign, especially American, capital strengthened the process. A far-reaching weakening of the working class and its organisations was the result. A storm attack against the social achievements of the proletariat began.

On the land, the agrarian policy of prewar times was simply continued. Supported by tariffs and subsidies, the Junkers continued to grow cereals instead of turning their attention to high-class products which would tend to make German agriculture capable of meeting competition and self-supporting without state aid, simultaneously reducing German imports. No benefit accrued to the peasants, for neither did they get subsidies worthy of mention, nor did they derive any tangible advantage from the tariffs. No wonder many of them fell under the wheels of capitalism, and the number of victims sold up increased constantly.

The reparation payments imposed upon Germany in consequence of its defeat in the war, which had been brought about by the criminal policy of her statesmen in the time of the Kaiser, increased the economic misery of the people. While the impoverished state continued to give millions by way of subsidy to the agrarians and heavy industry (700 million marks of 'compensation' for the Ruhr magnates and 300 million marks for the swindling concern of Flick, which latter had been allotted by Brüning[31] shortly before the breakdown with the silent assent of the Social-Democrats, and paid out by von Papen), the masses were sinking into poverty. Workers and employees were suffering from wage cuts and unemployment; peasants and small shopkeepers from the reduced purchasing-power of their customers; intellectuals and artists from the increasing inability of the masses and municipalities to spend money on cultural objects.

Those very Junkers and industrialists who were the real gainers from the Weimar Republic took great pains to stir up the discontent of the masses, to put them against the state and to build up from their ranks a prætorian guard for its overthrow. It was they who financed, a decade before, the monarchist *Orgesch*, and the Ehrhard brigade. From their coffers, always well filled, thanks to the Republic and its policy, the Brown gangs were equipped and paid, and on their shoulders Hitler could now climb to power.

Thus the Republic and Social-Democracy, on whose shoulders it rested, always felt themselves threatened. The more it yielded to the pressure and made concessions, the stronger grew the Communists on the other side, and menaced them from the left. The result was a vacillating, opportunist and indecisive policy. The discontent of the proletarian masses with this development, by which they found themselves cheated of the fruits of the revolution, added fuel to the fire of the Communist movement, increasing the pressure from the left.

And so Social-Democracy was compelled to defend itself on two fronts. This led, not only to a vacillating policy, to a zigzag course, reminiscent of the Kaiser, it also resulted in a desire to look round for support from other quarters, which grew out of a feeling of innate weakness. Instead of Liberty and Equality, it now inscribed Law and Order on its flag. For ten years the question, wide coalition or narrow, was one of the main problems of German politics. For German Social-Democrats it was no longer a question *whether* they should form a coalition with bourgeois parties, but merely with *which* of them. Even the German People's Party, the party of the magnates of capital, was acceptable as a coalition partner. To keep these coalitions alive, by which they hoped to strengthen the Republic, they made concession after concession. The systematic piecemeal destruction of the social and political achievements of the proletariat followed. The eight-hour day was sacrificed, the social welfare services were depleted, the various benefits cut down, the wages reduced. Meanwhile, expenditure on armaments, tariffs and indirect taxation increased, while the capitalists succeeded by means of the wage tax to make even the payment of direct taxation a privilege of the working class.

All these measures naturally did not add to the security of the Republic. The Communists hated it. The supporters of the Republic outside the Social-Democratic ranks were shrinking more and more.

Social-Democracy never lost the feeling that the Republic was in danger. For that reason, it never dared to entrust it to anybody; it was always struggling to keep in office. However, as a result of this, in the eyes of the people, all the responsibility for the large capitalist and great landowner policies, for Versailles and its consequences, for the *Reichswehr* and its secret rearming, for the social and cultural depletion, for the corruption and mass-misery, finally even for the crisis, fell upon them.

Certainly, the Republic, in the first years of its existence, under the leadership of Social-Democracy, had created all that which it was now partially destroying. The social state with its widespread welfare institutions was the work of their hands. The universal franchise system, the extensive liberty of speech, meeting, demonstration and press, the right of political asylum – all these cultural attainments, which had been the far-off dream of millions in the time of the Kaiser, it had struggled for, built up, and fortified. But now, when Social-Democracy – like Penelope[32] – was pulling to pieces by night what it had been weaving by day, the masses were willing to see only its guilt of today, not its service of yesterday. Honesty demands today the recognition that its retrograde movement in the social, cultural and political field was not simply 'treason', but an attempt to save the Republic, by way of a dangerous operation – an operation like the one about which the doctor telegraphed: 'Operation successful, patient dead.'

To protect its sick child, the Republic, Social-Democracy tried to turn Prussia into a fortress; the less they could trust the inner strength of the Republic, the more they placed all their hope on the Prussian police.

In this field they attained considerable success. Under the Kaiser, the police had been so hated that no dog would take a bone from them. The Social-Democrats civilised this body, transformed it, and brought it into a normal relationship with the public. They soaked it with the Republican spirit and turned it into a reliable instrument of the Weimar Republic. In this regard, they had made all preparation for a successful defence of the Weimar state. The police force was well organised, splendidly armed (with armoured cars, machine-guns, hand-grenades, machine-pistols, carbines and tear-gas bombs), and for street fighting was superbly trained. The fact that it was more seldom used against the foes of the Republic on the right than against radical workers on the left, and that the misguided Social-Democratic Police President, Zörgiebel,[33] on 1 May 1929, employed it against workers celebrating May Day, thus causing the Neukölln massacre, was not the fault of its organisation, but of the policy of the government whose obedient tool it was. To keep the Prussian police in their hands, the Social-Democrats were willing to make any sacrifice. The sly Centre could, as their partner in the Prussian coalition government, squeeze one concession after another from them, both in the cultural and political spheres.

Through their policy of forming coalitions with non-republican parties, the republicans had their hands tied in their struggle with the right. During the terms of office of both Gessler and Groener, the *Reichswehr* had received only reactionary elements into its ranks. While the police was strictly republican, the *Reichswehr* was sternly monarchist. The unofficial military organisations it had created, the *Stahlhelm*[34] and '*Schwarze Reichswehr*',[35] with its notorious murder gang, 'St Vehme', flourished. The National Socialist prætorian guard of the heavy industries in 1923 made an armed rising, which called for little courage in this indulgent Republic. The *Reichswehr* division, led by General von Lossow,[36] sent against the insurrectionists, exercised friendly neutrality. In contrast with that, General Müller, with his troops, sent by President Ebert against the constitutionally-elected red government in Saxony proved very energetic.

Even after the Nazi rising in Munich in 1923, the republican government took no effective steps against the armed counter-revolutionary gangs. They were able to continue their terrorism against working-class meetings without hindrance. Thus, both Communists and Social-Democrats were compelled to take counter-measures – the *Rote Frontkämpfer-Bund* of the Communists and the *Reichsbanner* created by the Social-Democrats with the support of other republicans quickly developed into powerful defensive organisations. While the *Rote Frontkämpfer-Bund* proved themselves determined fighters in the struggles in the street fighting in German towns, which took place not always without their initiative, the big *Reichsbanner* was possessed by an almost Tolstoyan spirit – as regards internal strife; on the other hand, they felt themselves as a reserve of the *Reichswehr* and defenders of the Fatherland as the 'Young Guards of the German Republic' ...

The Social-Democratic Prussian Minister for Internal Affairs, Severing,[37] considering himself under an obligation to the bourgeois coalition partners for the maintenance of law and order, felt himself 'compelled' to prohibit the *Rote Frontkämpfer-Bund*, while the semi-military organisations of the Nazis and the *Stahlhelm* were allowed freely to develop.

In the defensive struggle against the Communists, who did not always employ straightforward methods, Social-Democratic ministers and police presidents, who had been caught in the bureaucratic machine, were frightened into using measures which later came back like a boomerang and hit their own heads. Prohibition of demonstrations and meetings; censorship of plays and films; suppression of newspapers and the scandalous expedient of compulsory insertion in newspapers of governmental statements which had to be printed by the newspapers in a prescribed position without comment; increased penalties for libelling ministers; the institution of a special state court whose brutal sentences were again chiefly directed against the left – all these measures, in the long run, could not but prove scourges against the entire working class.

While the right as well as the left were eulogising dictatorship and trying hard to practise it to the best of their abilities, the Social-Democrats fervently desired to be a strong rampart of democracy. Unfortunately the measures they adopted to this end proved fatal to the very democracy they were intended to protect.

Even institutions which to the superficial observer appeared to be the very perfection of democracy proved in practice to be anti-democratic. This applies to the direct election of the President by the people, but not less to the system of proportional representation, an old plank of the Social-Democratic platform. It is true that election by the party list permitted a distribution of parliamentary seats which exactly reflected recorded votes. But it had certain other effects which no one had intended or foreseen, and which greatly assisted in lowering the prestige of parliament in the eyes of the people. The close ties between members of parliament and their electors prevailing in other parliaments vanished as though by a wave of the wand. This, it is true, made members independent of local wishes, but it entirely destroyed all contact with their electors, and brought them into complete dependence on their party caucuses, to whom alone they now felt responsible. It was the party caucuses who in reality appointed the members. Outstanding personalities disappeared from parliament. The politically unorganised electors found themselves powerless – they could influence the composition of parliament only as regards the strength of the various party groups, but no longer as regards individual members. The personality of the candidate ceased to play any part. Thus it became possible that the Nazi Party put forward ex-criminals and that they were elected. In this way the level of the German parliaments sank to a degree that would have been quite impossible under the single-member system. But no Socialist voice was raised against this system – the party machine, the real beneficiaries of this system, controlled the press. However, it must be said that the prestige of parliament was certainly not raised by the free fights so dear both to the Nazis and Communists. A parliament having such a weak hold on the people could easily be set aside. So early as 1923, the first breach was made in the parliamentary system, when the *Reichstag* surrendered some of its powers to the capitalist Stresemann[38] Cabinet, empowering it to issue decrees.

This system of government by decree, by setting aside the weak parliaments, later on, under Chancellor Brüning, who was tolerated by the Social-Democrats, degenerated into an orgy. Limitation of elementary political rights, reduction of wages and unemployment benefits, fixing of prices, subsidies for Junkers and capitalist concerns running into millions ('Osthilfe', 'Danatbank',[39] Flick), usurpation of the functions of local government, imposition of new taxation, and finally the whole budget – all this was done by decree. When, in the name of the saving of democracy, the country for two years had been governed by dictatorial methods against the interest of the people, an emergency ladder had been constructed, then a Papen, a Schleicher, and finally a Hitler, could climb into power.

III. The Internal Decay of the German Labour Movement

The World War had changed the psychology of the international working class. One might indeed speak of a mental reversion to savagery. The human being, the individual, counted for little. Only when it was lumped together into regiments, divisions and armies, it might expect to get the attention accorded to one single grain of rice in a bag. Up till then, collectively-minded socialism had taken from individualistically-minded liberalism its humanitarian notions – its respect for the right of the human being as such. Now there was a danger of a barren barrack-like collectivism developing, which contemptuously ignored the rights of man. For several years human lives had been destroyed by machine methods; all the world over people had got used to reading day by day of thousands of killed and wounded; sensibilities had been blunted, people had lost the capacity to feel for the individual victim. That resulted in a general callousness. The soullessness of modern labour, which had reached its climax in consequence of the rationalisation, became the outstanding feature of the whole period. In every sphere of life the same tendency to the massive, the heaped-up, the organised and soulless, was noticeable. Everywhere mechanisation and rationalisation, the constant contact with automatic machines, turned a whole generation into automata, the loudspeaker overwhelmed the voice of humanity.

In Germany, during the war, a neglected, fidgety, underfed, hysterical, precocious, young generation had grown up, lacking not only in guidance but also in an inner calm and modesty, which might have induced them to learn and work out conceptions of their own. They wanted to get their views ready-made for them, like 'reach-me-downs'. Smart and quick they got hold of socialist catchwords, then very much in fashion. Now this 'turnip youth' (a term reminiscent of the 'turnip period' of the war) living in this rationalised world, soon got into the habit of ridiculing such notions as honesty, truthfulness and loyalty, as 'old-fashioned prejudices'.

The ideals that inspired the working-class movement before the war meant nothing to this new generation which seemed so different. The feeling of friendship and warm-hearted comradeship between the members of the party disappeared. The readiness to take up the fight against all injustice, against any oppression of man by man, wherever and in whatever form it might appear, had vanished. This generation was devoid of the sincere enthusiasm for the future free socialist commonwealth that would abolish all class distinctions, all oppression, and would guarantee to the proletariat and to mankind generally liberty of development of personality and its creative powers. It was striving only for immediate practical aims, and desired striking, simple slogans. While in prewar times every revolutionary worker had been incessantly learning, trying to become a worthy fighter for the great cause of socialism, for this postwar youth all means were good enough to attain its ends. Lies and slander, disloyalty and forgery, and the use of violence against opponents were regarded by them as legitimate weapons. They were fully convinced that the end justifies the means.

The gulf between Social-Democratic and Communist conceptions widened. The growing enmity between the two sections destroyed class solidarity.

While in the Social-Democratic ranks extreme revisionism predominated, according to which the ultimate object, socialism, is nothing and the 'half-loaf' is everything, while the Social-Democrats turned from Marx to Lassalle, idealised the capitalist state, the Communists on the other hand were idealising violence and dictatorship as it materialised in Russia. Their ideal was not the 'dictatorship of the proletariat' as advocated by Marx during a short transitional period from capitalism to socialism, when the proletariat as a class uses political power in order to abolish all class distinctions, and to reorganise society on a basis of equality. Their ideal was the dictatorship of a party, its executive, its general secretary, as it developed in Russia, as a form of government for long duration based upon a strong militarised oppressive state machinery.

However, the most dangerous feature of the Communist Party of Germany was that its policy was not the result of the application of Communist principles to the changing economic and political conditions of Germany, but always followed the line taken by the governing caucus in Russia in accordance with the demands of the foreign policy of the Soviet Union. For their policy and tactics were not laid down by leaders chosen by the members of the German Communist Party, but by the department of the Russian government, the Comintern. Every team of leaders that dared to show signs of revolt was unmercifully turned out. Such 'palace revolutions' were frequent. Under the motto 'Bolshevisation of the party', all honest, thinking elements were driven out of leading positions and the party was placed under the command of a numerous corps of party officers which extended its rule also over all Communist auxiliary organisations.

The more the Stalin dictatorship oppressed the masses of the people in Russia, the more the existence of democratic liberties in neighbouring countries appeared to them as a menace. 'It must be night where Stalin's stars are shining.' Consequently Moscow was carrying on a systematic struggle against the supporters of German democracy, while the friendship with the reactionary elements in Germany was as strong as it is with Mussolini. That may sound paradoxical, but an unbiased analysis of the Russian foreign policy and of the policy of the Comintern of the last decade will confirm this. All European Communist parties and their parliamentary groups are carrying out this policy, sometimes without even themselves noticing it.

At all elections, in the press, in meetings and in parliaments, the attacks of the Communists were directed chiefly against the parties of the left. The struggle against reaction seemed to them of minor importance. We need only recall to mind the curious conduct of the Communist Party during the Kapp Putsch, when they in the beginning declined to support the general strike that defeated the *putsch*. In this connection it is also interesting to note the friendly article by Karl Radek in *Pravda*, the central organ of the Russian Communist Party in those days, wherein he assured the Kapp government of the friendly cooperation of the Russian government.[40] Strangely enough, this article escaped public attention abroad. Yet from there a clear line can be traced to the negotiations between Radek and the Nazi leader Reventlow[41] during the Ruhr occupation in the Schlageter[42] case, the supply of armaments to Germany, and the friendship between the chiefs of the Red Army and the *Reichswehr* up to the extensive commercial relations in the first months of the Hitler rule between Stalin and Nazi Germany; relations which the inspired press tried to conceal from the poor Communists who were tortured in the Hitler hell.

In theory the Communists advocate a clear anti-national point of view. They do not divide mankind vertically into nations, but horizontally into classes. The worker has no country, he therefore has to consider every question solely from the point of view of the interest of the working class, which is identical in all countries. In international conflicts the question has to be decided in each case whether the workers of a given country should remain neutral, or actively support their 'own' country or its 'enemy' in order to defend the class interests of the proletariat. This clear international idea of class struggle as advocated by Lenin during the World War, as practised by those German Communists who in 1918 fought in the ranks of the Red Army against Germany, leaves no room for any sentimental patriotism.

However, in reality the policy of the German Communist Party had quite a different appearance. In order to catch votes, to gain influence on unenlightened elements, yes, just to further the interests of the Russian government at the French frontier, the German Communist Party did not shrink from using nationalist slogans at times, from advocating a purely nationalist policy and even from cooperation with nationalist elements, in order to attain definite objects. We need only mention the actions of the Communists during the occupation of the Ruhr, the so-called 'red plebiscite' which had been initiated by the monarchist Steel Helmets jointly with the Nazis, in order to turn out of office the Prussian government made up of a coalition of the Social-Democrats and the Catholic Centre.[43] At the outset the Communists had, along with the Social-Democrats, opposed this plebiscite. Suddenly they received counter orders from Moscow and they immediately wheeled round, and called the fascist plebiscite a 'red plebiscite' and harnessed themselves as the third horse to the fascist carriage. When the Nazis began to develop into a mass movement the Communists tried to dish them by excelling them in nationalism. In their propaganda during the last elections of the Republic they made extensive use of nationalist slogans. It was a despicable race between Nazis and Communists for the palm of demagogy. When in the winter of 1932 the Nazis, out of a far-seeing counter-revolutionary policy of theirs, found it opportune during the election campaign to provoke a strike at the Berlin municipal transport institutions, in order to gain influence amongst the transport workers and thus later on to make a general strike impossible, the Communists in their blind hatred against the Social-Democrats walked into the trap.

As is generally known, the parliamentary system, as a form of government, was repugnant to the Communists, who wanted to replace it by the soviet system. Nevertheless, compelled by circumstances to participate in parliamentary work, they could have used parliament to do good work by sharp but honest criticism. Instead, they took every opportunity to destroy parliament, to undermine it, to discredit it in the eyes of the people. They were the first to interfere deliberately with the work of parliament by free fights and cat-calls, thus degrading the forms of public life generally. The Nazis, who though from different motives were just as hostile to parliamentarism, need only follow the road paved by the Communists, but going the whole length when they became stronger. Consequently, Communist and Nazi tactics frequently coincided, and this always caused much justifiable indignation among the parties of the left. Less justifiable was such indignation in the case of collaboration of the two extreme parties for the securing of amnesties. Under the prevailing judiciary, which threw thousands of Communist workers into prison for long terms, while systematically protecting criminals of the right, it would be dishonest to reproach the Communists for this.

The general degradation of political usage caused by the Communists had a destructive influence on the entire political life of the country. Lies and slander in the press, systematic breaking up of meetings, disruption of labour organisations, man-handling of opponents – all this destroyed the old democratic forms of public life.

The big political mass meetings with free discussion, to which the German proletariat had been accustomed for many decades, disappeared. They were replaced by a stereotyped form of 'demonstration', where, with much flag-waving, stereotyped speeches of the official nominees of a party were delivered, friends and opponents being precluded from expressing any opinions. This development just suited the interests of a labour bureaucracy which estranged itself from the rank and file and which had good reason to fear public open criticism.

The same methods led to similar consequences in labour organisations not constructed on party lines, when these disruptive tactics were continued. The forming of factions by the Communists, their efforts to cause splits, the disruptive activities of their agents, had a paralysing effect on all organisations. All labour bodies became emasculated, their internal life stagnated. Here again, the consequence was an increase of power for the bureaucrats, who could now denounce every disagreeable critic as a Communist, and expel him or put him out of action. Stagnation in all labour organisations was the consequence.

Jesuitism, elevated by the Communists to a principle, their hero-worship, their admiration for violence, the confusion created by their nationalist slogans, their deliberate discrediting of parliamentarism, their practical annihilation of liberty of speech, their disruption of labour organisations – all these assisted in preparing the soil, psychologically, for fascism.

It must, however, be borne in mind that the Communist Party of Germany, though in a certain sense a road-builder for fascism, has also prepared the struggle against it. It was the Communists who kept alive in the minds of the German proletariat the idea of revolution surrendered by the Social-Democrats, and emphasised the socialist aim, although not in its classical form. In their organisations, at their demonstrations, throughout their actions, there was noticeable a virile and fighting spirit for which one might search in vain at Social-Democratic meetings and demonstrations. It is true that, being internally corrupt, completely dependent on the Russian foreign policy, they also failed at the decisive moment; but mitigating circumstances have to be admitted. Had the Communists, at the time of Papen's or later Hitler's ascent to power, placed themselves at the head of an armed mass resistance, they would have been met, not only by the storm-troops of the Nazis, as would have been the case in such an action led by the Social-Democrats, but also by Severing's police, by the Steel Helmets and the *Reichswehr*, while the entire middle class at home and abroad would have been seized by the fear of the spectre of Communism. And the fact that, at the present moment, the Communist Party in Germany has taken up the struggle, all along the line, with revolutionary heroism and tremendous sacrifices, shows what a sound proletarian kernel it contains.

★ ★ ★

The breakdown of German Social-Democracy before the assault of the Hitler gangs can only be grasped by laying bare the cracks in the building, for long noticeable, and what caused them.

Before the war, the Marxian tendency was predominant in the German Social-Democratic Party. Since their disgrace on 4 August 1914, when they voted the war credits for the Kaiser, the party had hopelessly sunk in the morass of revisionism. It veered more and more to the right until it completely lost its Marxian compass. Since then it has drifted towards the most mediocre opportunism and the shallowest reformism. It regarded its revolutionary past with a contemptuous smile as a youthful sin. For decades the theorists of revisionism had tried to prove that the Marxist theory was obsolete and outworn. They declared that as a result of the development of capitalist combination, and the growth of trusts, there would be no more crises; that the theory of the concentration of capital and the increasing proletarianisation of the masses was refuted by the increasing stability of the medium enterprises, especially in agriculture, as well as by the 'diffusion of wealth' through the growing number of small investors; that class antagonism, far from becoming more acute, was decreasing, that there was no pauperisation of the masses. They therefore rejected the Marxian theory of class struggle and advocated collaboration with the capitalist class.

In postwar times there was an influx into Social-Democracy of new masses that were not class-conscious proletarians, coming chiefly from the civil service and the bourgeois intellectuals. These people were not revisionists – they could not wish to revise the Marxian theory, just because it was unknown to them. Thus the coalition policy became the alpha and omega of the tactics of the Social-Democrats, who were more and more falling into line with the capitalist state, while their socialist aim became more and more nebulous. Dozens of ministers, hundreds of prominent permanent officials, governors of provinces, police presidents and other high officials coming from the ranks of Social-Democracy and their following of middle-class job-hunters, suddenly found themselves in the administration of the capitalist state. To them it seemed that a gigantic revolution had taken place, that the state had become completely changed. However, what had changed was merely their own position in the state – for the masses of the people everything had remained as it was. To this stratum of Social-Democratic new bourgeoisie, numerous influential and excessively remunerative posts in the industrial undertakings of the state and municipalities also became accessible. In the party class distinctions had arisen, and became more and more accentuated.

In all working-class organisations, a powerful bureaucratic machine sprang into existence, and with it a new class of bureaucrat. This machine possessed an extensive power. It had in its hands the entire labour press; tens of thousands of posts were available in the Reich, in the states, in the municipalities and in their numerous institutions and enterprises, in social insurance, in the cooperative societies, in innumerable offices of trade unions and other labour organisations, in editorial offices and party enterprises, in the labour clubs, bookshops, libraries and welfare institutions of the working-class movement. In bestowing these posts the influence of 'the machine', the 'bureaucracy', was decisive. Thus hundreds of thousands of people became economically dependent in one way or another on this labour bureaucracy, or they hoped by its good offices to obtain a job for themselves or for a member of their family, be it only as night-watchman or scavenger. The bureaucrats knew quite well how to turn this economic power of theirs into political power. It was they who had the last word (thanks to the proportional system) in the composition of the parliamentary groups, they who directed the policy of the labour press.

This class of bureaucrats, which was nicknamed *Bonzen* (bosses), clung together like the ivy on the wall. By the aid of special pension and insurance societies they helped each other in dark days, and they were always ready to hush up any delinquencies of their brethren. Intermarriage among them was common, and they were in the way of becoming an hereditary caste, as they all tried to find jobs for their sons and daughters in the machine. As regards their relationship to the organised workers, they formed a compact mass, which, by and by, developed all those features which make the German civil service so unpopular. Precisely as the bishops of the early Christian Church developed from servants of their congregations into an international machine of enormous power which has been for more than a thousand years exploiting the masses, there was beginning to develop from the ranks of those who should have been the leaders in the struggle of the proletariat a new exploiting caste, separated from the mass by a quickly widening gulf. It is characteristic that the people found for this new caste the name of *Bonzen*, a word used in the Middle Ages to designate priests.

This development became especially pronounced in the trade unions. These old fighting organisations of the working class were scarcely recognisable. The struggle of the masses was more and more subdued; a new economic 'pacifism' tried to replace strikes by compulsory arbitration and to avoid labour conflicts. The conciliation system, with its compulsory arbitration fixing unfavourable wage scales, transformed the trade unions from militant organisations of free proletarians into appendages of the capitalist state. This development conferred on the trade-union 'leaders', who became more and more respectable, the halo of statesmen weaving secret diplomatic webs. In their luxurious palatial office buildings, with their beautiful equipment in the most modern style, an army of parasitic officials completely detached from the labour movement gathered. The total expenditure on this swallowed a very considerable part of the income of the trade unions, and the chief concern of these officials was to prevent the reduction of the funds by strikes. They used all their influence to prevent strikes. Of the old militant socialist spirit of the German trade unions no trace was left. It was characteristic that, while the most terrible crisis was raging, one of the best and most advanced of the German trade-union leaders, Tarnow,[44] at the last annual conference of the German Social-Democratic Party called upon the party to play the part of the doctor to cure sick capitalism, a statement which caused a storm of disgust amongst the workers. However, this declaration actually was the very quintessence of the entire policy of both German Social-Democracy and the trade unions.

This huge bureaucratic machine having become an end in itself had lost all contact with the members. Plato's aphorism of the two peoples living together but speaking different languages and unable to understand each other could be fittingly applied to the machine and the members of the German trade unions. The individual member counted for nothing. The mass of the members were regarded primarily as contributors. When in difficulty, the organised worker found a more humane attitude and more goodwill to understand his position at the municipal welfare institutions than in the shoulder-shrugging bureaucrats of his union. A characteristic case by way of illustration: a long-standing member of the Central Union of Clerks and Shop Assistants, an elderly woman who being unemployed had lived for a long time on temporary jobs, had paid for seven years the highest-scale contribution, without receiving any help of any kind. She retained her membership out of sheer loyalty. Her position got worse, so that she fell into arrears for several months. In accordance with the rules, she wrote within the prescribed period asking for postponement, and not knowing that she was required to send in her membership card failed to enclose it. She was expelled and when she complained she was told that as soon as her position improved she might rejoin as a *new* member, thus losing all her rights. When she told her story to a circle of trade unionists, another member of the same union exclaimed: 'Well, you have been lucky that they have not sued you for arrears, as they usually do.'

Another instance: a member of the juvenile section of the Metal Workers Union of Frankfort, a young Social-Democrat, had been unemployed for a long time, and when he was out of benefit he walked to Berlin to try his fortune there. Tired and hungry, with worn-out boots, he arrived and went to his union for assistance, hoping at least to find here a bit of warm food and a friendly reception, but he got the cold shoulder. He was told: 'You have no further right to benefit according to the rules of the union. Go and get a job, and pay your contributions again, then you may come back.' What was the outcome? In his despair, the boy went to the Nazi storm-troops. Here nobody asked him for documents or opinions; they gave him plenty to eat, let him rest, and gave him new boots. Only then they told him: 'If you like, you can join us ...' The trade-union bureaucrats could not see a hungry boy, they could see only their rules and regulations. A member has to pay contributions. If he cannot do that, and there is no clause in the rules according him further rights, this sucked orange will be thrown on the dump. Let the Nazis pick it up if they like. And the Nazis did pick them up – in masses ...

Throughout the German working-class movement, democracy was little by little abolished, giving way to a more and more avowed dictatorship of the machine. While in the small provincial towns frequently a local democracy continued which made the central despotism more endurable, in the big towns the rights of the members were surrendered more and more to the 'body of functionaries', in which the number of those economically dependent in one way or another on the central body was especially big. Everywhere, the machine got control of the press; usually it also controlled the appointment of lecturers to various meetings, as well as the selection of subjects – whoever was suspected of having ideas of his own could be easily muzzled and systematically excluded from lecturing and expressing his views in the press, even on questions where there was no difference of opinion, just to prevent him from getting influence. That applied to the trade unions as well as to the party and the cultural organisations. The consequence was a degradation of the press and of the internal life of the organisations, while the meetings became devoid of life. The youngsters stayed away. In the branch meetings of the Social-Democratic Party the discontented faces of elderly people noticeably predominated; they frequently offered criticism, but were powerless against the machine, which worked with the precision of an automaton. The existing latent opposition in the party could never get its own way at annual conferences. The strong parliamentary group had until lately a decisive vote without being elected as delegates, thus being available to the party caucus as 'voting cattle'. If, in spite of all this, in any organisation a dangerous opposition appeared, it was denounced as Communist, or was arbitrarily dissolved, as was the case with the *Jungsozialisten* (the Young Socialists) throughout the country, or in 1932 the Spandau branch of the

'Free-Thinking Youth'.

The trade unions, cultural and sporting societies greatly suffered from the disruptive tactics of the Communists. The Social-Democratic majorities of those bodies often retaliated by expelling the Communist minorities, which in such cases formed parallel societies of their own. Thus every society with a Social-Democratic bias soon had a Communist counterpart, while both continued to declare that they were organised on non-party lines.

It is essential to have a thorough acquaintance with the German working-class movement to understand the consequence of this dualism. Even in prewar times German Social-Democracy had striven to extend its influence over all spheres of life of its members. A Social-Democrat was discouraged from joining any colourless bourgeois society. All his aspirations should be satisfied by his movement, even when they consisted of hiking, fishing, singing, sport of any kind, the study of languages, shorthand or chess. Freed from the pressure of the old regime, this network of societies and groups spread, and, wherever possible, juvenile and children's sections were formed. The fact that in the first years after the war the political working-class movement was split up into three parts – the Social-Democrats, the Independent Social-Democrats, and the Communists – made the non-party form of these societies appear the natural one. Now this network of societies broke into two parts, a stronger Social-Democratic one and a livelier Communist one. Thus for the politically unorganised worker to join any of these societies or sports clubs actually meant a tacit choice between the Social-Democratic and the Communist tendencies. As a result the gulf was widened. The position of those elements consciously standing between the two parties became increasingly difficult.

In the guerrilla fighting of this fratricidal struggle the Communists, as the attacking party, often introduced the most despicable methods. The Social-Democrats at first were highly indignant about it, but soon tried to copy them. However, while the Communists could justify the use of dictatorial methods, as being in harmony with their conceptions, the Social-Democrats, who stood for democracy, in using dictatorial and autocratic methods put themselves in a false position, thus creating confusion among the workers, and disillusionment among their own members. As a consequence, the leading circles of societies under Social-Democratic influence were scared of any kind of opposition, however constructive, of any different opinion, of any new idea, of any free word. Frequently, under such circumstances, they refrained for months and years from calling members' meetings, replacing them at best by open lectures without any possibility of discussion. The limit was reached in this direction by the Social-Democratic Secular

School Society, which split without consulting the members. In some cases, functionaries and delegates were appointed from above. Finally, lecturers and contributors to the party press were not recognised as functionaries, and were thus excluded from participating in the meetings of functionaries called to decide matters of policy.

Thus the Social-Democratic masses were also psychologically prepared for dictatorship. The suspension of parliament by the Brüning government, governing by decrees setting aside parliament, accustomed the masses in the country to the methods of dictatorship. So yet another ladder was set up for a Papen, a Schleicher and a Hitler to climb to power.

The Social-Democrats were living on the mistakes of the Communists, and the Communists on the mistakes of the Social-Democrats. There was much swinging from side to side among the electors of the two parties – they were not satisfied by either of them. Even among the membership there was much fluctuation; the number of those who had crossed over and come back was by no means small. As regards the Communists, the fluctuation reached at times over fifty per cent of their membership. Large masses were and remained unsatisfied, many of them sank into apathy, or they left general politics alone, and devoted themselves to a special branch of cultural or similar work.

★ ★ ★

Under these circumstances, it would seem strange that between the two parties a third alternative did not evolve. Attempts at this were made, but they never succeeded. Various groups which had been expelled from time to time from the Communist Party sank into the quicksands of a barren political sectarianism, devouring each other in academic quarrels. When one of these groups was financially strong enough to run a daily paper, *Arbeiterpolitik*,[45] it remained without any influence whatsoever on the working class. About two years before the Hitler disaster, when an expelled Social-Democratic opposition group tried to form a new party, their attempt aroused much interest, and attracted a considerable number of discontented youths. However, after a few weeks, the larger part of these youths were disillusioned and rejoined the old organisation. The new Socialist Workers Party,[46] strengthened numerically by the entry of a section of dissident Communists but morally weakened by the formation of factions, soon became the scene of endless internal strife, and, in spite of very valuable proletarian elements, it soon led the shadowy existence of a hair-splitting sect. It united the faults of both the Social-Democratic and the Communist Parties. The wide gulf that splits the German working-class movement went right through that party.

All groups and factions with anarchist leanings remained also without influence. It is true they rendered a service in creating in many places possibilities for discussion, where open-minded workers of different creeds could honestly discuss political and theoretical questions. But their own views did not gain ground among the masses. In the German Republic the state appeared to the workers more as a welfare institution than as a means of oppression. This made them little susceptible to anarchistic ideas.

IV. The Crisis

The outbreak of the world crisis ought to have shown to everybody the correctness of the Marxian theory. The productive forces had outgrown the economic framework. Starvation and misery prevailed because *too much* food, *too many* goods, had been produced.

The present crisis is different from the crises of the nineteenth century, not only in its dimensions, but also in its essence. It is not simply one of the recurrent capitalist crises, it is a crisis of capitalism itself. In the nineteenth century the raising of the standard of living of the workers in consequence of the victorious onslaught of the trade unions, the creation of new demands, the acquisition of new markets, the capitalist absorption of new countries, still made a certain adjustment to keep pace in some degree with the rapid development of the productive forces. And when there were no further markets to conquer, no new territories to be brought into line, there came the World War. And it hastened the economic development of what had been colonial countries, thus turning them from markets into competitors.

In the postwar period, the enormous power accumulated by the trusts, and the weakness of the trade unions, hampered the development of the internal market; there was no rapid rise in the wage level necessary for an increased purchasing-power. In addition to that, steam power, which had given employment to many hands, was displaced by labour-saving electricity, and this, together with the increasing mechanisation and rationalisation of the enterprises, brought about a quick increase in the number of unemployed.[47] The purchasing-power of the masses decreased, consumption declined, and the consequence was a crisis of unprecedented dimensions.

One might think that, in such circumstances, the masses would flock round the Marxian theory, or rather round those organisations that advocated it. However, the contrary happened. The objective factors for a social change were mature, yet the subjective factors were missing. The oft-repeated idea that the crisis, with its increased mass misery, would have a revolutionising effect and just lead automatically to socialism again proved wrong, as it had so often done before. The well-worn joke of Bernard Shaw: 'Socialism would long ago have arrived, were it not for the socialists', assumed a very modern and sinister meaning.

The two working-class parties which should have been a support to the masses sinking into misery, which ought to have shown them a clear aim, and rally them round their banner in a struggle for that aim, failed, and they had to fail. A big moment had found little minds. The machines of the Social-Democratic organisations that had become respectable recoiled from revolutionary aims. As the ancient Christians, when they became respectable, had done with the 'millennium', they would have liked to put off the 'socialist commonwealth' into another world beyond the grave. Unwillingness to proclaim the socialist order as the object of a revolutionary struggle of the present day made them timid and uncertain in face of the masses. For the same reason they could not resolve on energetic action for drastic palliatives that might cure unemployment for a time (a thirty-hour week, the raising of the school age, etc). Instead, they crept under the wings of reaction, seeking protection. As regards the Communist Party executive, they failed to take their own revolutionary socialist phrases seriously, and they acted merely as agents of the Russian state interests. Thus the social and economic crisis could not but lead to a political crisis, and this in a reactionary, not in a revolutionary, direction.

A general cultural and social decline set in; the period of cultural and social advance under Social-Democratic leadership closed; the downfall of the government of Hermann Müller[48] in the spring of 1930, which died from the poison of the reactionary snake it had cherished in its own bosom, was the turning-point.

The *Reichswehr* clique, together with big industry, always ready for wage cuts, who just now had in their hands the reins of the old war-horse Hindenburg, managed to get together the 'Cabinet of the Front-Soldiers', under Brüning's leadership. Its first attempt to lower the standard of living of the masses by an emergency order was wrecked by the two proletarian parties in the *Reichstag*, but in the following election campaign the Social-Democrats failed to find their way to the hearts of the masses. They did not show any inspiring aim, nor any visible way out of the mud, nor did they call upon the masses to exert all their strength for the defence of liberty and democracy. Their chief concern was how they would work together with the Catholic Centre Party in the new *Reichstag*. No wonder that a part of their electors went over to the Communists. But in this election, for the first time, a new power earnestly competed for working-class votes – the Nazis.

The capitalists had recognised the danger of this crisis, and were looking for sheep's clothing to dress their wolves in, so that they might get near to the workers. They showed themselves open-handed as regards finance for Nazi propaganda, and the American magnates of capital, who were annoyed about the German social legislation, were not stingy. The six million votes that the Nazis received were a foreboding of coming storm. The terror with which the Social-Democrats were stricken did not turn them back, but led them on to the disastrous road of a toleration of Brüning, throwing them in the end into the moral abyss of the Hindenburg election. For, just as in 1918, the Social-Democrats did not now dare to trust themselves and their Republic to a mass action of the proletariat. They turned rather to the right, whereby in the end they completely sawed off the branch on which they sat. Thus Social-Democracy was compelled as the serf of its overlord to demolish, stone by stone, the proud building of the democratic Republic, the work of its own hands. The rights of parliament, the liberty of the press, the wage level, social insurance, unemployment benefit, municipal self-government – all this was systematically crippled by way of emergency orders, and the responsibility for all the deeds of the Brüning government was thrust on to the shoulders of Social-Democracy in the eyes of the workers. 'The Brüning government is the most hated government, and with it Social-Democracy', declared a Neukölln Social-Democrat in a meeting of functionaries.

Simultaneously with this, a similar process was going on in the municipalities, and here again the responsibility rested on the Social-Democrats. The crippling of the social welfare services, affecting millions of proletarians, and especially youth, at the time when these services were the last hope of the masses sinking into poverty, synchronised with cuts in the municipal expenditure on education, which hit them no less hard. School feeding was cut down, children's holiday homes were closed, school excursions were abolished, the number of children in a class increased, the medical school service was restricted, textbooks and stationery were refused, teachers dismissed. Everything the unemployed man had been brought to regard as his and his children's right, in times of emergency was to be taken away from him. However, the excessive salaries of the directors of municipal enterprises remained intact for a considerable time. That might appear to be of little consequence to the municipal budget, but the psychological effect on the masses was by no means insignificant.

The number of unemployed grew. In Germany the crisis raged worse than in any other country. The war and the inflation had already created a strong slum proletariat. The elements who, after the war, failed to find their way back into civil life were joined by the declassed of the lower middle class who were ruined in the inflation. These elements were discontented; they had no ideology of their own, at one time they held the Allies responsible for their position, at another the Republic, and they were longing for the flesh-pots which in the time of Wilhelm their families had possessed. Now, ever-new masses of proletarians, declassed by unemployment, were in danger of sinking into the slum proletariat. Hundreds of thousands of skilled workers, up till now well paid, suddenly found themselves consigned to constant unemployment, robbed of their economic power without hope of an improvement in the near future. The dividing-line between proletariat and slum proletariat threatened to disappear; instead, a gulf began to appear between employed and unemployed. In a most difficult position were the juveniles, who had scarcely entered the process of production before they were unemployed. They were resentful, and, inexperienced as they were, they were searching for a way of escape.

Not less discontented were the peasants, who had to look on while Junkers, like Oldenburg-Januschan,[49] Count Kalkreuth and Hindenburg, grew fat on 'Osthilfe' subsidies, while they themselves got only pence, or nothing. Large numbers of farms were sold up and that led to spontaneous riots, whereby the unfortunate auctioneer got at times a good hiding, until nobody dared any more to make a bid.

Under such circumstances there was no lack of inflammable material. Large masses of despairing people were searching for a new ideology for comfort and hope. The working-class movement had failed. Social-Democracy had no influence on these declassed. The Communists with their violent phrases and their revolutionary romanticism were nearer to them. But neither could they hold this shifting mob, though most of them had at some time passed through one or other of the Communist organisations. Many of them tried the Church, the Salvation Army or other religious sects. But there again they did not find what they wanted. Peculiar things happened. An expectation of a Messiah gripped large numbers of people. Business-like prophets seized their opportunity. One of them, a man named Weissenberg,[50] who pretended to cure sick people by anointing them with cream cheese, attained power and got rich. Fanatical crowds hung on his words; his little paper *Der Weise Berg*, in which he wrote senseless stuff, had a large circulation. One had a feeling of having awakened in the Middle Ages, or rather in the time of the decaying Roman Empire.

The growing Nazi movement understood how to take advantage of this widespread longing for a saviour, and some of them proclaimed Hitler as a 'second Christ'; the 'Heil Hitler' had an electric effect and made the mediocre figure of the Bavarian soldier from Austria appear, in the imagination of his followers, as a hero and a saint. At last, here in real life, as in a trashy novel, there was a case of a nonentity playing the part of a great hero. And he played it well.

The cunning politicians who stood unseen behind Hitler did not overlook the economic or the military side of the movement they had fostered. They let the successful mob-orator Hitler promise everything to everybody – to the peasants high prices; to the workers cheap bread; to the landlords high rents; to the poor people cheap flats; to the small shopkeepers the abolition of the cooperative societies and large stores; to the consumer cheap commodities; in a word, to everybody the fulfilment of his heart's desire. They had leaflets distributed to the unemployed, with nebulous reactionary contents, but purely Communist language, as well as new reactionary words for well-known socialist songs. They were wallowing in money and used it to establish barracks, where they kept mercenaries bought for two marks a day, giving them shelter, nourishing food prepared by the Nazi women hordes, and brown uniforms.

The state looked on in inaction. It had proscribed the Communist *Rote Frontkämpfer-Bund*; here it failed. Hitler's Brown army, the storm-troops, was growing and growing. It was well armed and knew how to use its arms. Political collisions and street fighting became daily occurrences. Social-Democrats and Communists were never sure of their lives; at any street corner they might be attacked by armed Brownshirts and mown down. Even at home they were not safe. The fact that the Social-Democrats nevertheless failed to arm their defensive organisation, the *Reichsbanner*, effectively, which worked in close contact with the Prussian police, and could have counted on its arsenals, is not an honourable page in their history. Generally speaking, the *Reichsbanner* was trained exclusively for the defensive and was devoid of all initiative, in contradistinction to the *Rote Frontkämpfer-Bund*, which was armed within limits, trained for street fighting, and imbued with a very militant spirit. Against the latter, even when the Nazis were more numerous, they were knocked out, provided that republican police did not come to the rescue in time. The *Stahlhelm*, in reality merely an illegal section of the *Reichswehr*, seldom participated in these fights. The police, whose chiefs were Social-Democrats, took no serious measures against the Brown gangs, while being very energetic against the Communists. It tried to prevent, as much as possible, street fighting between political opponents, to separate the fighters, occasionally to disarm small groups, but it never took any systematic action against the Brownshirts. Had these Brown gangs met with serious resistance and been forced into the defensive, they would soon have dispersed – only against opponents who showed no fight were they brave fellows.

With these mercenary hordes, Hitler would never have been able to gain power through an armed rising; the constitutional way appeared more reliable. After all, the elements for a successful counter-revolution were already present. There were the monarchist President Hindenburg, the *Reichswehr* command who were keen to enter politics, the reactionary officials, the monarchist nationalist judges, the reactionary capitalist parties, the impotent, discredited parliament, the *Präsidial-Kabinett* (President's Cabinet – a cabinet dependent more on the confidence of the President than on parliament), which could at any moment be dismissed by a stroke of the President's pen; Big Industry, with its millions and powerful press. So there was a wide field of manoeuvre. When the curtain had fallen on the parliamentary stage, those cliques who were acting behind the scenes gained the mastery. Why should the wire-pullers who had put a Brüning on the stage not be able to replace him by a Papen, a Schleicher, a Hitler? Of course, it still remained to arrange for a reliable *claque*.

An enormous propaganda apparatus was set to work; an army of agitators and scribes led an energetic attack against the 'system'. A magic word this – the reactionaries of all shades meant the democratic Republic by it; the hungry masses, however, understood by it the capitalist system, which they held responsible for their starvation, while caring little for the democratic Republic. Now the task was to make use of the rage of the masses directed against capitalism, and divert it for the struggle against democracy. Their slogans – against the 'system', against the 'bosses', later on against 'the government of the fine gentlemen' – that is to say, slogans appealing to class hatred, served the purpose. Here, the nationalist slogans served only to increase the confusion. Greater was their effect in other circles – among the middle-class youth, among numerous relics of the officers and petty officers of the Kaiser's time, among those elements of the officials who came from the *Militäranwärter* (ex-non-commissioned officers rewarded by state employment), as well as among the declassed coming from the middle class. These last, especially, squeezed out of all class communion, were clinging to nationalism, which seemed to offer them a new spiritual home.

The next objective was the Prussian government, the most important bulwark of the Weimar Republic. For fourteen years the Social-Democratic Party had made every imaginable concession to the Centre and the other middle parties, in order to keep the Prussian government, and therefore the Prussian police, in their own hands. And they really had succeeded in keeping in their hands during the whole period the positions of the Prussian Prime Minister, the Minister of the Interior, and the Berlin Police President, as well as many other police and administrative posts in the provinces. At the same time, they had been striving to republicanise the police from the bottom upwards. The crisis, with the general disintegration which it brought in its train, was undermining the position of the Prussian government. Thus the storming of Prussia was made easier for the reaction. The old middle-class parties were rapidly shrinking, while the Nazis grew stronger from election to election.

Finally, Nazis and *Stahlhelm* joined forces for a storm attack on the Prussian government, attempting to bring about its downfall by a plebiscite in August 1931, though the electoral period of the Prussian Diet was already nearing its end. As we have before mentioned, the Communists had by order from Moscow lent to the Nazis and *Stahlhelm* their assistance, though they could not fail to see that a downfall of the Prussian government at this juncture must needs help reaction into the saddle. It is true large sections of the Communists declined to participate in this treasonable action, the plebiscite received only nine million votes and so failed to overthrow the Prussian government, but it weakened the Communist Party, thus proving after all an asset to reaction.

The crisis deepened and the growing despair of the masses had to assert itself politically. The emergency orders of the Brüning government fell on the starving masses like so many blows. The Brown flood rose. The capitalist parties melted like snow. Both Social-Democrats and Communists saw only the beam in each other's eye, but neither of them chose to notice the not less prominent beam in his own eye. Instead of standing together against the common foe, they carried on a desperate fratricidal war.

One election campaign chased another – more and more the workers were thrown back on the defensive. When Hindenburg's term of office was drawing to a close, there was danger that Hitler might be elected in his place. Instead of using the opportunity to unite all the forces of the proletariat in one clear common action, while the Communists insisted on a candidate of their own, the Social-Democrats put all their hopes on the idea of chasing the devil Hitler by Beelzebub Hindenburg. Their electors maintained their discipline, and a coalition ranging from the Social-Democrats to the big capitalist German People's Party carried through, on 10 April 1932, the re-election of Hindenburg, who received nineteen million votes. Some naive leaders of the Socialist International congratulated German Social-Democracy on its 'victory'. Yet, when these good wishes arrived in Berlin, Hindenburg's treason had already become evident. He did not repeat his oath on the constitution – servile legal authorities declared the taking of the oath again to be unnecessary. Neither the Social-Democrats nor the Communists attempted to make him repeat it, or to draw the attention of the people to this breach of the constitution. They let him alone, though they could not fail to understand the significance of this, taking into consideration the character of the old soldier. Now, in the hands of a reactionary clique, Hindenburg was completely degraded into a puppet.

In the following election campaigns – the election to the Prussian Diet on 24 April 1932, and the three elections to the *Reichstag* rapidly following one another on 31 July 1932, 6 November 1932 and finally on 5 March 1933 – while ever-new crowds of indifferent electors were brought to the ballot-box, both the working-class parties failed to show a practical way out of the crisis, to inspire the poverty-stricken despairing masses with new hope and courage, and rally them to the struggle for a brighter future. The Communists repeated their old worn-out slogans and directed their attack mainly against the Social-Democratic Party, while the contented Social-Democratic bureaucrats could not find a common language with the suffering masses of the people. They desired to preserve the existing political and social order – the masses were eager to trample it down and pull it to pieces.

At the Social-Democratic election meetings, mostly taking one monotonous form of 'demonstrations', gloom reigned supreme. There was a palpable gulf between speakers and audiences. There was much dissension even over the mode of address. In a meeting in Saxony, Severing, one of the biggest guns of the Social-Democratic Party, was shouted down when he commenced: 'Ladies and gentlemen' – a few days later Hitler spoke in the same hall, addressing the meeting: 'German men and women', and was cheered. In many Social-Democratic meetings the speakers would repeat the Nazi formula *Volksgenossen*, inspiring the socialist audiences with contempt. These external trivialities showed how wide the cleft between leaders and masses had grown.

Instead of an incisive criticism of the capitalist system and the policy of the government, anxiously awaited by the masses; instead of demanding drastic measures against unemployment and misery; instead of holding out a prospect of a bright socialist future, the Social-Democratic apologists generally confined themselves to a purely negative criticism of the contradictory programme of the Nazis, and to a rejection of the Communist slogans. Their positive proposals seemed petty and insufficient, or gave the impression of no more than pious hopes, since there was the feeling that there was no serious intention of immediate action behind it.

In these exciting times the branch meetings presented a similar picture. The appointment of speakers as well as the selection of subjects was in the hands of indifferent employees at party offices, the slaves of red tape. A Social-Democratic woman lecturer complained to us that she had been asked to address a Berlin women's meeting on 'Socialism in the Family' just before the breakdown ... The youth ignored these meetings. The elderly people, bound up with the party for a lifetime, remained sulkily in their seats. It brought to mind Heinrich Heine's little story of the two old people who from their childhood had been used to praying before the image of a saint painted in glowing colours in a niche. Now the image had faded, the niche was in ruins – unmindful of this, they continued to pray.

If one further considers that, up to the very height of the present crisis, one would search in the Social-Democratic press in vain not only for socialist ideas, but even for the word socialism, then there can be no wonder at such a lack of enthusiasm.

Still, the fact must be emphasised that however great might be the turnover between Social-Democrats and Communists, the Nazis for a long time failed to make any breach in the Marxist front. The increase in the Nazi vote came in the first place from the bourgeois parties, and also from people who had never before taken the trouble to vote.

After the Prussian elections on 24 April 1932, the Nazis became the strongest party in Prussia. However, with the German Nationalist Party and the German People's Party added together, they still had no majority. There generally was no working majority in the Diet. There was only a negative majority. No majority could have been formed without either the Communists or the Nazis. The Communists with the Nazis and the other reactionary parties carried a vote of censure and turned out the coalition government led by the Social-Democrat Braun.[51] The government tendered their resignation, but remained in office as an interregnum government until a new government could be formed, in accordance with the constitution. This short-sighted action of the Communists greatly weakened the government for the approaching struggle, and this is the only excuse that the Prussian government can urge for its disgraceful behaviour in the decisive hour. The Communists, however, were not yet satisfied with their laurels – together with the Nazis they demanded in the Diet the immediate removal of the government, whereby the road would have been open to the Nazis. Really, the proletariat were on the horns of a dilemma, having to choose between the criminal short-sightedness of the noisy Communists and the criminal weakness of the Social-Democratic 'statesmen'. No wonder that, in these circumstances, large numbers of electors lost their heads, and like a flock of sheep at a fire, deprived of the bell-wether, ran right into the flames of Nazism.

The critical hour came nearer and nearer. In the Reich, the Brüning cabinet was kicked out, although it had a majority in the *Reichstag*. Its place was taken by the 'Cabinet of the Barons', led by von Papen, a cabinet that had almost the whole *Reichstag* opposed to it. It was understood that the first act of this cabinet would be the dissolution of the *Reichstag*. Yet the *Reichstag* would have still had the power to vote it down and so compel the Nazis to show their hand, thus tearing off the mask from these demagogues. However, here the Social-Democratic President of the *Reichstag* failed, and with him failed also the constitutional parties – instead of voting down the government, the *Reichstag* tamely submitted to be sent home by von Papen, and this without the fixing of a date for a new election. Only after some vacillation, 31 July was fixed for a general election.

Thus, on the one hand there was the Prussian interregnum government, which, although it had been voted down by a Diet with a strong Nazi element in it, still kept a firm grip on the Prussian police – on the other hand, the Reich government led by von Papen, whose constitutional standing was very questionable, together with President Hindenburg, only recently re-elected with nineteen million votes, but who had already, since then, been guilty of two breaches of the constitution, and the generals of the *Reichswehr* – these opposing forces were confronting each other. Papen could, in case of need, rely also on the Steel Helmets and Nazi storm-troops; the Prussian government could rely on their police, the Social-Democratic Party, the Social-Democratic auxiliary organisations, the trade unions, and the *Reichsbanner* – in case of actual hostilities, perhaps also on the Communist masses.

In this situation, balancing the forces on both sides, it was by no means clear from the outset who would arrest whom. Just this moment was the time chosen by the Social-Democratic Prime Minister, Otto Braun, for a holiday. His place was taken by the Welfare Minister Hirtsiefer,[52] leader of the Catholic trade unions, with the support of the Minister of Internal Affairs, Severing, the 'strong man' of the Social-Democratic Party. To the latter all eyes were now turned.

★ ★ ★

On the morning of 20 July 1932, Papen invited Severing to a conference. He told him that for the sake of law and order, a Commissar of the Reich was to be put in the place of the Prussian government, and called upon him to surrender his affairs in a spirit of goodwill, as otherwise he would be obliged to declare a state of siege.[53] Severing indignantly rejected the insolent demand. He declared that only by force could he be removed from office, and left the conference under protest. Papen immediately proclaimed an order of the President, based on the notorious Article 48 of the constitution, declaring that the Prussian government was dismissed and Papen appointed Commissar of the Reich for Prussia. Papen relegated his powers to the Mayor of Essen, Bracht,[54] a member of the right wing of the Catholic Party. At the same time a second proclamation announced martial law in Berlin and appointed General Stülpnagel[55] as commander of Berlin.

In the city, which was in the throes of a violent election campaign, these proclamations, published by special editions of the papers, fell like a thunderbolt. Holding their breath, the people looked now to the Prussian Ministry of the Interior, where Severing was sitting, now to the Wilhelmstrasse, where Papen resided.[56] Motor cars filled with *Reichswehr* soldiers were patrolling the streets. Everywhere discussions were to be heard on the question whether the Prussian police or the *Reichswehr* were superior in street fighting. Bills were posted up inviting people to election meetings that had been arranged for that evening in all parts of the city.

Rumours sprang up — the police were called out — the *Reichsbanner* was mobilising, the police were arming the *Reichsbanner*. Every little detachment of the *Reichsbanner* that happened to be passing called attention, caused comment and gave rise to fresh rumours. All were waiting for further developments.

A special edition of the papers announced the dismissal of the Berlin police president, Grzesinsky,[57] and the vice-president, Dr Weiss,[58] by General Stülpnagel. Grzesinsky had refused to recognise the order, declaring that he would accept orders only from the Minister of the Interior. Thereupon an officer of the *Reichswehr* with four men appeared at the Alexanderplatz and arrested the two officials, taking them like sheep from the midst of their well-armed and entirely loyal police, while their subordinates, whom they were unwilling to order to resist, looked on in tears. The masses stood aghast, stunned, unable to understand. What would Severing do? In still greater excitement, they turned their attention to the Minister of the Interior. Surely Severing must have some deep scheme? Police patrol cars rushed through the streets. What is the Executive of the Social-Democratic Party doing? With great excitement people waited for the evening meetings.

It was said the famous lawyer Alsberg[59] had been instructed to defend the two arrested police presidents and that he immediately went to the military officers' prison where they were detained. However, he came too late. The gentlemen had been released after two hours' detention. (The fact that this release was due to the two heroes signing, even before the arrival of their lawyer, an undertaking to refrain from performing their duties, was not yet known.)

Meanwhile, the newly-appointed Deputy Commissar of the Reich,

Bracht, had come to Severing and had demanded the surrender of affairs. But Severing had declared that he would give way only to force. Suddenly the news became known. Herr Bracht had appeared again to Severing accompanied by the new-made police president, Melchior, and a few soldiers of the *Reichswehr*, who, however, remained outside – to this 'show of force' Severing had surrendered, and had retired into his private rooms, which had been graciously left to him.[60]

Nobody was willing to believe it. Yet it proved to be true …

What next?

People streamed into the meetings. Agitated audiences were sitting at Social-Democratic meetings waiting. Sellers offering the recently introduced badge with the three arrows found many customers. Everywhere, inside and outside the halls, fists were raised on high with the greeting: 'Freiheit!' ('Freedom!')

Finally the chairman's bell sounded. The speaker stood up. Expectation was on all faces. All eyes were on him. But soon expectation subsided – what came were the old well-worn shibboleths. Between the speaker and the audience a barrier arose. What he had to say on the events of this historic day seemed shallow. The prospect, the conclusions one had come to hear, were absent. No word of a general strike, nothing about the calling out of the *Reichsbanner*, no appeal to the republican police. Nothing about struggle – only law, order, discipline. Such music the workers had not expected.

Was this the last act of the drama? It was stated that the Executive of the Social-Democratic Party were holding an important meeting. Their decision was still outstanding. To this hope people clung. It is true that the meeting had been a wet blanket. All high hopes had evaporated – still, the party Executive was deliberating, the decision was yet to come.

In the large works, the workers waited all night for the order for a general strike. The Communists, during the night, distributed an illegal leaflet calling for a general strike, in support of the very government whose dismissal they had so recently violently demanded in company with the Nazis. However, they had so often called for general strikes that nobody took their calls seriously, they themselves included. Everybody ignored the cry of 'Wolf!'.

And the Social-Democrats? Long was the decision awaited. When it became known, it read: 'Our reply will be given at the election on 31 July.'

> The brave old Duke of York
> He had ten thousand men,
> He led them up to the top of the hill,
> And he led them down again.

A storm of indignation raged through the masses. They felt themselves to be shamefully misled, betrayed. But having been for long years bereft of any initiative of their own, these masses could not take action without their recognised leaders. So no hand moved, no shot was fired, not a single factory closed. The twentieth of July passed, and it had brought to the masses only a boundless discouragement. But many a fist was clenched in the pocket – it was not quite clear against whom … The dismissed Prussian government later on appealed to the State Court. But it aroused among the workers only a smile of contempt.

The election campaign continued its weary way. Reaction triumphed all along the line. In small towns and villages, the Nazis imposed a violent terrorism on the electors. The elections indeed brought an answer – the negative answer of the electors to the failure of the working-class parties. From this election the Nazis emerged as the strongest party of the *Reichstag*. Their votes had mounted up to thirteen millions, so that they obtained 230 seats, while the Social-Democrats had got only seven million votes and 121 seats. However, even in such a parliament, the Papen government could not long hold its power. By its subsidies to the rich, and its robbery of the poor, as well as by its threats against all remaining political liberties, it aroused against itself such hatred among the people that the Nazis dared not much longer vote for it. With a majority of four-fifths, the *Reichstag* voted against it. It dissolved the *Reichstag*, but the new election on 6 November 1932 brought little change. In this election, the Nazis experienced their first setback, losing thirty-five seats. That was the answer of the electors for their underhanded support of the Papen government.

Soon after his ascent to power, Papen had withdrawn the prohibition against the Nazi uniform. The Nazis felt themselves to be the masters of the situation and began to exercise an unbearable terror. Every day there were dead and wounded. In the working-class districts of the big towns they had to be careful of showing themselves, but in smaller places and in outer suburbs their murder gangs had nearly a free hand. The beastly murder at Potempa in Upper Silesia soon found many imitations. Hitler himself had praised and identified himself with the bloody bandits who had in the middle of the night torn an inoffensive worker from his bed, slaying him in a brutal manner in the poor home of his old mother. In Eastern Prussia, too, there were people anxious to earn such praise from their leader.[61] The week of terror at Königsberg and its neighbourhood called forth the indignation of the civilised world. But the same terror was raging everywhere, though in a lesser degree. Its climax was reached on election day, 31 July.

The workers, ignoring party quarrels, joined hands for defensive action.

In many factories, in many villages, and especially in the proletarian outer suburbs, defensive bodies spontaneously sprang up. In accordance with the character of the district, these bodies were organised either on party lines, or jointly. But in either case there was close contact. An extensive system of alarm signals within a given area, or for calling for help from a neighbouring area, was worked out. Night patrols were instituted. Every 'red' dweller in the huts on the outskirts of Germany's big towns kept axe and spade ready by his bed (if he had no revolver). Knocks with the hammer on a washing-tub or on a piece of hanging iron rail were the means of signalling. Everybody tried to get at the political complexion of his neighbour. All who were 'red' stood together. Within the settlement, the district or the village, the 'united front' had become a fact. Blood was still flowing, but the feeling of helplessness vanished, thanks to the neighbourly solidarity of all those who were threatened. The party Executives of both Communist and Social-Democratic Parties disliked this development. They tried hard to keep these defensive bodies, whose appearance they could not prevent, under party control, and on purely party lines. The Social-Democratic Party, especially, tried to dissolve them as soon as things seemed to quieten down after the election.

The masses vigorously demanded a united front. But the two bureaucratic party machines were united only in the rejection of a united front. The Social-Democratic Party had, together with the trade unions, the *Reichsbanner* and other auxiliary organisations, already united in the 'Iron Front',[62] forming in works and factories groups called *Hammerschaften*. Now they simply declared that the Iron Front *was* the United Front! The Communist Party, on the other hand, paid lip-service to the United Front, but they clouded the idea by talking about a 'united front from below', a manoeuvre which amounted to asking the Social-Democratic workers to quit their leaders and join the Communist organisation. This manoeuvre they accompanied by a fusillade of abuse against the Social-Democratic Party.

It was perfectly clear that the united front could grow only out of common action. But that was just the difficulty, because all Communist actions were in some way or another directed against Social-Democracy, while the Social-Democratic leaders had as great a dread of real mass action as the devil has of holy water – under such conditions common action was unattainable. The Social-Democrats propounded a curious plan. They wanted to replace the popular idea of a united front, for which the masses were clamouring, by a proposal for a 'non-aggression treaty'. That meant in reality that the Social-Democrats would do nothing, and the Communists would not attack them for it. The workers had at last recognised that their disunity was the cause of their weakness. They energetically demanded the tearing down of all barriers. But their leaders always met their demands with dishonesty, hypocrisy and sabotage. So it was with the Social-Democrats; so it was with the Communists.

However great the divergence of principles between Social-Democrats and Communists, considering the common class interest in face of the common foe, as well as the existing balance of power, they ought to have established a united defensive front. But instead of jointly beating the enemy they apparently preferred to be separately beaten.

In face of a proletariat so eagerly carrying on a fratricidal struggle, and so weakened in its power of resistance, the Papen government could keep in power. It was not the masses who brought about Papen's downfall, not even the *Reichstag* – the Papen government was kicked out by intrigues behind the scenes, where the War Minister, Schleicher, kept the wires in his hands. This general now decided to leave the darkness behind the scenes, and appear on the stage as the Chancellor.

★ ★ ★

General Schleicher is a unique figure in German politics, a figure whose part is probably not yet played out. A reactionary of the purest water, who, however, is by no means narrow-minded, and is prepared to learn from everybody: a clever far-seeing militarist. His ideal is an enlightened social militarist state. He was searching for a way to utilise the militarist element contained in Communism for his purposes, and to create for his aims a broad mass foundation in the trade unions. He understood that capitalism in its classical form was played out. Therefore he desired to build up his enlightened military despotism on a foundation of state capitalism.

With broad-mindedness unheard of in Germany, Schleicher attempted to draw to himself all the brains of the country, without caring in the least which camp they came from. From the War Ministry (whose organ was the *Tägliche Rundschau*) he spun his invisible threads which ran together in the *Tatkreis*,[63] a circle of political personalities of widely varying political creeds. Here all shades of opinion were represented, from far-seeing industrialists and military specialists to trade-union leaders and Communist intellectuals; behind the scenes there were the strangest interconnections.

Like Hitler, Schleicher also aimed at utilising the anti-capitalist driving-power of the masses, diverting it from its natural course. But while Hitler as an uncouth slave of capital desired to beat down opposition by brute force and unlimited demagogy, Schleicher was busy spinning a finer web into which he was cleverly weaving tendencies and currents prevailing in the working-class movement, a web which he hoped would prove more durable. While the Hitler movement with its rough hooligan mentality remained entirely negative, trampling down everything cultural, and always destructive, Schleicher had far-reaching constructive schemes designed to save capitalist society by reforming it in the direction of a sort of state capitalism. Anti-revolutionary-minded labour bureaucrats, whom he tried to win, and not without success, seemed to him the most valuable collaborators in his task.

Schleicher's economic schemes in agriculture were directed to taking over the bankrupt estates, and to dividing them into small holdings, where cooperative machinery and a combination of agricultural and industrial labour should play a part. The War Ministry therefore tried to get into contact with theorists on the agrarian question of all shades of opinion, especially with those of the Communist peasant movement and nationalist *Landvolk* movement.[64] In industry Schleicher thought of utilising the influence gained by the state by the granting of loans and guarantees to the banks, in order to exercise pressure on big industry for the purpose of a kind of planned industry under state control. Here his idea coincided with the German trade unions, on whose machinery he wanted to lean. Between them there were already secretly established very close relations, which found expression in the patriotic speeches of the President of the German Federation of Trade Unions, Leipart.[65]

The so-called 'socialist action' of the Social-Democratic Party and the trade unions with their 'planned industry' hardly went much farther than Schleicher's dreams. However, the brutal magnates of capital, whose real representative was Papen, as well as the brutal East Elbian Junkers, found the brutal methods of a Hitler more to their liking than the finely-woven nets of the clever general.[66]

Behind the scenes a severe struggle was going on. The many attempts made up till now to put Hitler by hook or by crook into power had failed. The Centre Party manoeuvred. In the Prussian Diet it elected the Nazi, Kerrl,[67] as President. It wished to keep all doors open, and not to break with anyone, in the face of this doubtful future. This 'Pillar of the Republic' did its best to recommend itself as a useful support to the coming power, whatever it might be.

The masses were seething with excitement; both Social-Democrats and Communists were grievously disappointed with their leaders. Nevertheless, they could not break away from the old ties. There were many demonstrations of mutual sympathy between the two parties, but even now no official agreement was reached. The small Socialist middle groups tried to play the part of the honest broker in bringing about agreement between the two big parties, but the latter put them contemptuously aside, fearing to increase their prestige.

Schleicher made all sorts of concessions to the Nazis. The uniform prohibition had been withdrawn already by the Papen government on his initiative. Now he gave them permission to hold a demonstration in Berlin, in the Bülowplatz. In the Bülowplatz, situated in the east of Berlin in an avowedly red working-class district, there was the 'Karl-Liebknecht-Haus', the headquarters of the Communist Party. The Berlin proletariat looked upon this demonstration as an unheard-of provocation. An enormous force of police, armed with carbines, machine-guns and armoured cars, had to protect the Nazis. There were numerous skirmishes between police and Communists, while the Social-Democrats as usual had asked their followers to stay at home and close the windows. But in spite of this, many Social-Democrats went on this day into the streets with the Communists, and it was proved that Nazi detachments could not show their faces in working-class districts without police protection.

The workers now energetically demanded that rights granted to Nazis should be granted to them also. Social-Democrats and Communists prepared for mass demonstrations. The Communists were the first in the field. On a weekday which happened to be one of the coldest days of the whole year, hundreds of thousands of Communists turned out. Underfed, poorly dressed, they tramped in thirty-five degrees of frost for hours and hours through the working-class districts of Berlin in order to march past the tribune in the Bülowplatz where their leaders stood. The presence of the prohibited *Rote Frontkämpfer-Bund* was felt, though there were no uniforms. A few small detachments of the *Reichsbanner* and of the Social-Democratic Youth, as well as many individual Social-Democrats wearing their three arrows, marched in the procession, and of course also the Socialist middle groups who joined in to the last man.

The Social-Democrats had arranged their demonstration for the following Sunday. The weather was more favourable. From all parts of the town, their processions marched to the Lustgarten. A number of Communist groups who wanted to join in were turned away at the entrance of the Lustgarten. Even the Socialist middle groups were not welcome. The procession of the Socialist Workers Party had to wait for hours before it was decided kindly to admit them to the Lustgarten. But they did not worry and did their best to arouse some fighting spirit among the passing Social-Democratic processions. Again and again they shouted in chorus: 'SPD, KPD, SAP, *müssen gemeinsam marschieren.*' ('Social-Democrats, Communists, Socialist Workers, must march together.') Every Social-Democratic procession marching past was cheerfully greeted. It was interesting to note how differently these processions reacted. Those from the working-class districts marching to spirited fighting-songs replied to the friendly '*Kampfbereit*' ('Ready to fight'), the greeting of the Socialist Workers Party, with a no less friendly '*Freiheit*' ('Liberty'), the greeting of the Social-Democrats. But the processions of the well-dressed coming from the respectable districts, arriving wearily without songs, did not reply to the greetings, or made sarcastic remarks: 'Why have you broken away from us, if you now wish to demonstrate with us?' The strong middle-class element in the Social-Democratic Party had never made itself so evident as at this demonstration, when the party had mobilised also those of its members who on other occasions would stay away out of snobbishness or indifference.

The difference between these two demonstrations separated by only a few days, but differing so widely both in composition and spirit, could not escape notice. In the *Vorwärts* an anxious article by Stampfer[68] appeared, pointing out that the political division that had sprung up between Social-Democrat and Communist might, through economic factors active in the crisis, be strengthened, and thus become permanent. These two demonstrations showed to all who witnessed them the political and social problem of the division of the working class into two socially differing sections, an ever-sharper cleavage, thus exhibiting to all observers the underlying difficulties of the united front problem.

Meanwhile, the struggle continued behind the scenes. The gentlemen around Papen wanted to manoeuvre Schleicher out and put Papen back into power. The *Reichswehr* threatened to prevent this, if needs be by force. It was widely imagined that Schleicher would strike a blow. Schleicher wobbled. He had made concessions to the Nazis, whose demonstration in the Bülowplatz, made possible by police protection, had weakened his position on the left. So he could not but fail.

Meanwhile Papen was negotiating with Hitler. The latter gave all desired guarantees that he, on assuming power, would not harm a hair of the heads of the Junkers, of big industry or finance capital. He also declared his willingness to accept in his cabinet Papen and Hugenberg,[69] as commissars, so to say, of big money, and to leave the economic ministries in their hands. Thereupon Papen managed to get the ageing soldier Hindenburg to appoint Hitler as Chancellor on 30 January 1933.

V. Under the Brown Yoke

Hitler's appointment as Chancellor by Hindenburg was a smack in the face to his Social-Democratic electors. In order to prevent the election of Hitler they had voted for Hindenburg in spite of the abhorrence they felt for him. Now it was that same Hindenburg who put Hitler into the saddle.

The appointment of Papen as Chancellor had caused general indignation. However, the press of the left, including the Social-Democratic press, could find no word of reproach against the violator of the constitution so recently elected with their aid. Schleicher's appointment was accepted with complacency – politicians of various creeds putting various hopes in him.

Throughout this time, the Social-Democratic leaders and their press tried to pacify the people: 'Hitler will not get into power; the "Iron Front" won't allow it.' The masses believed the oft-repeated declaration that Social-Democracy would, if need be, 'fight the fascists with the same weapons which they themselves use', that is, by force of arms.

Under Papen and under Schleicher, the Social-Democrats, as a constitutional party, could still hope to muddle through somehow, although with clipped wings. 'The party has overcome the anti-socialist law of Bismarck, it has gone through the war, it will get through this time as well'; so they comforted themselves.

But now that they were faced with the fact of Hitler's appointment as Chancellor, what hopes were left? Where were the 'Iron Front', the *Reichsbanner*, the general strike threatened by the trade unions in such an emergency? Nothing stirred ...

And the Communists? What was left for them to lose? Had they not been trained for civil war? Had their military experts not made all preparations? Had they no terrorist groups? Where was the *Rote Frontkämpfer-Bund*? Were they not sufficiently armed? Was it not clear to them that only one alternative was left for them – either to wait till they were slaughtered or to fight for life? Why did not they prefer to fight, hopeless as the situation was?

Had they perhaps no free choice left to them? Had Moscow forbidden them to fight? Surely there was no lack of willing fighters. No one who witnessed their demonstration in Berlin shortly before Schleicher's fall; who saw those hundreds of thousands tormented by hunger, without overcoats, poorly clad, with worn boots, marching through the streets in thirty-five degrees of frost, often held up for long intervals, standing in the terrible cold without leaving their places; no one who saw those resolute faces, those glowing eyes, could question the revolutionary fervour for fight of these masses who had gathered under Communist banners. Not below, but above, was the failure. Why did the Communist Party machine fail?

Were they perhaps under the illusion that they would be able to steer the organisation, reshaped for underground work, through a short fascist period, so that they might afterwards step into the shoes of the quickly played-out fascists, replacing their dictatorship of 'monopoly capital', by a 'dictatorship of the proletariat'?

★ ★ ★

Hitler dissolved the *Reichstag*, the Diets, the municipal councils. There was a hail-storm of newspaper suppressions. The storm-troops marched through the streets with the air of victors, in the manner of an army of occupation in newly-conquered territory. The new elections were fixed for 5 and 12 March. However, the working-class parties and their auxiliary organisations remained intact. Did the Nazis actually believe that they would succeed in getting a majority?

The prohibition of the Communist Party, the expulsion of its members from parliament, was expected. Some serious provocation was anticipated. Night attacks became as frequent as in July. The phrase 'St Bartholomew's Night', or 'a night of long knives', was in everybody's mouth. And the provocation came – but in a form which no one expected. Göring burned the *Reichstag* and tried to put the blame on the Communists. The attempt to involve the Social-Democrats also was soon dropped. In Berlin only a few were deceived by the clumsy trick, but in the provinces it caught on at first. Today all the world knows that Göring and Hitler were the incendiaries.[70]

The burning of the *Reichstag* was a beacon for the Nazi hordes. Right through the country swept a hurricane of terror against all spiritual culture, against every free idea. A crusade of extirpation against Jews and Marxists set in. The Brown beasts, with or without police escort, entered the houses of progressive and radical poets, writers, lawyers, politicians, trade-union officials, socialists and Jews, tore people from their beds, books from shelves, smashed furniture, took whatever they could turn to use – clothing, watches and jewellery, rucksacks, typewriters and musical instruments. They behaved like bandits in the houses of quiet, cultured people. There were wholesale pogroms. In the streets Jewish citizens were knocked down. The stolen books were afterwards publicly burned by the Nazis, amid the cheers of learning-shy, beer-drinking students and mobs of loafers. Meanwhile the captives were taken to storm-troop barracks or public houses turned into torture chambers.

Meanwhile, between Nazis and nationalists there was little harmony. Each of the two coalition partners was toying with the thought of taking possession of undivided power by force, and turning out the other. Among the semi-military forces of these two parties – storm-troops and Steel

Helmets – there was feverish activity. The fact that at the elections of the Diet of Lippe-Detmold, the nationalist electors had run over to the Nazis in crowds, had inspired the nationalist leaders with dread.

On 3 March a great procession of the storm-troops was planned to pay homage to Hitler. There were rumours that the Nazis intended to seize this opportunity to occupy the Wilhelmstrasse. Under pressure from the nationalist ministers, who had the *Reichswehr* behind them, Hitler cancelled part of the programme at the last moment, and agreed that storm-troops should not march through the Wilhelmstrasse, after the nationalists had promised that the Steel Helmets, for their part, who were to hold a demonstration in the evening of election day, would also avoid the Wilhelmstrasse.

The election day passed comparatively quietly in Berlin (but by no means all over Germany). The presence of strong mounted or motorised police detachments in the streets, and police or auxiliary police in front of the polling-booths, showed the great nervousness of the authorities. Only a few sandwich-men were to be seen there, generally a Nazi, a nationalist and a Social-Democrat. In most parts of the town the Social-Democrats had staunchly stuck to this right – loyally their sandwich-men stuck to their posts. The Communists, in view of the terror chiefly directed against them, could not retain these posts except in some of the most revolutionary districts. However, they had organised a disguised cyclist patrol service throughout the town. The election committees of the two working-class parties did not meet as usual in cafés, but secretly in private flats.

The four and a half millions of votes recorded on 5 March for the Communists in spite of the terror raging all through the Reich, as well as the seven million votes of the Social-Democrats, showed how loyally the proletariat stood by its old allegiance. However, the fact that in this election Hitler, who had succeeded in bringing to the poll all the apathetic, had received, together with his monarchist allies, 52 per cent of the recorded votes, caused immense discouragement. It is true the Nazis, in addition to their terror, which muzzled their opponents, had at their disposal a tremendous propaganda and lying machine. They had at their disposal the hoardings, the survivors of the press, the broadcasting and the cinemas, they had ample means and great technical possibilities. And yet, and yet ... how could seventeen million men and women vote for incendiaries, murderers and torturers? Fifty-two per cent of the electors voted in favour of being deprived in the future of all their political and human rights – what a terrible sign of humanity sinking into barbarism! This act of political suicide of a large part of the electorate acted on the minority like the paralysing gaze of a serpent.

In Berlin all sorts of rumours were circulated which were not a good foreboding for election night. Everyone who had been politically active in any way tried to find shelter for this night with relatives or friends. After the countless raids and arrests of the last week, the number of those forced to live underground constantly increased. The workers practised solidarity regardless of party distinction – the Communist harboured in his house the Social-Democrat, the Social-Democrat shared his own bed with the persecuted Communist, a member of the Socialist Workers Party found an abode with an anarchist. A common danger united all.

In the late afternoon of 5 March the Steel Helmets were marching through the streets in procession, as homage to Hindenburg. Hindenburg, however, was not there, as originally intended, to receive the salute. He spent this night under the protection of the *Reichswehr* at Döberitz.[71] Hitler had been informed that Hindenburg had been taken ill and could not leave his palace. 'The Nazis believed that the President was on the evening of 5 March in the Wilhelmstrasse', states a memorandum of the Chairman of the nationalist group of the *Reichstag*, Dr Franz Oberfohren, a document based on internal information and published in connection with the *Reichstag* fire.[72]

The Steel Helmets had brought into Berlin detachments from outside to attend the procession, and they remained overnight in the city, having been quartered there so as to surround the government offices. At the conclusion of the election, the Nazis also began to concentrate detachments of storm-troops from the provinces in the centre of Berlin. Everywhere their motor lorries packed with troops were hurrying through the city.

However, the *Reichswehr* had taken countermeasures. Dr Oberfohren states:

> The *Reichswehr* was not idle. From the Reichskanzler Square as far as the Kaiser Wilhelm Gedachtnis Church, an armoured wireless wagon of the *Reichswehr* was patrolling slowly through Kant Street and New Kant Street. Not only in this street, but in all important main roads leading into the city, this wireless car was to be seen, thus the general staff was constantly informed as to the strength and movement of all incoming forces and about their quarters, because every incoming column of the storm-troops was followed by an intelligence car of the *Reichswehr*.

In addition to that, the *Reichswehr* had occupied the most important public buildings.

According to Dr Oberfohren's memorandum, the Nazis had intended to take action at midnight. But an hour before this time a strong group of

Reichswehr officers led by General Blomberg[73] appeared in the Chancellery, where Hitler, Göring, Goebbels and Frick[74] had assembled as the general staff for the coming struggle. To them Blomberg declared that Hindenburg was in Döberitz, and demanded the immediate withdrawal of the storm-troops from the capital, under the control of officers of the *Reichswehr*. He threatened in case of a refusal to arrest all four of them as incendiaries.

The conspiring ministers collapsed – the storm-troops concentrated in Berlin were withdrawn, and the Steel Helmets, until then kept at the ready, were allowed to sleep.

★ ★ ★

The wirepullers of the puppet Hitler understood very well that the twelve million 'red' electors meant, in quality as well as in fighting value, incomparably more than the seventeen millions of voting cattle and mercenaries who had fallen a prey to Hitlerism. They knew also that the millions of deluded would one day turn against them. From this resulted the necessity for them to keep their followers always well occupied and in a state of excitement. Small and big festivities, parades and similar allurements were arranged to keep them in good spirits. They took for their model the Roman demagogues at the time of the decay of the Republic, who by games and public feasts kept the masses in good humour and bought the votes of the loafers of Rome at election time. Bread they could not give to the people, but they did not stint the games.

The Day of Potsdam was the first in the series of the oncoming festivities. This festival was meant to capture the imagination of the lower middle class. Here the Nazis showed their true colours – and there was a smell of the Middle Ages. The workers held their noses; the deep chasm separating the noisy followers of Hitler from the class-conscious proletariat was clearly to be seen.

The Nazis recognised the failure of their stage-management. In the following week, attempts were made to touch up a picture that had become too near to Nature. Their ridiculous motto 'Abolition of class struggle' was made their key-note. In the factories the Nazis carried on a feverish campaign. By economic pressure and terror they tried to induce the workers to join the Nazi factory groups. Members of shop committees were arrested and tortured. In this way, they hoped to make a breach in the twelve-million power of the Marxists.

Now that the Nazis had, unexpectedly to themselves, obtained the majority of the recorded votes, they naturally desired to make use of the position, in order to legalise, through parliament, the naked force by which they intended to govern in future. They understood that this would increase their credit at home and abroad. Still, they did not set their foot on this road without misgiving. To free criticism they could no longer expose themselves. The Communist group of the *Reichstag*, which, as experience had shown, refused to be muzzled, had to disappear. The very much tamer Social-Democrats it sufficed to intimidate. As regards the Catholic Centre, negotiations were possible. In these circumstances the *Reichstag*, already killed, could be galvanised into life with the object of voting full powers to the government.

Had the Social-Democrats possessed at least so much self-respect as to decline participation in the disgraceful farce, after the arbitrary disqualification of four and a half million Communist votes, they could have helped German parliamentarism to die at any rate an honest death. But for that they lacked courage. In the ranks of their parliamentary group sifted out by the party machine there was no Matteotti.[75] But there was a Wels.[76] In the name of the parliamentary group, Wels read a tame declaration which after some criticism of internal politics, and denying full power to the government, nevertheless supported Hitler's foreign policy.

The same leader, Wels, soon after gave in his resignation to the Socialist International. Later on he declared he had done this only to save the property of the party ... The leaders of the trade unions issued a declaration expressing their willingness to cooperate also with this fascist state. Also in order to save their property ... Dr Hertz[77] and other Social-Democratic emissaries travelled through Europe requesting the foreign socialist press to refrain from reporting the terrible tortures meted out to active members of the working-class movement in Germany. All this in order to save their property ...[78]

And at a time when thousands had been tortured, when no town, no village, was left where the Brown beasts had not raged, when the trade-union offices, party houses and printing presses had long ago been taken over by the Nazis, when hundreds of socialists had been brutally murdered, when tens of thousands had been imprisoned for months in concentration camps, subjected to humiliation – on 9 August 1933, there were still some German labour 'leaders' who felt no shame in asking the British trade unions to refrain from criticising German conditions ...

Twelve million workers had voted red in spite of the terror. They would have been prepared to fight. But after this complete failure of their organisations, many lost heart. If the proletarian organisations were unable to take the offensive, why did they not organise passive resistance? In most industrial enterprises the Nazis formed a negligible fragment. Now they suddenly wanted to force the masses of the workers into their factory groups. Of course, no terror could have compelled millions of anti-fascists to join fascist organisations if these workers in their own legal or illegal organisations could have found moral support. But that is exactly what was lacking. There was no one who called upon the masses to resist. Left entirely to themselves, nevertheless the great majority of the industrial workers, out of a proper class feeling, declined to join. However, many Communists remained loyal to their long-practised 'tactic of disruption' and joined the Nazi factory groups, in order to disrupt them from within, while others – Communists and Social-Democrats – did the like from egotism or cowardice. With the increase of the terror, there was an influx of Communists into the storm-troops, of Social-Democrats into the Steel Helmets. Soon it was impossible to distinguish between friend and foe – between heroic illegal workers, harmless cowards, and dangerous renegades. These well-meant tactics of disruption cut both ways and minimised the power of resistance of the masses.

The climax of the campaign to win over the factory workers was 1 May, with its processions and fireworks. In Berlin, on the Tempelhof Field, enormous crowds of people gathered. They came to see the biggest firework display Berlin had ever known, although they were supposed to demonstrate for the bridging over of class antagonism and the 'unity of the German people'. Very fitting, therefore, was the provision of good seats at £1 apiece for the smart set who had brought an ample supply of toothsome dainties, while the unemployed with hungry stomachs were crowded together down below. The following day poor women came to search for the fragments that remained, but were chased away by storm-troops lest foreign press photographers might find here a lurid illustration of the story of the abolished class antagonism.

Encouraged by the participation of such large masses in their 'German May', annoyed by the coldness with which the whole affair had been met by the industrial workers, reassured by the absence of any active resistance against the raising of the swastika flag on the trade-union clubs and other buildings belonging to the working-class movement, the Nazis, on the following day, began to 'take over' the trade unions. They took over the money-boxes filled with the hardly-gained pennies of working men and women, destroying by one stroke of the pen the rights of those who had paid their subscriptions for many years; they took over the trade-union offices, arrested the elected leaders and the more class-conscious ones among the technical staff, replacing them by bandits of their own, recruited mostly from the declassed Nazi 'intellectuals' or ex-non-commissioned officers.

The present members found themselves caught in a trap – they were not permitted to leave the unions. They were expected to continue paying contributions to maintain these gentry, but were to have no further say in the matter, as that would contradict the 'principle of authority'. Talk on wages and working conditions became taboo. Strikes were declared illegal. Of the trade unions nothing now remains but an empty shell. The only activity left to them is to control the workers during their spare time in order to deprive them of time and opportunity for any 'undesirable' activity – illegal work or even private thinking.

The Nazis then threw the trade unions of all political shades,[79] into one common cauldron, adding the employers' associations for seasoning, let their notorious Dr Ley[80] swim on top of it as a dumpling, and called the stew thus made the 'Labour Front'.

The chief activity of this 'Labour Front' is the organisation of Nazi parades. In a proclamation *To All Toilers*, issued in the autumn of 1933, it declares: 'According to the will of our leader, Adolf Hitler, the German Labour Front is not the place to consider questions arising out of the daily labour.' However, when a German newspaper, the *Oberpfälzischer Kurier*, stated that the trade unions were disappearing, it was compelled to publish on 10 December 1933 the following characteristic *démenti*: 'The statement "the trade unions are disappearing" is not correct. The fact is that the unions meanwhile continue their existence. Only when the leader of the German Labour Front, Dr Robert Ley, finds it necessary will they be liquidated.' The cooperatives were also taken over by the Nazis and are sharing the fate of the trade unions.

The political parties had to disappear. The Communist Party was followed by the Social-Democratic Party into Nirvana, the Democrats and the Catholic Centre vanished, even the parties of the right withered away. The parliamentary debris of the capitalist parties was sucked in by the Nazis.

On 14 July 1933, the Nazi government promulgated a law declaring all political parties except the Nazi Party illegal. It reads:

Clause 1. In Germany there exists only one political party, the National Socialist German Workers Party.
Clause 2. Whosoever undertakes to maintain the organisation of another political party or to form a new political party is liable to punishment ... by penal servitude up to three years or by imprisonment from six months to three years.

A crusade against culture commenced. All cultural institutions and societies of the proletariat were already destroyed. The municipal secular schools and the experimental schools, with their new libertarian methods for the development of personality, were destroyed, their teachers turned out or put in concentration camps. The elementary schools were turned into nationalist drill-halls. They were designed to bring up spineless mercenaries. Hitler had declared he would take the children away from the proletariat, and the Nazi school policy clearly aimed at that. The children of tens of thousands of tortured, arrested, kidnapped or murdered workers formerly active in the working-class movement were now compelled to cheer their parents' torturer by greeting their teacher with 'Heil Hitler'. In many schools, Jewish children were thrust into a ghetto corner, and humiliated. In the higher schools, again, fatuous drill was introduced. Military night-practice for the older boys took the place of serious schoolwork. Even part of the normal lesson-time was to be devoted to talks on protection against gas attacks and bacteriological warfare.

The universities were left completely to the mercy of the Hitler bandits. Jews and Marxists disappeared from their professorial chairs, as well as from the auditorium. A new spirit took possession of the universities – the spirit of fanaticism and brute force. Before this new spirit, the great minds of Germany had to flee across the frontier, and even there they were not safe from the bullets of brutalised fanatics.

Science was to be made a prostitute of the fascist state. Art met with no better fate. Not ability or knowledge but creed alone became the deciding factor. The best authors fled, the great artists followed them abroad. The famous stage-managers and cinema technicians hurried after them. The mediocre ones and those devoid of ideas rejoiced – their time had come.

The German press was brought down to the Nazi level – all German newspapers are now Nazi sheets. They have become so gloomy that people refuse to read them. While foreign newspapers are imported in ever-increasing numbers, the German press is dying.

According to the report of the *Institut für Zeitungskunde* (Institute for Contemporary Studies) of October 1933, the number of German daily papers decreased from 2703 in 1932 to 1128 in 1933; 1248 newspapers had been suppressed, while 327 died a natural death. The number of weekly journals was reduced from 348 to 217; fortnightly reviews from 96 to 47, and monthly journals from 183 to 102. In 1932 the monthly average of printed copies reached 1000 millions – in June 1933 it went down to 300 million copies, a decrease of 70 per cent! The number of permanently employed editors in 1932 was 19,200, in 1933 only 5341. Even the *Angriff*, the organ of the Minister of Propaganda, Goebbels, with all its subsidies and official booming, lost two-thirds of its circulation – from 60,000 in 1931, it dwindled to 20,000.

Germany's numerous good public libraries were 'purged' – all the treasures of libertarian thought they contained were sacrificed to Wotan, while a mob of ignorant students were the priests.

However, the ideology of the Nazis is by no means derived from the Wotan-worshipping times of Germanic paganism with its rough but honest brutality. It has more in common with the darkest times of the romanised Middle Ages, with their corrupt, sadist, cowardly cruelty, with their black superstition, their heresy hunts, witch-hunts, and bloody Jew-baiting.

Against the half-million of German Jews a 'holy war' was declared. Jewish scientists and artists, authors, publicists, organisers, lawyers and doctors were to be politically degraded, physically destroyed, economically ruined, morally humiliated. The mass of the Jewish population was delivered to the tender mercy of the storm-troops as an object for the gratification of their desire for social revenge. The Jews were to suffer for the sins of the Lahusens,[81] Stinnes and other 'Aryan' knights. Down even to the schools, where defenceless Jewish children were made to endure the whole brutality of future Wotan-warriors, this race-war was raging. Medieval superstition was revived, notions from the ancient blood cult; even the disgraceful ritual murder lie was dug up!

But the wildest hatred of the Nazis was directed against the Marxists. Thousands of men and women who had been active in the labour movement, in the political, trade-union, cooperative or cultural spheres, who had been working in the free-thinking school reform or peace movement, who as scientists, poets, authors or artists, had stood up for Communist, Socialist or liberal ideas, suddenly found themselves deprived of rights and protection, at the mercy of the Brown hordes. These creatures could by day or night enter their houses, just as they thought fit, to make 'searches'. Often such Nazi hordes passed through a town or village on motor lorries. In such places they rounded up Marxists, taking them into one of the torture houses, where they were themselves subjected to horrible torments, and compelled to witness the torturing of their fellow prisoners. Many of them were afterwards taken to hospitals with broken bones, or simply turned out into the street. But a large number remained under arrest and were taken to concentration camps, which had been established in all parts of the country. The number of political prisoners was constantly growing – in September 1933 the number exceeded 80,000.

In the concentration camps, the Nazi gaolers found a special pleasure in tormenting and humiliating especially their prominent prisoners. By order of empty-headed youngsters they had to stand to attention, to exercise, to shout 'Heil Hitler', sing the 'Horst Wessel' song, and 'Deutschland über alles'. The dirtiest and most repulsive jobs were always kept for them. The prisoners, especially the older ones, when at work were always made to run, driven with blows and kicks. Barbarians against cultured people! The object was the physical destruction of the spiritual part of the German nation – ill-treatment and humiliation were to break the spirit, lack of sleep and insufficient nourishment the body. If these means failed, revolver bullets followed. The number of 'executions' considerably exceeds the number of death sentences in court ... Heinrich Heine's aphorism of Germany as one huge prison has become cruel reality.

Having carried through the imprisonment, destruction or expulsion of cultural Germany, the remainder being driven underground, the way was now clear for the Nazis to build up their 'authoritative' and 'totalitarian' state.

All the authorities and institutions of the Reich, the states and the municipalities were *gleichgeschaltet* (Nazified) and reorganised on authoritative lines. In the words of the Weimar Constitution: 'all power emanates from the people'; now it suddenly emanated from 'the leader'. He appointed his lieutenants, who in their turn set up their underlings, and so to the bottom, until a Nazi net was uniformly woven throughout the whole administration. Every kind of private association was also Nazified or dissolved. All juvenile organisations were subordinated to the 'Hitler Youth'. All that was left of non-political social and economic societies had to conform to the totalitarian one-party state. The Church tried to maintain a certain degree of independence, but in vain. It found itself struggling in the same net.

The 'idea' of the 'corporative state', borrowed from Mussolini's 'classical' fascism, according to which the corporations are permitted to put forward lists of candidates from which a consultative body for the 'leader' is appointed, has up to the present proved in Germany to be the same farcical humbug as in Italy. In reality, it is the fascist or Nazi caucus that holds the reins of government as agents of big money; in their hands is concentrated the executive, the administrative power, and all the armed forces of the state. Everything else exists only on paper, and serves as a curtain to hide the reality.

★ ★ ★

Fascism has now become an article for export: no people can feel entirely immune from this plague.

Fascism is the modern form of capitalist reaction. It is the last attempt of the lords of money to keep economic and political power in their own hands, when this can no longer be achieved through democratic forms. Fascism means the domination of Big Capital over the proletariat, with the aid of the slum proletariat and the despairing lower middle class.

A characteristic feature of fascism is the use of popular socialist-sounding slogans (and even socialist emblems, songs, etc) to cover their anti-socialist deeds. It is a kind of militarised dictatorship of a completely new type, supported by militarised gangsters, terrorising the population. Therefore lies, dishonesty and brute force are an essential part of the ideology of fascism. The democratic principle of liberty and responsibility, fascism replaces by the principle of authoritative leadership. For freedom of thought, of speech, of the press, for liberty of art and science, there is no room under fascism. Whereas all tyrannies of the past demanded of the 'subject' only passive obedience, fascism demands of everybody, from the cradle to the grave, *active* support.

Fascism insists upon the totalitarian state. That means it does not admit the existence of any sphere of public or private life outside the control of the fascist state. Under fascism the 'subject' in his work, in his social relations, his political activities, his scientific outlook, his religious fervour, his artistic taste, his sexual behaviour, his physical exercise, and even his use of spare time, is under the control of the state. Neither ancient slavery nor medieval serfdom have ever known such a measure of bondage.

★ ★ ★

However 'totalitarian' the fascist state in Germany may appear, it nevertheless rules only the surface. Below, subterranean Germany ferments and simmers, undismayed and unconquered. Here are gathering the forces of resistance, all those whose most precious hope it is to put an end some day to Hitler barbarity, and to put Germany again into the ranks of civilised nations. The high walls separating the different sections of the German working-class movement are crumbling – common sacrifices in the common fight against the common foe are serving as a strong cement, however much some emigrated leaders and the Communist International may try to counteract it, A new rejuvenated revolutionary working-class movement is germinating.

It can, however, become dangerous to the fascist regime only when it shows new positive socialist objectives calling forth the enthusiasm of the masses. Neither a Communist dictatorship nor the Weimar Republic have any longer any attraction for the German people. Only when the revolutionary movement, by creating a new ideology of comradeship and revolutionary solidarity, becomes a new moral force, gathering and strengthening the masses, and thus helps to overcome the boundless discouragement resulting from the complete breakdown of the German labour movement – only then will German fascism be really menaced from within.

Probably in no country of Europe had socialist ideas become the common property of the masses as in Germany. The Nazi state is therefore threatened not only by the conscious enemies of the regime, but also by the large number of those who had voted for Hitler, because they took his socialist phrases in good faith. These people fell victims to the widespread superstition that the wielder of political power can arbitrarily overrule economic laws. They therefore expected that Hitler, to whom they attributed anti-capitalist tendencies, would soon lead them out of the economic crisis.

In Italy, fascism came at the end of a crisis, the incipient improvement of the economic situation (American orders!) therefore appeared to be its work. Hitler, on the contrary, is faced with a crisis, which in Germany shows no sign of decreasing. The very existence of Hitlerism aggravates and perpetuates the crisis. All the cooking of figures and swindling manoeuvres cannot alter the fact.

After their great victory the Nazi hordes felt themselves the new masters. They believed they could not only pose in front of the working-class population and the small Jewish shopkeepers, they were anxious to play the master towards the big capitalists. In the factories they lifted their heads, and a number of Nazi factory groups took it upon themselves to appoint 'commissars'. They counted without their host. The agrarians who could rely upon the *Reichswehr* and the big lords of industry with whom they were interrelated soon put an end to this. Not for this purpose had they suckled the Hitler movement on their fat wallets! They gave to Herr Hitler a few private lessons in political economy and so brought their pupil to the conviction that the affair was rather complicated. The consequence was Hitler's declaration: 'The revolution is at an end.'

While all arbitrary interference with industry was prohibited and disobedient commissars were threatened with the concentration camp, the power of the magnates of capital was greatly increased by the 'Law of Reorganisation of Industry' of 27 February 1934. Their organisations have been strengthened by the introduction of compulsory membership and have acquired dictatorial powers over all employers. Their rights and property remain free from state interference. The Nazi principle of leadership is introduced, but the appointed leaders require a vote of confidence to be carried annually by a 'leaders' council'.

The entire industry and trade of the country is divided into twelve groups, a leader being appointed for each of them, and a chief leader representing industry as a whole. Thus Philipp Kessler of the Siemens concern, Graf von der Goltz, late head of Ivar Kreuger's 'Union Bank',[82] Krupp von Bohlen of the armament industry, Albert Vögler of the Steel Trust, and similar knights of industry, are officially sanctioned as the real masters of Germany.

Meanwhile the Minister of Agriculture, Darré,[83] had to pacify the disturbed Junkers. With special emphasis on Hitler's agreement, he declared on 10 July 1933 that there would be no interference with the large estates, not even those most in debt. The Nazis had found a better solution of the agrarian problem — a land fund was to be formed for the creation of small holdings, and the great landlords were invited to make a gift of land for the purpose. And soon the Nazis were able to report that 'great achievement' — in a short time they had in this way obtained 500 hectares (about 1200 acres) of land 'in Prussia alone'.

These were, however, only preliminaries. Now we witness peculiar plans and experiments in the agrarian policy of Nazi Germany. They have taken a leaf out of General Schleicher's agrarian militarist schemes and set to work in order to create a caste of Cossacks on the lines so successfully practised at one time by the Czars of Russia.

Feudalism is to be revived in rural Germany. Out of the total of about five million independent smallholders, they wish to establish a special privileged caste of pure Aryan 'hereditary peasants' whose present estates of 7.5 to 12.5 hectares cannot be sold or divided. One-half to one million such new Cossacks are to be created, who, in return for these privileges, must undertake special military duties and political (even judiciary) functions. They thus become a new, important and reliable military force for war and civil strife.

For this purpose the Nazis now intend to utilise the land purchased during a number of years out of the taxpayers' money for the creation of small holdings. So, poor peasants will be robbed in order to increase the size of the estates of the new Cossacks. The estates of the Junkers remain intact and will be strengthened by the provision of cheap labour and the introduction of a kind of serfdom for rural workers.

The problem of unemployment was tackled by the Nazis in various ways. At first, attempts were made to decrease the number of unemployed through labour service, subsidies to employers, and by forcing additional labour on some employers. Then Goebbels came forward with his 'great plan' to combat the misery of the unemployed by collecting donations. The rich people were to sacrifice one meal, the workers in employment one hour's wage, bank depositors a small sum monthly. Now the chief efforts of the Nazis are directed to the increase of production of armaments and war materials and to the provision of public works consisting largely in building strategic roads. Women and young workers are replaced by older male workers and are taken to so-called 'labour camps' or handed over to the Junkers and rich peasants for exploitation. This is an ingenious way of taking them off the register, for as soon as they are considered 'agricultural labourers' they lose their right to unemployment benefit.

In November 1933, according to Herr Seldte,[84] Nazi Minister of Labour, there were 234,000 persons in labour service, 298,000 occupied on public relief works, and 165,000 so-called 'agricultural assistants'. The burden of these public relief works is borne chiefly by the local authorities. No wonder therefore that the latter have reached a stage of bankruptcy. The debts of German municipalities with a population of over 10,000 in May 1934 reached 9439 million marks, while they are already in arrears with a further 595 million marks.[85] Generally the national income is decreasing, the purchasing-power of the population is shrinking. Consequently the small shopkeepers are sinking into poverty.

The greatest success in combating unemployment the Nazis have achieved is undoubtedly on the statistical front. Their statistics 'prove' a constant decrease in the number of the unemployed. But the total earnings of the increased number of employed persons, as reflected in the revenue derived from the wage-tax, is decreasing. Herr Goebbels is right – the object of statistics in Germany is 'to create enthusiasm'! Meanwhile wages and unemployment benefit have been cut below starvation level. In theory the old wage agreements were supposed to remain. In reality there is a general reduction of wages, since there are no trade unions to protect the individual worker, and the workers are entirely at the mercy of brutal German employers. No general statistics on wages actually paid are available, as the statistics deal so far only with the old wage agreements which remain on paper. Some idea of the tendency towards a reduction of wages in Nazi Germany may be gained by taking actual cases. There are, for instance, the highly skilled and well-paid workers in the glass and china industry of Weiden and Neustadt. In 1928 their weekly wages reached 65 marks (£3 10s at par), in January 1933 they earned 45 to 55 marks, but in May of the same year their wages went down to 26 marks – a reduction of 42 per cent in five months of Nazi rule.

And the sinking wages are still further reduced by all sorts of compulsory reductions for various purposes. Thus, a worker earning 30.24 marks per week found his wages reduced by 0.90 marks for invalidity insurance, 1.02 marks for unemployment insurance, 1.24 marks for sickness insurance, 0.75

marks towards the state fund for the relief of the unemployed, 0.60 marks wage-tax, 1.50 marks citizen tax, 0.60 marks 'marriage assistance', 0.16 marks towards public works, 1.10 marks contribution for his bluff 'trade union' – leaving him with 22.37 marks (£1 2s 4d).

Having destroyed the trade unions and reduced the workers to slavery conditions the Nazis have legalised their system of slavery in a law establishing the subjugation of the workers to their employers. The Law for the Regulation of National Labour of 20 January 1934 is already known in Germany as the 'Slavery Act'.

The Nazis wish to 'abolish class struggle' by depriving the working class of all possibilities to struggle, delivering them to the mercy of the capitalists and proclaiming the identity of the interests of exploiters and exploited.

The first clause of this 'Slavery Act' proclaims:

In the enterprise the employer as leader, the employees and workers as followers, are working together for the advancement of the enterprise and for the common good of people and state.

The second clause reveals what is implied by these new terms – the employer as 'leader' fixes wages and conditions of labour, and the workers as 'followers', must obey and may not even grumble. It reads:

1) The leader of the enterprise decides for the followers on all matters of the enterprise so far as they are regulated by this law.
2) He has to care for the followers. The latter have to observe towards him the loyalty arising out of the fellowship of the enterprise.

Clause 27 still further emphasises this peculiar relationship, empowering the employer, 'the leader', to fix conditions of labour, wages, and to inflict fines by dictating the *Betriebsordnung* (factory rules).

Fearing that the capitalists might prove too generous, Clause 29 insists that the minimum wage should not be fixed too high so as to leave scope for special favours to loyal slaves. The trade-union rate is thus to be replaced by a sort of bonus system.

In enterprises employing over twenty people, there is to be formed a 'Confidence Council' elected by 'secret ballot' from a list of candidates put forward by the Nazi group in conjunction with the employer (Clause 5.10). In factories where there are no Nazi groups there can be no elections. In such and similar cases the members of the 'Confidence Council' are appointed by an official of the Nazi state described as *Treuhänder der Arbeit*.

The chief functions of the 'Confidence Councils' are to further 'mutual confidence' in the factory and to prevent conflicts (Clause 6). They have the right to appeal against decisions of the employer regarding wages and working conditions to the *Treuhänder der Arbeit* of the district (Clause 16). However, persistent complainants to that official may be punished (Clause 36). Such cases come under the jurisdiction of special 'Courts of Honour' (the latest Nazi invention!), and may be punished by reproof, fines, dismissal, etc.

This law supersedes most of the previous legislation for the protection of labour. It does away with collective bargaining. In short, it is a Nazi charter against labour. No wonder that dissatisfaction is growing all over Germany. Hitler, who wanted to 'abolish' class struggle, can keep in power only by intensified class struggle. He cannot carry on without terror. If, at the outset, he required torture houses, concentration camps, and gangsters to put down the opponents of the Nazi regime, today he needs them also to keep his disgruntled followers in check. The carrying out of the terror became more and more official, shifting from the storm-troops to the secret police, but the terror, sometimes diminishing, sometimes intensifying, retains its original cruel, sinister character. The imprisonment of complete detachments of storm-troops in concentration camps, the murdering of obnoxious lower-rank officers, are indications of the possibility of further developments.

Every dictator is compelled by circumstances to dismiss from the administration intelligent thinking men with a sense of responsibility. 'He thinks too much: such men are dangerous.' Only tools without will or character seem to him to be a guarantee for the uniformity of leadership for which he strives. In filling the various posts from the top downwards, not ability and honesty but obedience is the essential qualification. Therefore corruption and inefficiency are the characteristic features of fascist dictatorship, consequently its fear of honest criticism must constantly grow. The increasing suppression of criticism in its turn hastens the process of degradation, until the whole regime is immersed in the swamp, bursts from the inside, or is shattered from the outside.

Big Capital, the real master of Hitler Germany, does not want to permit economic experiments. The state capitalist tendencies of Schleicher appear to it suspect. Yet, under the pressure of the crisis and the fear of the awakening impoverished masses, Hitler might be driven to experiments in the direction of a certain 'planned economy' or state capitalism. Also as a measure of economic preparation for war, this might be conceivable – some clauses of the Nazi agrarian law can be explained only on such an assumption. Here are two conflicting tendencies at work, and it remains to be seen whether this will lead to the perpetuation of the zigzag course, or whether one of these two tendencies will get the upper hand.

State capitalism, as such, is endowed with dangerous poison fangs which can be drawn only by a genuine democratic control and by alert, compact labour organisations. As a basis of despotism, state capitalism becomes unbearable. Because an established state capitalism – as we see it today in Russia – makes the citizen in all spheres of his life dependent on the state: the state is his employer, his landlord, his tradesman, and by no change of employment or lodging can he escape from it. The state decides the admission of his children to higher schools, of members of his family to hospitals. A conflict with the state as employer might easily lead to reprisals by the state as tradesman, landlord or schoolmaster. A corrupt, petty, spiteful administration, which is a feature of every dictatorship, could not but drive the citizen to despair.

Nevertheless, the complexity of German economic life leaves little room for experiment by such unqualified hands – the incompetent bureaucratic machine of the 'totalitarian' state might, like the proverbial bull, destroy too much china.

Hitler therefore has solemnly renounced the 'second revolution', that is to say the nebulous socialist tendencies implied in his programme. This had done service in the propaganda, before the conquest of power. After dinner the world appears in a different light.

As the socialist pillar of the so-called 'National Socialism' (as the Nazis styled their movement) has collapsed, there remains only the nationalist pillar. On it now rests the weight of the whole structure, and it must be correspondingly strengthened.

The footings are there. Prussian militarism is alive – fourteen years' freedom from conscription have not sufficed for it to die out. By the system of *Militäranwärter*, this cancer has eaten too deep into the national life. Now the plague of militarism is to be injected even into the schoolchildren.

Adventures in foreign policy are designed to divert the attention of the masses from the internal misery, from the inability of the Nazis to get rid of the internal antagonism. In derision of all treaties, Germany is openly preparing for war. The entire population is put under some sort of military training. The Nazis are trying hard to work up a war psychology.

In all departments, feverish war preparations are in progress. The armament firms are laughing up their sleeves. Despite the Versailles Treaty, Germany is by no means defenceless. Already in the days of the Republic, German militarists knew how to turn the *Reichswehr* into a *cadre* army of the

American type. Germany has no lack of reserves. The twelve-year military service has remained on paper. The faces of the *Reichswehr* bore the marks of eternal youth – it would be necessary to include the 'Steel Helmets' in order to find the solution of this riddle.

Apart from that, Germany possesses a second military system – the militia. Since Hitler's ascent to power, the storm-troops – both Brown and Black – have received a thorough military training, and assumed the character of a state institution. They have been trained not merely in the use of machine-guns and hand-grenades for street fighting – already the strong air-squadrons organised from their ranks show that far-reaching objectives have been kept in mind in their training.

Recently the insatiable militarism of the Hitler regime has, further, made all preparations for the reintroduction of conscription. For the time being it is officially veiled as compulsory labour service. By the whip of hunger as well as by direct compulsion, young men are being pressed into this third army of the 'Third Reich'. As a result of these peculiar methods of recruiting, this labour army has a definitely proletarian character, so that the Nazis do not dare to arm it. But it is getting the necessary military training, to be turned to use at any moment.

To keep power, Nazism must have 'victories'. With all its might, it strives for the uniting of all Germans under the swastika. It presses forward and tries to impose its barbarity on Austria, Czechoslovakia, Switzerland, Alsace-Lorraine, the free Saar territory, New Belgium, Holland, Denmark, Lettland, Lithuania and Poland.

The existence of the Hitler regime therefore vastly increases the danger of war. Still, this regime has its Achilles' heel. In retrograde dictatorships, arms have an inclination to shoot backwards. In case of war at present large masses of the German workers would undoubtedly form insurrectionary forces that would attack the regime in its rear.

Many foreign pacifists have not yet realised this situation. They direct their fire, now as before, against the Versailles Treaty. However proper and progressive their demand for a revision of this treaty was during the existence of the German Republic, today it is reactionary and dangerous. A revision of the Versailles Treaty today would mean the strengthening of the barbaric Hitler regime, whose continued existence must sooner or later lead to war. They, therefore, resemble a man bravely marching forward – life turns him round, and he continues to go forward not noticing that he is moving backward ...

Hitler requires victories. The task of all friends of Progress, Peace and Liberty is therefore to see to it that in the field of foreign policy only defeat awaits him. Economic decay, humiliation in international politics, will soon open the eyes of Hitler's followers, and thus shorten the period of suffering of the German people. Concessions to Hitler increase the war danger – dogs bite when fear is shown!

The problem of the continued existence of the Nazi regime is not solely a German question. This plague-spot threatens all nations – all nations therefore are under an obligation to stamp it out.

★ ★ ★

The international proletariat must, if it does not want to go under, defend democracy. Democracy is not a bourgeois invention. It has been gained, developed and protected by the blood of the working class. But democracy alone does not suffice, it cannot appease the hunger of the unemployed, or do away with the crisis and its consequences. The best defence of democracy is a clear-cut socialist policy. Not socialist slogans, but a clear socialist policy in accordance with the changed political and social conditions.

The present world crisis with its unprecedented dimensions, duration and severity, has led everywhere to the declassing of large numbers of proletarians; it has weakened the fighting capacity of the working class. This wholesale declassing must be countered, even now under capitalism: a drastic shortening of working hours, the raising of the school age, are important milestones on this road.

Prevention of the wholesale declassing, merciless fight against all forms of corruption, democratisation of the working-class movement, education of organised labour to revolutionary responsibility, activity and initiative, education of the masses, and especially of the youth, to revolutionary thought and action – these are the most important measures to prevent the further spread of fascism.

The victory of fascism in Italy and Germany, and Austria, shows that not local but general causes are at the bottom of this phenomenon.

Great changes have taken place in economic life; the position of the working class in state and industry has undergone extensive change – but the working-class movement has not everywhere adapted itself to the changed conditions; it has become static in its old forms of thought and organisation, and, in some cases, has drifted away from the broad masses of the people.

It has been the failure of the working-class movement in times of crisis that has opened the door to fascism. This fact contains a lesson.

The working-class movement must readjust itself, it must again become a real force in class struggle, round which will gather the whole working class in their work, their struggle, and their aspirations. It must become again virile and ready for action – it must show to the working class a prospect of a better, socialist future, and it must lead them in the struggle for the attainment of this object, making it the primary question of the day.

The epoch of steady, peaceful growth is past. A new period of hard fight confronts the proletariat. Not growth and preparation for life are now its task, but life itself – the decisive fight. This demands a change of psychology. The working class in the middle of the twentieth century cannot fight *only* by the ballot-box and resolutions – it must get back to its revolutionary starting-point. It must take the offensive in the decisive battle for socialism.

NOTES

Notes have been added by Paul Flewers except where mentioned.
1. *Der wirtschaftliche Wiederaufbau der Union der Sozialistischen Sowjet-Republiken* (Handelsvertretung der UdSSr in Deutschland, Berlin, 1924); *Die wirtschaftlichen Entwickelung der Sowjet-Union* (Handelsvertretung der UdSSr in Deutschland, Berlin, 1926).
2. The *Reichsbanner*, 'The Flag of the Reich', was the Social-Democratic self-defence organisation. All its assets were seized by Hitler on 10 May 1933.
3. The *Deutschnationale Volkspartei* (DNVP – German Nationalist People's Party) was formed in 1918 by means of a merger of the German Conservative Party, the Free Conservative Party and the hard-right faction of the National Liberal Party. It was chaired by Oskar Hergt (1918–24), Kuno Graf von Westarp (1924–28) and Alfred Hugenberg (1928–33). Virulently opposed to the Weimar Republic, it lost support to the more populist National Socialist German Workers Party (NSDAP), and finally ended as a junior partner of the Nazis in Hitler's government of 'National Concentration' in 1933 before dissolving itself.
4. The *Deutsche Volkspartei* (DVP – German People's Party) was formed in 1918 from the right wing of the National Liberal Party. It was led by Gustav Stresemann (see note 38). Its initial opposition to the Weimar Republic softened somewhat under Stresemann's leadership, but returned after his death.
5. Hugo Stinnes (1870–1924) was a German industrialist. Starting off in coal-mining, he diversified into shipping, transport and electricity supply. He was a founder of the DVP, and was elected to the *Reichstag* in 1920. He subsequently built up a publishing empire, and made a fortune during the hyperinflation by borrowing huge loans and repaying them when they were vastly depreciated.
6. August Thyssen (1842-1926) was a leading German industrialist who built a huge iron and coal conglomerate. Politically he was a conservative nationalist. His son Friedrich 'Fritz' Thyssen (1873-1951) played an important role in the family business and took control of it after his father's death. He was a member of the DNVP, supported Hitler financially from 1923, and joined the NSDAP in 1933. He fell out with Hitler during the Second World War and was interned.
7. Albert Vögler (1877–1945) was a German industrialist. He worked in the iron and steel and mining industries and took over Stinnes' empire in 1924. He was a founding member of the DVP. He financed Hitler during 1931–33, and played a leading role in

the wartime munitions industry.
8. *Pensionsberechtigt* – having a right to a pension [Author's note].
9. The Vendôme Column was erected in the Place Vendôme in Paris to commemorate the French victory in the Battle of Austerlitz in 1805. It was demolished on the order of the Paris Commune in 1871, and was rebuilt after the Commune was suppressed.
10. The Kapp Putsch was an attempt in March 1920 by right-wing forces to overthrow the Weimar Republic. Although its nominal leader was the East Prussian civil servant Wolfgang Kapp, its prime mover was General Walther von Lüttwitz, a *Freikorps* leader and commander of the Berlin *Reichswehr*. The coup collapsed after it was countered by a massive general strike called by the trade unions.
11. The *Orgesch* was the popular name for the *Organisation Escherich*, a right-wing paramilitary organisation led by the Bavarian Georg Escherich (1870–1941). It was set up in 1920 and disbanded by the Allied occupying authorities in 1921. Escherich subsequently set up similar organisations. The Ehrhard Brigade, or *Marinebrigade Ehrhardt*, named after Hermann Ehrhardt (1881–1971), was one of the *Freikorps* groups, and was set up by German naval personnel in the aftermath of the First World War. Numbering about 6000 men, it played an important role in suppressing left-wing activities across Germany, and participated in the Kapp Putsch. Many of its members subsequently joined the Nazis.
12. Otto Karl Gessler (1875–1955) was a founder of the right-wing liberal *Deutsche Demokratische Partei* (DDP – German Democratic Party), and was Minister of Defence during 1920–28.
13. Johannes Friedrich von Seeckt (1866–1936) was a career army officer. He was in charge of rebuilding the German army after the First World War, and was determined to subvert the military restrictions imposed by the Versailles Treaty upon Germany, including by way of secret military cooperation with the Soviet Union. After Hitler's victory, he became a military advisor to Chiang Kai-Shek.
14. See note 4, p. 35.
15. See note 23, p. 38.
16. The Dawes Plan was drawn up in 1923 by a team under the US Republican Vice-President Charles Dawes, and the Young Plan was drawn up in 1929 by a team under the US lawyer Owen Young and was ratified in 1930. Both were intended to regulate the payment of the reparations that Germany was obliged to pay under the Versailles Treaty.
17. Walther Rathenau (1867–1922) was a German industrialist. He became chairman of the *Allgemeine Elektrizitäts-Gesellschaft* (AEG) combine in 1915, and played a major role in organising Germany's industrial war effort. A staunch nationalist, he was a founder of the liberal German Democratic Party, and was appointed Minister for Reconstruction in 1921 and Foreign Minister in 1922. He was in favour of economic collaboration with the Soviet Union, and engineered the Treaty of Rapallo. He was assassinated by an anti-Semitic gang.
18. Alexander Niedner (1862–1930) was President of the Senate of the Supreme Court and Chairman of the Constitutional Court to Protect the Republic during 1924–28.
19. See note 15, p. 37.
20. Louis Eugène Cavignac (1802–1857) was a French general and statesman. He was Minister of War and then Head of the Executive Power in 1848, and led the crushing

of the Paris workers' insurrection of June 1848.
21. See note 5, p. 35.
22. See note 3, p. 35.
23. See note 22, p. 38.
24. The potato crop in Germany failed during 1916, and an attempt was made to compensate by means of the late sowing of turnips, hence the 'Turnip Winter'. The potato crop failure, combined with the British naval blockade, resulted in severe food shortages.
25. The *Kulturkampf* (Culture Struggle) was a series of discriminatory measures against the Roman Catholic Church introduced by the Prussian government under its Prime Minister Otto Eduard Leopold von Bismarck (1815–1898). It was brought to an end because of resistance from Roman Catholics and Bismarck's recognition of the need for new allies in his opposition to Social-Democracy.
26. See note 24, p. 38.
27. The House of Wittelsbach reigned in Bavaria for 738 years until its abdication in November 1918.
28. Otto Wolff (1881–1940) was a German industrialist who co-founded Otto Wolff AG, a German steel company which branched out into other metals, coal and electrical manufacturing during the 1920s. It manufactured munitions during the Second World War.
29. And all the rest of them.
30. Friedrich Flick (1883–1972) was a German industrialist. He ran an extensive coal and steel conglomerate, and was a prominent financial supporter of Hitler from 1933, donating some seven million marks to the NSDAP.
31. See note 21, p. 38.
32. In the Greek myth, Penelope was bothered by dubious suitors whilst her husband Odysseus was absent. In order to keep them at bay, she pretended to be weaving a shroud for his old father, promising to choose one when she has finished it. Each evening she unravelled some of what she wove during the day, but her subterfuge was eventually discovered.
33. See note 26, p. 39.
34. The *Stahlhelm, Bund der Frontsoldaten* (The Steel Helmet, League of Frontline Soldiers) was the paramilitary force of extreme right-wing conservatism, generally allied with the DNVP. Founded in December 1918, by 1930 it had half a million members. In 1934, it was renamed the *Nationalsozialistischer Deutscher Frontkämpferbund* (Federation of the National Socialist Frontline-Fighters) and integrated into the SA, and dissolved in 1935.
35. The *Schwarze Reichswehr* or Black Reichswehr was a collection of paramilitary bodies assembled by the German military leadership as one of the means to subvert the tight restrictions placed upon the country's armed forces under the Versailles Treaty. Its membership often overlapped with those of the *Freikorps* groups.
36. Otto von Lossow (1868–1938) was a career army officer. He was one of the leaders of the postwar *Reichswehr*, and was head of the military area containing Bavaria at the time of Hitler's Beer Hall Putsch. He favoured the idea of a nationalist coup, but did not support Hitler's bid for power.
37. See note 25, p. 39.
38. Gustav Stresemann (1878–1929) was an industrialist who played a major role in forming the DVP from the right wing of the National Liberal Party. One of the very few outstanding personalities of the Weimar period, he was Chancellor and Foreign

Minister in two cabinets during August–November 1923, ending the hyperinflation of the mark and thus stabilising the economy, and calling off resistance to the French occupation of the Ruhr and thus defusing international tensions. His policies were to revise the Versailles settlement by negotiations with other great capitalist powers.

39. *Osthilfe* (Eastern Aid) was set up in the late 1920s by the Reich government to give financial assistance to bankrupt estates in East Prussia, in order to maintain political support amongst the Junker landowners. A scandal ensued when it emerged that certain Junkers used the funds for their personal comforts. The Darmstadt and National Bank (Danatbank) was formed in 1922 by a merger of the Darmstadt Bank for Trade and Industry and the National Bank of Germany. By the time it crashed in 1931 it was the second-largest bank in Germany. Its collapse was a massive blow to the country's economy.

40. According to Jean-François Fayet, Radek wrote in *Izvestia* for 16 March 1920 that 'a victory for the insurgents' – the Kapp putschists – 'could have positive consequences for Russia by obliging France to use Poland against Germany and no longer against the Soviets': Jean-François Fayet, *Karl Radek (1885–1939), Biographie politique* (Peter Lang, Bern, 2004), p. 352; thanks to Ian Birchall for this reference.

41. Count Ernst Reventlow (1869–1943) was a career naval officer. He responded positively to Radek's speech on Schlageter (see note 42), developed National Bolshevik views, and had material published in the KPD's *Rote Fahne*. He formed the *Deutschvölkische Freiheitspartei* (DVFP – German Völkisch Freedom Party) in 1924, and in 1927 took a faction of it into the NSDAP, aligning with Gregor Strasser's current.

42. Radek's speech on Schlageter was delivered to the plenum of the Executive Committee of the Communist International in June 1923: Karl Radek, 'Leo Schlageter: The Wanderer into the Void', *Labour Monthly*, Volume 5, no. 3, September 1923, pp. 152ff. Albert Leo Schlageter (1894–1923) was a Freikorps member who became a hero for the German nationalist right after he was executed by the French occupation authorities for his sabotage activities during the occupation of the Rhineland in 1923.

43. The KPD leadership initially opposed the 'passive resistance' campaign in 1923, but soon turned to support it, and considered, in Thalheimer's words, that 'the German bourgeoisie has emerged as objectively revolutionary'. The 'Red Referendum' took place in August 1931.

44. Fritz Tarnow (1880–1951) was a carpenter. He rose up the ranks of the woodworkers' union, and was its chairman during 1920–33. He became an SPD deputy in the *Reichstag* in 1928. Arrested after the Nazis' seizure of power, he was released after fellow SPD *Reichstag* deputy Hans Staudinger, masquerading as a senior Prussian official, intervened.

45. This was the paper of the *Kommunistische Partei Deutschlands (Opposition)* (KPDO or KPO – Communist Party of Germany (Opposition)). The KPO was formed in December 1928 by a group of expelled KPD members, and was led by August Thalheimer and Heinrich Brandler. *Arbeiterpolitik* was published on a daily basis from 1 January 1930, but had declined to a weekly within two years.

46. The *Sozialistische Arbeiterpartei Deutschlands* (SAPD – Socialist Workers Party of Germany) was formed in October 1931 by former members of the SPD. It soon attracted members of the USPD, KPD and KPO.

47. From 1929, industrial production fell catastrophically and in 1932 it stood at 40 per cent of the 1929 level. Unemployment rose from 1.6 million in October 1929 to 6.12

million in February 1932, by which time 33 per cent of the workforce was unemployed.
48. See note 20, p. 38
49. Elard Kurt Maria Fürchtegott von Oldenburg-Januschau (1855–1937) was a Junker, a staunch monarchist and a Conservative member of the Prussian *Landtag* during 1901–10 and the *Reichstag* during 1902–12, and a DNVP *Reichstag* deputy during 1930–32. He was a friend of Hindenburg and he encouraged him to appoint Hitler as Chancellor in 1933.
50. Josef Weissenberg (1855–1941) was an occultist and mystic healer who founded various small religious sects.
51. See note 25, p. 39.
52. Heinrich Hirtsiefer (1876–1941) was an official of the Christian trade unions and a member of the Centre Party. He was a member of the Prussian State Parliament and Minister for State Welfare for Prussia during 1921–33. He was held in concentration camps for a time after the Nazi takeover.
53. This was in the wake of 'Bloody Sunday' on 17 June 1932, during which confrontations between Communists and Nazis in Altona, near Hamburg (the Reich government had lifted a ban on the SA and SS some two weeks earlier), had led to 19 deaths and nearly 300 wounded; von Papen accused the Social-Democratic government in Prussia of being unable to maintain order.
54. Clemens Emil Franz Bracht (1877–1933) was a lawyer and a member of the Centre Party. He became Mayor of Essen in 1924, and was appointed Deputy Commissioner for the Interior of Prussia after von Papen dismissed the Social-Democratic Braun–Severing government on 20 July 1932. He was a minister in both von Papen's and von Schleicher's cabinets.
55. Otto von Stülpnagel (1878–1948) was a career army officer. He played a key role in the *Reichswehr* during the Weimar period, and was military commander in France during the Nazi wartime occupation.
56. During the time of the Weimar Republic, the Reich Chancellor and the Reich President both had their official residences in the Wilhelmstrasse.
57. Albert Carl Grzesinsky (1879–1948) joined the SPD in 1897. He held various posts during the Weimar period, including President of the Berlin and Prussian police, and Minister of the Interior of Prussia during 1926–30. He banned the KPD's *Rotfrontkämpferbund* in Prussia in 1929. He went into exile following his being stripped of German citizenship by the Nazi regime.
58. Bernhard Weiss (1880–1951) was a lawyer. A liberal nationalist, he became deputy head of the Berlin criminal police in 1918, and deputy head of the Berlin police in 1927. His Jewish background made him an especial target of Goebbels. He went into exile after being stripped of German citizenship by the Nazi regime, living in Britain from 1934.
59. Max Alsberg (1877–1933) was a lawyer, author and playwright. He defended the pacifist Carl von Ossietzky in a famous treason trial in 1931. Victimised under the Nazis' campaign against Jews in the legal profession, he went into exile in Switzerland, where he committed suicide.
60. Later on Severing declared at a Social-Democratic meeting at Lichtenberg that he could not have called upon his men to defend him – they would have lost their pensions! [Author's note]
61. On 9 August 1932, at a time of rising political violence, von Papen issued a decree

imposing the death penalty for people found guilty of killing political opponents. On 10 August, a group of SA men brutally killed Konrad Pietzuch, a Polish KPD sympathiser, in his home in Potempa, Upper Silesia. Five SA men were found guilty of murder and were sentenced to death. Hitler openly condemned the verdict and threatened widespread violence, von Papen backed down, and the sentences were commuted to life.

62. The Iron Front was formed mainly of organisations associated with the Social Democratic Party and the ADGB union federation, including the *Reichsbanner Schwarz-Rot-Gold*, the SPD's paramilitary group, which claimed a membership of around one million.

63. The *Tatkreis* (Action Circle) was a right-wing current that promoted the romantic anti-capitalist, nationalist and autarkic programme that was typical of the Conservative Revolutionary movement. Under the editorship of Hans Zehrer, its magazine *Die Tat* (*The Deed*) enjoyed a circulation of some 30,000 in the early 1930s, mostly amongst middle-class people.

64. The *Landvolkbewegung* was a militant peasant movement that arose in the late 1920s in Schleswig-Holstein in response to the worsening conditions facing small farmers. It engaged in both passive resistance and terror tactics, and its right-wing, often anti-Semitic populism enabled the Nazis subsequently to gain much support in the area.

65. Theodor Leipart (1867–1947) was a woodworker. A right-winger in his union, he rose up the trade-union apparatus until he became Chairman of the ADGB in 1921. He was a forthright opponent of the concept of workers' control of industry during the German revolution. In 1932, he recommended that the ADGB unions distance themselves from the SPD, with which they had customarily been close. In a desperate attempt to stave off the destruction of the unions by the Nazis, Leipart offered Hitler the services of the German trade-union movement, but his proposals were rebuffed, and he was interned in a concentration camp for a while.

66. Since the foregoing paragraphs were written, General von Schleicher has been assassinated by the Nazis [Author's note].

67. Hanns Kerrl (1887–1941) was President of the Prussian *Landtag* during 1932–34. A strong believer in Christian–Nazi unity, he was appointed *Reichsminister* of Church Affairs in July 1935, his job being coordinating the Christian organisations with the Nazi regime.

68. Friedrich Stampfer (1874–1957) was a journalist and worked on the SPD's *Vorwärts* from 1902. He was an SPD *Reichstag* deputy during 1920–33, and was on the party's Executive in exile after 1933.

69. Alfred Hugenberg (1865–1951) joined the Prussian finance ministry before being appointed by Gustav Krupp as chairman of the board of directors of Krupp Armaments Company in 1909. He owned the film company UFA and a number of provincial newspapers. With Hugo Stinnes he founded the DNVP, and he funded campaigns against the Versailles Treaty, the Locarno Treaty and the Young Plan. He gave money to Hitler and was Minister of Agriculture and Economics in the very early days of the Third Reich, but resigned after six months.

70. The responsibility for the *Reichstag* fire remained a matter of conjecture for a long time; authorities now agree that the Dutch left-winger Marinus van der Lubbe was solely responsible for starting the fire, and that the Nazis took full advantage of the event in order to reinforce their rule.

71. A large army depot to the west of Berlin.
72. Ernst (not Franz) Oberfohren (1881–1933) was a teacher and a member of the DNVP, which he represented in the *Reichstag* during 1920–33. He became leader of the party in December 1929. He resigned his *Reichstag* seat and retired from politics at the end of March 1933. His death on 8 May 1933 has not been explained: either he committed suicide or he was murdered by the Nazis and the killing disguised as suicide. A memorandum on the *Reichstag* fire, a translation of which was published in the *Manchester Guardian*, was attributed to Oberfohren, although it has been considered by some historians, including AJP Taylor, that this document was a product of Willi Münzenberg's publicity organisation.
73. Werner Eduard Fritz von Blomberg (1878–1946) was a career army officer. He gravitated towards the Nazis at the end of the 1920s, and was appointed Minister of Defence in the first Nazi government. He purged the *Reichswehr* of Jews, and introduced the military oath of allegiance to Hitler. In 1935 he became Commander-in-Chief of the German armed forces. Disagreements with Hitler's strategic policies and a faction fight with Göring and Himmler led to his dismissal in 1938.
74. Wilhelm Frick (1877–1946) was a lawyer. He took part in the Beer Hall Putsch in 1923, and became an NSDAP *Reichstag* deputy in 1924. He was appointed Minister of the Interior in the first Nazi government, but he tended to lose out in power struggles with other top Nazis, and he was replaced as Interior Minister by Himmler in 1943. He was a defendant in the Nuremberg Trials and was duly executed.
75. Giacomo Matteotti (1885–1924) was an Italian Socialist Party deputy who publicly condemned electoral malpractices during the rigged elections in 1924. He was kidnapped in June 1924 by a gang attached to the Interior Ministry who were responsible for many attacks upon left-wingers, and was found murdered. The only response of the Socialists was to leave parliament in protest, the Aventine Secession.
76. Otto Wels (1873–1939) was an upholsterer. He joined the SPD in 1891, and became a union and SPD official. He was the Chairman of the SPD from 1919 and a *Reichstag* deputy during 1920–33. He was the leader of the SPD's *Reichstag* faction, and the last to protest in the *Reichstag* against Hitler's absolute power. Stripped of his German citizenship by the Nazi government, he was Chairman of the SPD in exile until his death.
77. Paul Hertz (1888–1961) was a member of the right-wing faction of the Independent Social-Democratic Party and returned to the SPD in 1922. He was a *Reichstag* deputy for the USPD and then the SPD during 1920–33. He was editor of the exile papers *Zeitschrift für Sozialismus* and *Sozialistische Aktion*, and his siding with the *Neu Beginnen* group led to his leaving the SPD in 1938. He worked as an official in West Germany after his return in 1949.
78. An émigré Executive Committee of the SPD was set up in Prague and it published a weekly paper, *Neuer Vorwärts*, the first issue dated 18 June 1933, which called for resistance to the Nazi regime. Most of the party officials in Germany opposed this line, and on 19 June at a meeting in Berlin a new Executive Committee was formed which disavowed the Prague course. Three days later this attempt to work out a *modus vivendi* with the new regime was scotched when the government outlawed all activity by the SPD: see Donna Harsch, *German Social-Democracy and the Rise of Nazism* (University of North Carolina Press, Chapel Hill, 1993), pp. 237–38.

79. There were in Germany five types of union: Socialist, Communist, Catholic, etc [Author's note].
80. Robert Ley (1890–1945) was a chemist. He joined the NSDAP after the Beer Hall Putsch, and rose rapidly up its hierarchy, eventually replacing Gregor Strasser as its Reich Organisation Leader in late 1932. He led the Labour Front once the Nazis were in power. The general militarisation of labour during the Second World War saw his eclipse by Albert Speer and Fritz Todt. He committed suicide whilst awaiting trial for war crimes.
81. Georg Carl Lahusen (1888–1973) was the owner of Nordwolle, a giant textile concern in Bremen. He was arrested after Nordwolle became bankrupt in June 1931. In 1933 he was arrested and subsequently jailed for falsifying financial records and issuing misleading information to creditors.
82. Ivar Kreuger (1880–1932) was a Swedish entrepreneur who was known as the Match King because of the international cartel he established in the match industry, but he also built up large concerns in a wide range of sectors, often using highly unorthodox and risky financial methods. He shot himself when his business empires started to unravel.
83. Richard Walther Darré (1895–1953) was a paganist advocate of 'blood and soil' theories concerning the German peasantry, detailed in his two main works *Das Bauerntum als Lebensquell der nordischen Rasse* (*The Peasantry as Life Source of the Nordic Race*, 1928) and *Neuadel aus Blut und Boden* (*A New Nobility of Blood and Soil*, 1934). He joined the NSDAP in 1930, and was Minister for Food and Agriculture in the Nazi government from 1933. Although his romantic theories keyed in with the Nazi quest for lebensraum in the east, they also clashed with the industrial requirements of the Third Reich, and he was replaced in 1942. He served a short sentence for war crimes.
84. Franz Seldte (1882–1947) was the founder of the *Stahlhelm* and a member of the DNVP, joining the NSDAP in March 1933. He was appointed Minister of Labour in January 1933 and remained in that post until the end of the Third Reich. He was captured and died in hospital before he could be tried for war crimes.
85. *Der Deutsche Volkswirt*, no. 31, May 1934 [Author's note].

The Tragedy of the German Proletariat
Defeat Without Combat, Victory Without Risk

Hippolyte Etchebehere

Berlin, November 1932
We arrived in Berlin on the first day of November 1932. 'You must live in the Westen, the best district for foreigners', we were told in Paris by some who knew Berlin. But we chose the Alexanderplatz, a centre bubbling over with life, heated by the anguish of the young Berlin unemployed.

The streets are full, full of cries, full of people. First surprise: on the pavement, young men or young women are shaking large collecting tins, making the pennies jump up and down inside: 'Give for the electoral campaign of the Communist Party ...' And straightaway, another voice alongside: 'Give for the electoral campaign of the National Socialist [Nazi] Party ...'

We stopped for a long time looking at them. It is obvious that these collectors are not alone. It is obvious that everyone knows that they are protected by some friends. But this is not apparent. You only see this extraordinary thing: side by side, face to face, Communist militants and Nazi storm-troopers are collecting for their parties, occasionally looking at each other with hatred, but without arguing. We are in a political truce. This German discipline!

The elections have been fixed for the 6th, and Berlin is decorated. Everyone declares his political opinion on his window with a flag. In the working-class districts the flags form an unbroken red line over grey façades. Red is the flag for the three parties which compete for the German working class. The white circle with the black swastika in the middle on a red backcloth stands for the Hitlerites, and it bears the number '1'. The Nazi party is the first party in Germany by its number of votes. The three arrows of the 'Iron Front' and the number '2' are printed on the red banner of the Social-Democrats. The hammer and sickle and '3' show Communist windows. The words 'Vote for list 1' and 'Vote for list 3' inscribed on the flags address their appeals to passers-by.

Political passion dominates the streets. Talking goes on everywhere. Little groups form on every corner. Cyclists stop their bikes. Women, young and old, are locked in discussion. Every door, every lapel, has the distinctive sign of its party. All attempt to convince, argue, and accuse the leaders, but exempt the rank and file. The tone rises: everybody wants to say a thousand things to the contrary at the same time; words become hard; but there are no fights. We are experiencing a political truce. Any breach of order is severely punished. Hands are stuffed tightly in pockets, and discussion goes on. The arrival of the *schupo* (police) puts an end to the meeting.

A transport strike has broken out in Berlin.[1] All the means of transport belonging to the Berlin Transport Company (BVG) are halted. Trams, buses and tube trains remain in their depots. The strike was decided upon by the great majority of the personnel. But they were about 500 votes short of the three-quarters that the law requires before a strike is considered legal. So the reformist unions have not supported the strike ... We asked a Social-Democrat:

> – How is it that the leadership of your unions does not approve of a strike decided upon by so overwhelming a majority of the personnel? Haven't 16,000 workers out of 22,000 voted for it?
> – You do not understand, because you do not know German law. Here in Germany we have a law that allows the government to seize trade-union funds when a strike is not strictly supported by three-quarters of the votes. There must be three-quarters, three-quarters exactly, not a vote less ... You know, we have a law ...

But the Berlin worker also has a law, proletarian solidarity. Tube stations remain closed, and not a tram nor a bus comes out into the street from the first day. Cycles run in thousands on the roads. The strike is solid.

One day, two days, three ... The passive reformist unions are sabotaging the strike. Once the elections are over the Nazi leaders start to negotiate and give up the strike. It is necessary to go back. And back in they go. Two thousand workers, the most militant and the most conscious, are fired. The company wants no more of them. But the strike has sown fear in the ranks of the bourgeoisie. The German working class appears to have regained its will to struggle.

The Elections of 6 November 1932

Election day. We will spend it in the working-class districts. This is the first time we have been to Wedding. We expected to see narrow streets, but we found large asphalted avenues, with many balconies, and little gardens in front of large houses of four or five stories. Wedding is nonetheless the district of barricades. Wedding is Berlin's Communist fortress. From these pleasant little balconies the Nazis have received flowers (very often accompanied, it is said, by the heavy pots in which they grow, which annoyed the Nazis ...). The Nazis don't have an easy life in Wedding.

The flags are red. In the new Wedding, full of open modern houses, swastikas are to be seen. These are the houses inhabited by the clerks and the petty-bourgeoisie. The hammer and sickle predominate in old Wedding.

Occasionally, in the middle of a façade or a street that only carries swastikas, the number '3' of the Communist list stands out. Occasionally there are the three arrows. Elsewhere a swastika dares to exist among the Communist banners.

How do we explain this spectacle in such a red hot atmosphere? Did the militants, Communist, Socialist or Nazi, have such extraordinary personal courage? We think that on 6 November an equilibrium of forces existed in Germany, and that each militant also felt it. With a strong party behind you, victory belonged definitively to nobody. The future was wide open.

At the doors of the beer halls where the vote is being held are living adverts, men carrying placards on their chests: 'List 3', 'List 2', 'List 1'. The voters come in, pass through the bar where beer is drunk, and go to place their votes in the room at the side. The silence is unbroken. You don't see many Nazis in Wedding. A group of six, wearing uniforms, passes near a *Reichsbanner* (Flag of the State)[2] headquarters. The *Reichsbanner* youth, also in uniform, who are at the door, taunt the Hitlerites: 'Hey ... heroes, don't run like that. Is your leader waiting for you? Come here, we have something for you ...' The Nazis do not reply.

The Communists gained 700,000 votes. The Social-Democrats lost 700,000. The Nazis lost two million.[3]

Vorwärts[4] commented on the Nazi defeat: 'For ten years we have predicted the failure of National Socialism, we wrote it in our journal in black and white ...' *Die Rote Fahne*[5] celebrated the Communist victory, and announced that Nazism was beginning to disintegrate: 'Everywhere there are SA[6] who are deserting the ranks of Hitlerism and placing themselves under the Communist flag. Hitler is beginning to be disowned within his own movement.'

The discontent that manifested itself within the Communist Party after its defeat in the Presidential elections has now been stilled.[7]

The government has emerged from these elections completely defeated, in the sense that it has yet again shown its narrow social base; and a long crisis ensues ending with the fall of von Papen[8] and the coming to power of Schleicher.[9]

Die Rote Fahne, recalling the BVG strike, interpreted these facts thus: 'The offensive of the proletariat made Papen fall!', which was not true from two points of view. In its entirety the proletariat was, and remained to the end, on the defensive, even if the Berlin transport strike had shown a revival of combativity. Profiting from the general passivity of the proletariat, the factions of the bourgeoisie took their time fighting each other for power; with the rise of Schleicher, the big landed bourgeoisie was defeated for the time being.

Waiting …

Now we are still in a state of political truce, and Christmas is coming on. The Berlin worker didn't want to be starving on Christmas day. He wanted his kids to be happy on that day, and he wanted his Christmas tree decorated and lit up, and the tree had to be a pretty little fir tree. 'Our Christmas dinner will not be very rich', said Frau Müller. 'I have bought the meat. We will have a little roast lamb. But the tree! Oh, the tree will be amazing!'

Frau Müller's husband has been unemployed for more than two years. They live on a dole of 360 francs a month. Their daily nourishment consists of potatoes with margarine, some slices of sausage and a few dried vegetables. As far as Frau Müller is concerned, the Christmas tree is no longer a matter of religion. In her life, as in the lives of millions of German unemployed, it represents the need for hope. It recalls 'the good times', when you were working and earning a wage.

Winter is here. Suicides are increasing. The gas pipe solves problems quickly.

The courtyards are full of singers, of dancers, and of acrobats. Occasionally it is circuses that come along: a thin and shaggy pony and some dogs, none too skilful. The pennies rarely fall. The square is almost entirely inhabited by unemployed …

The End of the Political Truce

Petty trading goes on in the streets. Shoelaces, buttons, toys and sweets are sold. In this corner two unemployed youths are displaying a cathedral 2.8 metres high that they have made out of wood. Further on there is a Dornier X, an aeroplane made out of matches during a year of unemployment. And now a little wooden house, sitting on top of two bicycles …

The talk is about the winter. The government has said nothing yet about help for winter. The Communist Party launches the slogan 'Coal and potatoes! Open the depots, distribute the stocks to the people!' There are small demonstrations in the working-class districts.

The new year opens with the murder of five workers by the Nazis. The political truce has ended. The Communist Party organises a demonstration for 4 January in the Lustgarten: 'Red Berlin will come en masse on 4 January.' It is a rainy day. The workers come from the furthest districts. Women and children, young and old, all march, calmly and seriously, with set expressions. It is raining. Many of them do not have a coat.

The speech delivered by Florin[10] is made up of the usual clichés: 'Show Schleicher how many we are. He wants the German Communist Party to be illegal? Working-class Berlin knows how to reply to him ... Look at Russia! No unemployment there ...' And so on and so forth ...

The mass listens quietly. It is waiting for a perspective, a way out. It returns empty handed.

On 15 January the Communist Party calls the workers to the graves of Rosa Luxemburg and Karl Liebknecht. The Social-Democratic councillors of Lichtenberg, where the cemetery is situated, have voted to forbid marching in front of the graves. Only a delegation of flag bearers is to be allowed. The Social-Democrats have discovered that demonstrating in front of the graves of Karl and Rosa upsets the other visitors and infringes their rights ...

The Communist Party denounces this, and appeals to the Socialist workers to demonstrate against their leaders, but, as always, remains alone. It was decided that the columns would assemble at the Wagner Platz to listen to the speakers. There the procession of flag bearers will form up to go to the cemetery.

The 15th is a freezing day. The thermometer indicates sixteen degrees below zero. The pavements are crowded. The Communist columns advance to the middle of the large Frankfurter Allee. Discipline is perfect. One formation with its leaders and cadres is marked out as a distinct body among the mass that marches alongside it. Songs mount up, powerfully. Their slow rhythm controls the march. They mount up to the windows of the proletarian houses, and the windows open. All the windows are open on the Frankfurter Allee. The refrains show a stubborn hope: '*Wir siegen trotz Hass und Verbote.*' – 'We shall triumph in spite of hatred and repression.'

The cold wind carries the clear music of the tunes far afield. Drums open the march. The streets are fuller and fuller. The *Spartacus* song is sung. The flags are like red veils. From time to time the trumpet sounds a long fanfare. From columns, pavements and windows comes the response: '*Rot Front!*'[11]

It's a bit theatrical, but it is very impressive.

Arriving at the Alexanderplatz, the flag bearers and delegations begin to form up for the procession. They are waiting for the speakers. The cold has become insufferable. You must keep moving. It is too cold, clothing is too light, and the dole money does not allow you to assuage your hunger. You have set off with only a cup of hot water coloured with coffee and a thin slice of bread. Splendid children fall fainting. That's hunger, that's cold.

The procession of flags sets off towards the cemetery. A hundred, two hundred, a thousand red flags, swell up in the wind. Towards a horizon punctuated with factory chimneys, along the main street of the workers' town, advances, pours a stream of red flags and a growling storm of red songs.

The clique of heavy industry and the landed bourgeoisie, driven out by the rise of Schleicher and Papen, returns, but accompanied by Hitler and Hugenberg.[12] Schleicher has a trump card to play against Hitler: the *Reichstag*. If the Nazis refuse their support to the government in the *Reichstag*, he can call for new elections. Hitler fears new elections. He has serious difficulties within his own party. Strasser[13] has just abandoned him, and the stormtrooper divisions are not happy. The *Führer*'s prestige is suffering as a result. The *Führer* needs to polish up his image, and to show, as against Schleicher, who wants to come to an understanding with Leipart,[14] that he, and he alone, is capable of subduing the working class. Their *coup d'état* requires a reconnaissance of the terrain; what will be the response of the proletariat, and to what extent? And in addition, if there is a bloody response, that will be an opportunity for plunging the Communist Party into illegality, so carrying out Schleicher's threat.

The Nazis on the Bülowplatz

One day the Berlin workers read on the front pages of their newspapers the following unbelievable thing: '*The Nazis will be assembling at the Bülowplatz ... the Nazis will be marching in front of Karl Liebknecht House ...*' Nobody wants to believe it. The provocation is so clear, so monstrous, and a bloody result is so sure, that from one moment to the next a denial is expected from the police. The denial does not come. The Nazis will be parading in front of Karl Liebknecht House. With their flags, their music and their songs, they will be defiling the streets of the working-class quarter. They will be shouting 'Death to the Commune' in front of the Communist citadel. They will be chanting 'Our knives must be red with the blood of the Yids' in that part of the ghetto where Bülowplatz stands.

In factories, in the labour exchanges, in the streets, in pubs, among schoolkids, among women in the marketplace, everywhere, everywhere, there is no other subject of conversation than the march of the Nazis on Sunday, 22 January on the Bülowplatz, in front of Karl Liebknecht House, the headquarters of the Communist Party. *Die Rote Fahne* cries:

> Berlin workers. Make the government withdraw. Demonstrate in the factories and at the labour exchanges. Send letters of protest! Socialist workers: remember that the Communists rushed to the defence of the threatened *Vorwärts. Now it is your turn!*

The Communist Party did everything: canvassing for a counter-demonstration, approaches to the Minister of the Interior to halt the Nazi demonstration, and a conference of the German and foreign press to receive 'very important' declarations of the parliamentary fraction: 'The Communist Party holds the authorities responsible for what will happen on the Bülowplatz, and reserves the right to act accordingly if working-class blood is shed ...'

It did everything, everything that amounted to threatening, threatening – and appeals to the rank and file over the heads of the leaders. It did not forget to act. How we felt in those days the impotence of this boasting and empty policy in the face of a real danger! In front of Karl Liebknecht House little columns led by Communist groups kept coming up. The leader would stand out and make a little speech: 'Send letters of protest to the Prefect of Police, speak with the Nazi proles in the factories at clocking off time!' And off they went again, indoctrinated. They discussed in little groups: 'They will not dare ... I bet that at the last minute the police will forbid the demonstration.' One old man said: 'No, they will go ahead. They cannot retreat any more. But blood will flow.' The others said: 'Obviously blood will flow.'

It was Saturday the 21st. What will happen on Sunday? The Social-Democratic Party on this occasion is consistent to the last: 'This provocation is possible because the Communist Party is keeping the working class divided.' And in its appeal: 'Socialist workers are disciplined workers, and, as ever, will only follow the directives of their leaders. Socialist workers will abstain from demonstrating on Sunday!'

And to cap it all the *Reichsbanner* troops, as if by chance, were mobilised to carry out a long exercise march – read 'out of the way' – this Sunday, outside Berlin ...

The bourgeois liberal press was speaking openly of the provocation, not only to the Communist Party, but to the whole of the working class. The *Berliner Tageblatt* advised the police to go into reverse and refuse the

Nazis the right to demonstrate on Sunday the 22nd in the Bülowplatz, and not to allow themselves to be carried away by false ideas of authority. The headquarters of the reformist trade unions addressed the Minister of the Interior, affirming 'that this provocation towards the working class could have the gravest consequences'.

The right-wing press (the *Deutsche Allgemeine Zeitung*, the organ of heavy industry) and the Schleicher government also began to get concerned. On the 21st the *DAZ* declared that:

> Rapid decisions are not always the decisions of good government; that the present economic and social situation in Germany above all demands calm and tranquillity, and that casualties in the Bülowplatz [it was convinced in advance that there would be casualties – HE] are obviously not going to contribute towards assuring this.

But it added:

> Schleicher should speak with the Minister of the Interior, Dr Bracht,[15] and should concern himself personally with tomorrow's demonstration. It is said that he should forbid it. We do not see it this way. In any case, it is necessary in such circumstances to think hard as to the best way out.

Schleicher spoke with his minister. He needed an hour to show him that there would be no incidents. 'The police are in command of the situation', the Prefect of Police said in effect. Then a fresh argument came from *Rote Fahne*: 'To satisfy the provocative wish of the Nazis, the government is going to subject the policemen to an additional burden and risk their lives!'

Our landlady, a respectable petty-bourgeois, advised us to lay in some food: 'This Sunday will be a bloody day. The dead will be counted in dozens. Strikes will break out, perhaps even a general strike. You can't trust the workers. Follow my advice, and buy in provisions ...'

Sunday morning. There is no way of getting near the Bülowplatz. Access is barred by the police. Guns in hand, the police close off the streets over a very wide area. We mingle with groups of workers who are standing around everywhere. They discuss unceasingly. What should we do? What should we have done? Is there anything we should do? There is a profound disorientation.

The police throng the streets. An armoured car noisily makes its appearance. The grey muzzles of four machine guns are greeted with contempt by the workers:

— They need a stunt like that to come among us ...
— They should let us demonstrate in front of the *Angriff*.[16] We wouldn't ask to be protected by armoured cars.
— They wouldn't need to block the streets either ...
— Nor put the cops on the roofs ...

Indignation, shame and rage swell up in the district.
Three arrows on some lapels mark the supporters of the 'Iron Front'.[17] These are Socialist workers. They are discussing, surrounded by Communists.

— Yet again your leaders are playing the game of the Fascists. They told you to stay at home today. They have moved the *Reichsbanner* away. We want unity, we want you to struggle with us ... Do your leaders want unity?
— Our leaders, our leaders ... It is always the same tune. Are yours leading you any better? What are your leaders doing today? They told you to come here shouting '*Red Front!*'. You shout, you only shout ...

A column has just formed up with an attempt at a demonstration: 'Down with the government! Death to Hitler!' The cops rush up. Truncheon blows. The cops are booed from the windows; they train their guns on the houses and demand: 'Close the windows! Close the windows!'
A group is talking. An old worker is speaking to people who have just returned from shouting:

Children ... this is nothing ... Nothing is done by shouting. Where are we, the 800,000 who voted Communist? Come down from all the districts, fall on the spot where they have now assembled and wipe them out like maggots.

And his thin fingers wiped out the maggots.

— The party should have ordered us to concentrate in the districts to prevent the Nazis from setting off towards the Bülowplatz ...
— The party told us to gather near the square to demonstrate.

What did the party really say? Those in charge confirmed this last order to us.
How many were we on the vast perimeter that surrounds the Bülowplatz? Thirty thousand, 40,000, perhaps 60,000. But you only saw groups; they

talked, and they called out until the arrival of the police. And that was all. Nothing but groups, impotent groups. Working-class Berlin did not respond to the appeal of the Communist Party. *During the danger the Communist Party remained alone and did not have the confidence of the masses.* The bourgeoisie had just established this in a decisive fashion.

Everything was over by about half past five. The last Nazi columns, almost invisible behind the police columns that were guarding them, left the area of the Bülowplatz. Rather than a Nazi demonstration, it could be said that a demonstration of the police, armed with all its weapons, had taken place on the square and its environs. On their way back to their homes the militants drew scant consolation from this observation.

Six o'clock in the evening. We arrive at Karl Liebknecht House. Cops armed with rifles are still guarding the pavement. With empty hands and defeat in our hearts, we go off with some workers. The cry that had resounded in our ears all day still follows us: 'Keep moving ... keep moving ... keep moving.' And now, in the Alexanderplatz, some Nazis, two or three isolated groups, who have also returned there after their 'feat of valour', pass among the workers. They boo and whistle at them, and that is all ... The Bülowplatz was a climax, a decisive moment in the German tragedy.[18]

The Social-Democratic leaders went on to circulate this scandalous justification:

> The Communists reproached us with having given up the Prussian state on 20 July without resistance, but did they not allow their guard at the Karl Liebknecht House to be sent away by the police in the same way on 22 January?

Hitler Chancellor

Events were now going to unfold at an increasing rate. On the 25th the Communist Party 'replied' with an anti-Fascist demonstration that filed for four hours in front of the Karl Liebknecht House. One hundred and twenty thousand workers came from the furthest districts of Berlin in the freezing cold. The anti-Fascist cadres were composed of magnificent young people.

There was a briskness, an enthusiasm and a decisiveness that we had never seen before. These working-class troops passed in front of us with their streamers. We tried to estimate the number of serviceable fighters per column. Ninety-five per cent of them were of the right age, and their deportment indicated to us that they were militants ready for armed struggle. Yet again, what a formidable impression! Only, this Bülowplatz ... and in spite of all, that was the dominant impression among us whilst waiting for the functionaries to repeat, on the arrival of each column opposite the rostrum where the Central Committee of the Communist Party was standing, the cry: 'Red Berlin greets the Central Committee of the German Communist Party headed by Comrade Thälmann with three cheers for the Red Front!'

That same day, the 25th, in a hall where an anti-Fascist meeting called by the Communists was being held in Dresden, the police fired on those present, killing nine workers and wounding thirteen. There was no effective response to this incredible act: a local general strike could not be got off the ground.

Schleicher asked Hindenburg for power to dissolve the *Reichstag*. But his fate had already been decided. Hindenburg refused him,[19] and called for von Papen. Negotiations commenced with Hitler, Hugenberg, etc, who like the rest of them seemed to want to drag them out at great length.

On the 29th the Social-Democratic Party for its part also went on record in the Lustgarten 'replying' to the provocation of the 22nd:

> Berlin remains Red! Social-Democrats, maintain your traditional discipline! You may perhaps be called upon to use your final energy! Social-Democrats, be calm!

But there was a new sight on this demonstration. The Sozialistiche Arbeiterpartei[20] organised in an independent column, raised the portrait of Rosa Luxemburg, and with a chant untiringly repeated called for a united front: '*SPD, KPD, SAP must march together!*' The left is giving us hope ...

And then, on the unconcern of those parties who talked about a *coup d'état* without thinking seriously about it, there fell like a flash of lightning on Monday, 30 January the news: '*Hitler is Reichskanzler!*' The Bülowplatz has found its echo, its result!

That same night we hastened to the 'Masch', the Communist Party's Marxist school. The atmosphere was gloomy. We anxiously accosted the first comrades of the Communist Party whom we met:

— What are you going to do?
— What do you want us to do?
— Are we going to allow Hitler to install himself in power?
— Who can stop him?
— But do you believe that the working class will remain passive?
— Obviously ... Perhaps a few partial strikes.
— But the party?
— What can the party do?

This is a body blow. But we do try to show them the immense hope, the enormous attention, the supreme attention with which the proletariat of the entire world is following their attitude ... but that discourages them even more. Others arrive. The circle gets bigger. There are factory workers, unemployed and students there. There is bitterness there, the anger of unbearable impotence:

— We have no party, we have no leaders! What can we do? On 20 July the party called a general strike, and did the factories stop? We determined nothing ... without the Socialist workers, we can do nothing.
— Anyway, Hitler will be rapidly worn out. He cannot keep his promises.
— Hitler means war, and war means revolution.
— The Nazis will not dare drive the party into illegality.
— He may do it, but that will be for the best. The party will come back all the stronger.
— The masses need the experience of Nazism, and afterwards they will come to us.

And one of them sketches out a fantastic scheme involving the USA, Poland, Romania ... Not only do they not have an idea in common, but each of them has four or five different ideas that he expresses in turn ...

The party did not have a policy. Everything was Fascism as far as it was concerned. Brüning[21] was Fascism, Social-Democracy was Fascism. Von Papen was Fascism. Schleicher was Fascism ...

A functionary broke in: 'Yes, that was Neumann's policy, which has already been severely condemned within the party.'[22] Confusion, disarray, an utter lack of confidence in their party and in their leaders ... And beneath our very eyes the formidable German Communist Party, Berlin's premier party, the most powerful section of the Communist International, dissolves like a sugar-cube in water.

Tonight, we received in the street, in the Alexanderplatz, from the hands of the Socialist youth, the most extraordinary sheet of paper just published by the Social-Democracy. And taking it, we ask: 'What's this? *"Jetz, abwarten."'* That means: '*Now, wait.*' Their deceitful formula! We read on the page:

Faced with the government threatening a *coup d'état*, Social-Democracy and the whole Iron Front will stand with both feet on the ground of the constitution and of legality. *Social-Democracy will not make the first move to leave it.*

Lackeys, faithful lackeys!

On the other side of Berlin, the Nazis carried out their 'heroic' 'March on Rome' promised long ago by their *Führer*. Concentrated in haste on the Tiergarten, they 'conquered' Berlin, marching in through the Brandenburg gate.

On the 31st the *Rote Fahne* calling for the preparation of a general strike was confiscated. *Vorwärts* prophesied: 'To carry out a general strike now would be to waste the ammunition of the working class by firing into thin air.' The reformist unions preached *'coolness and prudence'*.

Hitler launched – and that's the word for it – his programme by radio on 1 February. The next day it is read on the billboards: Communist disruption must be overcome. The workers' movement must be destroyed (later he will say this more forcefully). There will be two four-year plans. Four years from now the peasants will be happy: another four years and so will the workers. In the meantime, there will be compulsory labour service, the dissolution of the Reichstag, and new elections on 5 March.

In all the working-class districts of Berlin and throughout Germany the Communists organised demonstrations that didn't have much of a response. The refrains spoken in some factories called for the preparation of the strike. The demonstration called by the Communist Party for 3 February in the Lustgarten was forbidden by the police ...

A Social-Democratic MP was imprisoned in Lübeck.[23] The response of the Lübeck working class was a unanimous one-hour general strike. In Berlin the news had extraordinary repercussions. The workers drew from this spark a new surge of hope and confidence. This powerful German working class had so little on which to nourish itself!

On 6 February this was repeated at Stassfurt. The Social-Democratic town mayor was killed. And once more, on the day of the funeral, a unanimous strike closed factories and shops. The workers commented avidly on these two events, recalling 1918-19 and saying: 'All is not yet lost. Things can begin like that, little by little. Strikes can spread from town to town, one flame here and another there, and the fire can engulf all Germany.'

On the 7th the first mass meeting under Hitler took place in Berlin. Social-Democracy demonstrated in the Lustgarten. The head of the Communist fraction in the *Reichstag*, the MP Torgler,[24] requested permission to read in front of the Socialist masses an appeal for a united front that the Communist Party had addressed to them. He was refused, and the matter, of which we only learnt the following day, was closed. In his speech Otto Wels[25] defended the policy of the Social-Democracy since 1918, and finished by saying to the masses: 'The people have the opportunity, once more on 5 March to take its destiny into its own hands!' Three '*Freiheits!*'[26] saluted the speech of the Socialist leader. Their echo had not yet died out when from the other side of the square a powerful '*Red Front!*' called out by thousands of voices broke out like thunder. Movement, surprise:

— The Communists are here!
— United ... We march together ...
— These people have only come here to create disorder.
— Don't talk nonsense!
— Unity ... unity ...
— All the Communist workers must vote for the Social-Democratic list.
— It is certain that their party will be declared illegal.

Künstler,[27] one of the Socialist leaders, said a few words:

Brothers and sisters, do not spoil this magnificent demonstration with incidents. And above all do not allow yourselves to be provoked. The lives and safety of the Berlin workers are too dear for us to put them at risk lightly. We must keep them for the day of combat. And now let us sing our Socialist marching song.

We fight not with the weapons of barbarians.
We want no guns, we want no spears.
The banner of right, the sword of spirit
Will lead us to victory.

The meeting is over. They start to withdraw. Some shouts are still heard: '*United Front!*', '*Unity!*' And a group of militants with cries of '*Death to Hitler!*' and '*Down with the government!*' take off via the Bruderstrasse. They become more and more numerous. They now advance by the large Rosstrasse. They have filled the street, they have filled the pavements, people rush up from all sides, and it becomes a veritable flood which runs unceasingly. The police watch it pass without intervening. You can see the three arrows and the hammer and sickle on the lapels: '*Down with the government!*', '*Red Front!*', '*Liberty!*', '*Death to Hitler!*', '*Berlin remains Red!*' And on the corners it is said with surprise:

— They are marching together!
— The SPD and KPD have united!
— God be praised. Now we fear no Hitler.

It was a little old lady who said this. She lifted her fist: '*Red Front!*', and her eyes were full of tears. Ever they advance. Now they are taking over the Dresdenerstrasse. Four *schupos* are on guard in front of a Nazi headquarters. We see a mass of brown shirts pressing themselves against the glass of the closed doors. And we are witnessing this extraordinary thing: on 7 February an illegal, spontaneous demonstration in which Socialist and Communist workers are marching under Hitler's government is shouting in the faces of the Nazis shut up in their headquarters and guarded by four *schupos*, '*Death to Hitler!*', '*Down with the Fascist government!*'

Going Back

Let us go back some days earlier to be present at an event that opened up an entire epoch of the policy of the Nazis in power.

30 January: Midnight. After the 'torchlight parade' under the Brandenburg Gate, an élite stormtrooper detachment came back into the city. It entered precisely – and why? – the Wallstrasse in Charlottenburg. The street, from one end to the other, from basement to roof, was Communist. There were fights and shots. Maikowski, the Nazi leader, and Zaurits, the *schupo* who accompanied the column, fell. Did they fall in the fighting? Did the Nazis kill them? It was later known that Maikowski had had incidents with his superiors; and as for Zaurits, he was a good guy, said to be a friend of the workers ...

The government took away the two bodies. Fate had sent them. The doors of the Dome, Berlin's imperial cathedral, were opened. Police delegations and stormtroopers formed up elbow to elbow. The cabinet, the whole lot of them, was there. A solemn mass took place 'for the *schupo* and the member of the SA who symbolically fell together under the bullets of the Communist scum'.

It was necessary to win over the hearts of the brave *schupos* who perhaps still shared the views of Severing[28] and Grzesinski,[29] as the Social-Democrats claim, and to reconcile the *schupos* and the men of the SA. It was all the more necessary to reassure the police who feared for their livelihoods, to tame them, and to weld them to their new masters. This is what Göring, the Minister of the Interior for Prussia, was to concern himself with for the whole of February. This is what was to inspire many of his famous decrees.

31 January: The *Berliner Börsenzeitung*, the journal of monopoly capital, publishes a paragraph of praise for the attitude of the Social-Democracy: 'Whilst the Communists were calling for the preparation of the general strike, Social-Democracy does not seem to be inclined to fight the government by any other means than speeches, leading articles and appeals.'

This inescapably reminds us of the speeches that Mussolini delivered in the Italian parliament after the murder of Matteotti[30] in July 1924:

> What are our adversaries doing? Are they unleashing demonstrations in the streets? Are they trying to provoke revolts in the army? Nothing of the sort! They are restricting themselves to press campaigns! They are incapable of doing any more than that!

Do we have to listen to this in every language?

We are staying with Frau D—, a fat person obsessed with the idea of eating. Her husband is a commercial traveller. They have known better days. Frau D— sums them up in a phrase: 'We lived off the fat of the land.' At present they are living through long periods of unemployment, and Frau D— has become a ferocious anti-capitalist. She votes Social-Democrat, but after the November elections, and particularly since she knew we were Communists, she is in favour of violent solutions: 'The workers have to understand once and for all. They have to take by force all that they need. Myself, I'm a Communist to the tips of my fingers.'

But events were moving fast. Schleicher fell, and already there was talk of Hitler's coming to power. Frau D— asked:

— Do you think that the Nazis will come to power?
— They will do if the workers do not block the way.
— Then civil war is inevitable, for the workers will not allow it to happen.

Hitler is already Chancellor. Frau D— is sure that he could not hold on, he would fall like the others. She goes to get information in the locality. She talks with the grocer, she listens to what the baker says, she discusses with Frau Bartel. She is no longer quite so sure about Hitler's fall. 'The people are so enthusiastic about him! And after all, why not give him the opportunity to fulfil his promises? Who knows? A man who has succeeded in building up such a movement!'

We tried to make her understand what Hitler represented: the most monstrous reaction that Germany had ever known, the destruction of the organisations of the working class, the lowering of wages ...

— But he will provide work! Reaction ... I don't care a damn about reaction. There was less freedom in the Kaiser's time, but we ate better. Work is what we want. And Hitler already has a plan which will stimulate business, increasing the armed forces. Who knows? He might even bring back compulsory military service, and that will bring commerce back to life. The army has to have thousands and thousands of pairs of boots, and thousands and thousands of uniforms. All these people will have to be fed. And then, yet again, there's this: all these well-paid NCOs get married. Look, in the past a young girl like Frida [Frida is the maid, who has not been paid a penny for a year – HE] could get married to a non-commissioned officer, with a lovely home for herself and an escape from want for her entire life. Now what do you think she can do? Marry one of the unemployed?

— But you are forgetting Hitler's anti-Semitic programme, Frau D—, and you are nonetheless Jewish.

— The Nazis are not against the German Jews. They want to drive out all the Yids that came in from Poland and Austria, the lousy Galicians[31] in the Grenadierstrasse. They should chuck them out! They came here after 1914, and they profited from the misery of the German people. Myself, if you please, when I see one of these Polish Jewesses studded with diamonds choosing the plumpest chicken in the markets, feeling it with fingers full of rings, I want to spit in her face. They have all the money, all these dirty Yids. They are dirty, dirty, they never wash!

Towards the United Front

Hitler is in power. The threat is there, stark and brutal. Then, in the working-class camp, comes a period of obscure manoeuvres. It is difficult to find your way even with the help of notes taken on the spot.

On 31 January Breitscheid[32] declares in a meeting of the Executive Committee of the Social-Democratic Party: 'The struggle against Fascism has entered a new phase. All our hopes are that our relations with the Communist Party will also enter into a new phase.'

A motion proposing a Non-Aggression Pact with the Communist Party was rejected by only one vote. The utmost of confusion, diplomacy, and manoeuvre. Nonetheless, this pact remained at the centre of debate to the very last.

The initiative for united action seems to originate, and remains in the hands of the reformist leaders; action that could only be extra-parliamentary and revolutionary ... in the hands of leaders who said: 'It is necessary to wait! Wait until Hitler goes outside the constitution [!!!].' That means until such a point that everything is lost.

The Central Committee of the Communist Party was incapable of putting an end to this game, of posing the question clearly, bravely and firmly. The theory of 'Social Fascism'[33] tied it hand and foot. The *Rote Fahne* of 2 and 3 February published in full the speech of Manuilsky,[34] the President of the Communist International, in reply to Otto Bauer[35] in which the theory of Social Fascism was yet again enlarged upon. He intention was to reply to German Social-Democracy.

And behind the backs of the masses the Central Committee of the German Communist Party sent Torgler to talk with the leadership of the SPD and with the leadership of the ADGB (the German trade-union confederation). It sent Münzenberg[36] to speak secretly with Künstler. The latter took courage, became impertinent, and refused.

Naturally, you did not learn all this through the usual, normal channels, the organisations of the Communist Party and its press. No. You got it by indirect routes.

Torgler attended the Social-Democratic demonstration on the 7th, and demanded to read an appeal to the masses. They replied to him:

> You ought to have come beforehand and submitted this to the regular organs of the party. Also, if we concede the rostrum to a Communist, the police can dissolve the meeting.

By way of reply on the 9th we found the idea of an *aggression pact* against Fascism proposed 'to the workers who are in the SPD'.

On the 16th appeared an enormous announcement on the Berlin billboards, which read:

> The RGO[37] appeals to the ADGB, proposing to call a joint conference of the factory councils in order to organise the movement against the Fascist reaction, the formation in all the factories, labour exchanges and workers' districts of committees for the defence of working-class life and property.

The poster ended: '*This proposal has been rejected, but it will be repeated.*' On its side, the ADGB published a declaration: 'On a notice that passers-by could read, there is mention of a proposal that was made to us. We declare that we have not received it.'

On the 17th it was a proposal of the Young Communists to the Socialists. The latter replied by referring to a well-known 'agreement', and advised the Young Communists to address themselves directly to the leadership of the party. The reformists ended all their trade-union and electoral meetings with an appeal for the unity of the working class: 'A real united front, with no manoeuvres. Communist workers, we extend to you a fraternal hand. Reaction is here, let us unite to fight it.'

On 19 February a meeting of the factory committees of the ADGB and the AFA (the white-collar trade unions) of the Berlin-Brandenburg district took place in the great hall of the Trade Union House. It deserves a more detailed account. The Regional Secretary addressed the hall:

> We must have a united front, but that cannot be a united front that begins with lies against the leaders of the trade unions, any more than a united front that is announced on billboards. The RGO promoted by the Communist Party is not a serious partner for us. In addition, the slogan for a Soviet Germany is not acceptable in a united front with the workers of the free trade unions. We reject, on both a local and a district basis, all negotiations for such a united front.

A short speech from Dr Gusko,[38] who spoke in the capacity of a general reporter, ended with these words:

> It must be said, on the subject of the united front, that the Communist Party does not take its slogans too seriously. The Communist Party leadership knows that fifteen days ago Leipart, the President of the free trade unions, declared himself ready to respond to any immediate direct appeal for a united front addressed to him. But the Communist response to this honest proposal has not up to now been heard.

The conference ended by approving unanimously a resolution which said:

> Reaction has found support among the RGO and the organisation of Nazi factory cells. The workers and clerical staff must understand that the best defenders of their interests in the workshops are the factory councillors of the free trade unions.

That was the language that Leipart and Co dared to put before the workers on 19 February.

What is the point of going on – for the whole month of February these were dark times.

The revolutionaries were trailing behind, waiting for the decisions of the reformist leaders. The masses who could have been decisive were with them. And their slogan was: '*Abwarten!*' – '*Wait!*' Little by little the impression that the Communist Party could do nothing, and counted for nothing, conquered the streets. People stopped bothering about it. That emerged on 5 March in the election results. At this decisive moment the 'treacherous, reformist' party, held on far better to its voters than did the 'revolutionary' party.

The United Front in the Cemetery

On the 17th we accompanied three bodies to the Friedrichfeld cemetery where Karl and Rosa lay. They were three young Communists, Berner, Kollasch and Schulz.

A few details on Berner. It is midnight at the *Reichsbanner* headquarters on the corner of Fulda and Wessel streets, in Neuköln. A young man calls the neighbouring Communist headquarters on the telephone: 'Things look threatening.' They are being attacked by the Nazis. The Communists rush up, Erwin Berner among them. When they get to the threatened corner there are revolver shots. The Nazis, lying in ambush, fire. Berner falls there.

The police have forbidden funerary processions. On the way out of the house an officer inspects the wreaths, seizes one that bears too explicit a wording, tears it up, and tramples on it.

We take the underground, and wait at the entrance. The afternoon is cloudy and very cold, on a pale crossroads. There is a flurry of snow, and tiny white flakes fall thickly down. There are considerable forces of police. Finally, here they are. Three cars, fifteen metres apart, come up, bouncing on the paving stones. The cemetery pathways are well known. There is a stream of flags, but this time, on the left, with fists raised in silence, the workers of the *Reichsbanner* are saluting the cortège. Young Socialists and young Communists are carrying the coffins of the fallen comrades.

There's the united front – the united front in the cemetery …

In the Berlin districts, and in every corner of the Reich, little local agreements for action take place, sparsely and laboriously. But the great agreement at the centre, the only one that could have decided things, from which the resistance of everyone could be born, the mass response which the bourgeoisie fears (you have only to read its newspapers), that never takes place. And it never did.

The Electoral Campaign

The electoral struggle 'for the last elections' is begun by the Nazis. It is a huge poster, '*Against the November Criminals!*',[39] against the Marxism and internationalism 'that have governed and destroyed Germany for the last fourteen years', '*Against Marxism, vote Hitler!*'

Two days later, in the same place, is another no less imposing poster printed on white with red letters and streaked with black – the colours of the old imperial royal family:

> Germans, soldiers of the Great War, remember that the Social-Democrats also bled on the battlefields in defence of the fatherland. That in 1918, when the Kaiser fled, it was they who prevented Germany from sinking into a chaos similar to that in Russia. And now we are insulted, dismissed and persecuted. And that is our thanks from the fatherland!

The *DAZ* comments:

> Everything about this poster, the colours, the tone, and the appeal to the soldiers, suggests at first glance that it is a matter of the black-white-red nationalist bloc. But no, it is a question of the SPD. No matter how hard you try, Messrs Social-Democrats, you can always be recognised under the new skin.

The following day, on a new poster, the Social-Democrats reaffirm their right to be considered as true Germans and honest patriots, by quoting the declarations of Duesterberg, the leader of the Stahlhelm:[40] '*There are also in the so-called Marxist parties frontline soldiers who did their patriotic duty along with the best of them.*' Then the Nazis stick up this question in big letters: 'To what party did "Comrade" Crispien[41] belong, who said: "*Social-Democracy knows no country called Germany.*"?'

But here is Pieck,[42] one of the most prominent members of the Central Committee of the Communist Party, who goes in for saying at an electoral meeting in the Sportspalast on 23 February:

> Hitler is pretending to create the unity of the nation. How can he say this when he wants to eliminate from the unity of the nation the greater part of the German people by denouncing the 13.5 million voters of the SPD and the KPD as non-Germans and anti-Germans, against whom he must lead a struggle of destruction?

The battle goes on. The Nazis are attacking the previous fourteen years as forming one whole bloc of Marxist policy! Out of these fourteen years, five of them were occupied by Hugenberg, their own ally. So much the worse for him. What is required for agitation is bold, simple lines, as Goebbels says. Their programme is: '*The Destruction of Marxism.* One of them has to be the victor, Marxism or the German people. In ten years, there will no longer be a single Marxist in Germany.'

Hitler is devoting all his eloquence to developing these formulæ, and nothing but that. When they ask for more clarification from him, he says: '*Our programme is to do the opposite of what you have done!*' Word for word.

One day there is a huge poster against Soviet Russia, a sly attack of brutal hatred. It ends thus: '*We German workers coming back from Russia declare: it is better to live in a German prison than to be free in the Soviet paradise!*' That night many of the billboards in the working-class districts bearing this poster are set on fire.

We discuss the future ban on the Communist Party with the Social-Democrats:

The Communist Party is certainly going to be banned. If this is done before the elections, its votes will have to be concentrated on our party. The Communists would join us en masse. In any case, I do not support allowing them all in without conditions ... a year's candidate period would seem necessary to me.

All this smacks of sinister speculation and stupidity at one and the same time:

So you would allow the Communist Party to be struck down without moving? And you will continue to affirm that Hitler is keeping within the limits of your Weimar constitution? Listen, this petty malice has had its day. Your skin is up for sale along with ours. First of all it will be the Communist Party, and then it will be your turn. In any case, your little calculations do not take account of the resentment and contempt that the revolutionary workers will direct at you. You will be sacrificing any possibility of agreement forever.

Then we talk with the left Social-Democrats:

— Then what will you do? Are you also banking on the elections on 5 March?
— No way, we are preparing. We are seeking to set up an illegal liaison network. We know very well that the struggle will become an armed combat in the streets. Only it is for them to attack first. For us, it is the general strike ...

— But what do you mean by that? When, and how, do you think you can unleash this strike?

— I don't much know … maybe when our leaders are arrested. When the restoration of the monarchy takes place in Bavaria … I don't much know.

— But you don't need reasons: you have them all the time.

— That isn't enough.

We don't feel that they will do anything. It all comes down – and this is serious – to conceding time to the enemy, to abandoning the initiative to him. Here we get the essence, the cunning mechanism of that legalist and non-revolutionary mentality which doesn't even offer those among them who want to fight a point of departure. Each isolated event isn't enough reason to unleash the struggle. But every lost opportunity worsens the situation even more and makes the way out more difficult. While one has the strength one waits. And then it is lost. And when defeat is here, there is no longer any possibility of struggle. By this 'prudent', 'calm' and 'waiting' strategy, so dear to the reformist leaders, in the end there is only a bitter and shameful defeat.

The Last Spasms

In our notes we find:

7 February: Essen's 'Iron Front' has decided to carry out a demonstration, *a demonstration in force*. The Nazis turn up at the spot half an hour before, occupy the place, close off access from the neighbouring streets and wait around singing their battle songs. The 'Iron Front' leaders discuss it. They quite simply decide to change the route of march and the place fixed for the meeting. That is how they are preparing the morale of the anti-Fascist fighters.

8 February: The elections for the factory councils that have taken place all over the Reich do not show a definite movement towards the revolutionary list. In general, the reformists are maintaining their positions.

The newspapers are recounting the exploits committed by the Nazis the night before. They surprised three young people who had come out of a meeting with badges on their lapels. They tore them off them. One of the youths was thrown against the wall, and they knocked out all his teeth. Then they dragged him by the hair for more than a hundred metres. The other was badly wounded by knife thrusts. The third comrade fled and sounded the alarm.

Today we look at the lapels. Here we find a sign of the state of morale. The badges bearing the two flags of 'Anti-Fascist Action'[43] and the three arrows of the 'Iron Front' remain in place.

The same phenomenon persists for months. Such courage, such extraordinary individual political bravery; but in class terms, an unbelievable paralysis. But there we are, isn't that a matter of parties, and of organisations?

14 February: Two o'clock in the morning. We are coming back from the Sportspalast where the Red Sports Federation has been holding its ice-skating festival. Berlin is all white. The snow that has been falling for hours and hours is playing games with the statues in the Potsdamer Platz. It has blown out their cheeks, put bizarre wigs on them, and dressed them up in heavy white furs. It has given the trees a sharp outline, part white, part black.

It is too late to take the tube. Groups of workers are walking, pushing their bicycles.

— Did you see it?
— They didn't dare ...
— Obviously they didn't dare. We were over 10,000 strong.

We were over 10,000. Perhaps even more. The hall was already full at seven o'clock. You had to go in between a double row of self-defence boys; for at least fifty metres they formed a long corridor of careful lookout.

In spite of the ice rink it was warm in the hall. We had to squeeze up more and more to make a place for those who were still arriving. The pickled-cucumber sellers had to push their way through with difficulty. Eating went on while we waited. A few sandwiches, an apple. The number of sandwiches distinguished the unemployed worker from the worker who was still in a job.

The slogans stood out on the red streamers: '*Against the Fascisation of Sport!*', '*Against Compulsory Labour Service!*', '*For the Unity of Red Sport!*'

The strains of a beautiful song of hope, 'Brothers, towards the sun, towards liberty', began to rise up. The slogans of 'Red Sport!' were taken up by 10,000 mouths. Some words were said about the role of proletarian sport, then an appeal to vote for 'list 3' in the elections of 5 March, and the loudspeaker announced the procession of the participants.

Sliding softly on skates, the column advanced. It covered the ice rink, withdrew, and the signal was given for the festival to begin. There were hockey matches, races of all types, Viennese waltzes danced marvellously on the ice, and the hours passed. The public took careful note of all the results.

On the stairs we heard sharp, military footsteps. The self-defence guards were being changed.

There had been almost six hours of ice sport, and not an incident. Fascism had been in power for fifteen days, but its people didn't dare come to the Sportspalast. It was one in the morning when we left. The workers who lived some way away went off in groups. Some of the self-defence detachments assisted these groups to form on the pavement.

19 February: A 'Free Speech Congress' is being held in which the left Liberals participate; it was organised by courtesy of the Communists; Einstein and Thomas Mann[44] send their support. When Dr W Heine declares on the rostrum that the swastika has been found in Palestine in Jewish tombs that dated from the time of Jesus, the meeting is dissolved by the police.

The *Reichsbanner* organises an imposing demonstration on the Lustgarten, under the black-red-gold banner of the republic. Its leader, Hölterman,[45] reiterates that they, too, are Germans: 'We fought for Germany's freedom during the War, and we will fight, we will defend our liberty against all the enemies within, and we swear: "*Better to die than to live as slaves!*"'

When the demonstrators get back to their districts, there are incidents with the Nazis nearly everywhere.

Repression

For the second time since Hitler's coming to power the police carry out a search of Karl Liebknecht House. The defence guard, eight Communists, is sent away. The House is ransacked from floor to roof. Furniture is smashed. They are looking for illegal publications and, above all, for weapons. That same day on the billboards there is the usual red police message bearing the title '*Reward*', which promises a thousand marks to whoever could provide precise information on where Communist pamphlets and leaflets are being printed, and where weapons can be found.

That afternoon the Nazis repeat their exploits of 22 January on the Bülowplatz. The police are occupying all the roofs in the district, and under the rifles of the *schupos* the Nazis hold a concerted electoral propaganda meeting in front of the Karl Liebknecht House.

22 February: We went to see Comrade S— in hospital. He is an old Spartacist, a well-built man with gentle eyes in a rough face. We knew him at the Silvesterfest at Fichte. He is warm and comradely. He says *Genosse*[46] fervently, as if he were saying brother. He was badly hurt in the war, a wound that left him with painful complications. There he lay with his head bandaged, suffering terribly, and having difficulty breathing. But all he does is ask painfully, word by word: 'How are things going outside? If only I could get out! Just long enough for me to give you a hand. These Fascists ...' He makes a gesture of wringing a neck. Some other comrades come to see him. Soon we are a Communist 'cell' around his bed. These are bitter words, painful to listen to: 'Cell meetings are less frequent. Comrades are discouraged, they are abandoning the work ...' One of them concludes: '*I prefer to wait for illegal work ...*'

23 February: Karl Liebknecht House has been occupied for the third time since Hitler came to power. A huge contingent of police guards turns up in the afternoon. Five people are arrested. The headquarters of the Central Committee and the offices of *Rote Fahne* are closed, and seals put on the print-shop. A detachment of *schupos* remains to guard the headquarters. The newspapers announce that this time the occupation is to be final, and that the Karl Liebknecht House will be closed.

25 February: An election meeting of the Communist Party in the Sportspalast. An hour before the meeting opens the immense hall is full. It is Pieck who takes the rostrum. He says these words on the question of the united front:

> We address ourselves to all the Social-Democratic workers, the *Reichsbanner* and the supporters of the free trade unions, we extend a fraternal hand, we are ready for any united front that will have for its prime aim the defence of the working masses ...

But when he talks about measures taken against the state schools, the police declare the meeting dissolved, because the speaker 'has spoken contemptuously about religion'. The hall greets this order with an emotional '*Rot Front!*'. There are no incidents on the way out, but in some districts isolated workers were truncheoned and stabbed.

Anticipation

We are at the university among comrades of the Communist group there. We talk in low voices: '*What are we going to do?*' The same question obstinately coming up again. They cannot, they do not want to admit that all is lost in advance, that nothing can be done.

— Nothing. We shall go into illegality. The party will lose fifty per cent of its forces. The best will remain. The work will go on ...

— Today, when we got to the headquarters where we used to hold our cell meetings, we found it occupied by the Nazis.

— And what is '*die stimmung*' [the state of morale – HE] among the intellectuals?

— Bad. Many are afraid. They want to suspend all work till better times.

— But now, what do you think about all that? Who is to blame for this state of affairs?

— Social-Democracy. That's what has held back the masses. It didn't want to fight. It has betrayed yet again.

— But it is consistent in that! This argument could have been valid before the foundation of the Communist parties. Hasn't 1914 already shown us what Social-Democracy was capable of? What else could you have expected of it? The question posed for revolutionaries is the following: How has it come about that Social-Democracy has been able to keep the most important masses with it in spite of its betrayals, in spite of its cowardice, in spite of the deep economic crisis, when a Communist Party existed? Do you think that the party's leadership and its policy has been for nothing?

— *Yes, mistakes have been made …*

She stops for a minute, and then declares: 'We lack leaders …'

The Burning of the *Reichstag*

On 27 February the Social-Democrats are holding a meeting in the Sportspalast to commemorate the fiftieth anniversary of the death of Karl Marx. We wanted to go there, but we were waiting to meet our comrades from the 'Masch'.

The 'Masch' has moved out. It is now in the Neue-Friedrichstrasse, an old street in old Berlin. The district, a centre for the wholesale cloth trade, goes to bed early. The shadows are long on the deserted pavements. The streets are wide, the side alleys narrow. 'Masch' now lives in this big grey house. The old staircase smells of mildew and cats' piss, the smell given off by every wooden staircase in all the old houses in the world. The school is cold and silent. The painful impression of a house to let arises from its corridors without pupils.

Our course, which has held up quite well, tonight includes no more than ten comrades. We are waiting for the teacher. It is already half past eight and he is not here, he isn't coming. We are discussing, as always, the political situation. Our friends are depressed and discouraged. Comrade F—, a party activist, displays a resigned pessimism: '*Die Proleten werden es sehr schwer haben* [It will go very hard with the proles – HE]', he tells us when we ask how things are going in his district.

> — Did the party expect anything else of Fascism?
> — Obviously we know, but all the same, things have happened at such a speed!
> — Myself [says Comrade B—], I think that the party has kept silent for too long, and has hidden itself too much. You never see it. You don't know what to say to those who question you on each occasion.
> — And what do you want it to do? It's being hunted down! All its meetings are forbidden.
> — The meetings of the SPD are very often forbidden, but they manage to hold some of them, all the same.
> — Yes [accepts F—], they demonstrated in our district today, and you had to admit that it was quite good. There were more than 300 people. In times like these ...
> — And us? Why do we do so little?
> — So little, so little ... We are hunted like wild beasts. You make a move and you have the truncheon immediately on your back.
> — Myself [persists B—], I think that the Social-Democrats control their masses better. They can count on them better than our party. Would you have me say anything else? I hope our party gets made illegal as soon as possible.

We all protest indignantly, but he goes on:

> Yes, yes, as soon as possible, because it is certain that it will be declared illegal. It is possible that our leaders, now softened up by well-paid posts, need to come back to the hard realities of difficult days.

Then we go on to talk about the elections. Comrade B— continued:

> — I think that we will lose votes.
> — Obviously.

Practically everybody agrees with that.

> — Myself [said a young man], I think that the Nazis are going to win fifty per cent.
> — You are stupid ...

Our teacher didn't come, and it is already time to go. We go down and walk, as usual, with a few of the comrades who often go along with us as far as Neuköln. When we arrive at the Königstrasse, there is something in the street that alters its normal look, something, I know not what, a slight unease. We hear running behind us. It is a group of young people. When they catch up with us they blurt out:

— The *Reichstag* is in flames!
— You're joking!
— No joking. It is burning beautifully and well.
— I just can't believe it [continues F—], who would think of setting fire to the *Reichstag*?
— Who? [and the voice of the young man hisses hatefully] The Communists. Obviously it's the Communists.
— What have the Communists got against the *Reichstag* building?

Our objections are not to their taste. They stare at us with a provocative attitude, exchange glances, and finally take off.

We ask a *schupo* if it is true that the *Reichstag* is on fire. 'I know nothing about it', he replies to us, 'A lady has just asked me the same question.'

We decide to see for ourselves, and we set off. When we got to the Schloßplatz, we deliberated: Maybe this is a Nazi provocation, a trap. It is so incredible. We didn't go on.

On the following day Berlin is in turmoil. The news of the burning of the *Reichstag* has reached the furthest districts. A procession of bikes and pedestrians goes up by the Unter den Linden towards the Brandenburg Gate. There is a cold curiosity among the majority: to see, to ascertain the action of the flames. The police prevent the formation of groups. You talk a little, and discreetly.

The entire Communist press is banned for four weeks. There is protective custody for all the Communist Party functionaries, and a detention order against two of its MPs 'suspected of complicity' in the burning of the *Reichstag*.[47]

The entire Social-Democratic press also falls under the blow of a ban for fourteen days. Van der Lubbe[48] had confessed to 'links with the SPD'.

There are mass arrests. It is said that Torgler has given himself up at the police prefecture accompanied by his lawyer. And this ferocious terror evokes no response, no organised resistance.

The *Vorwärts* offices are occupied by the police. Leaflets and pamphlets are seized. After four hours of occupation the police depart.

The newspapers publish the puerile tale by Göring of the plans of the Communist Party. In it there are bridges blown up with dynamite, trains derailed, kilos of poison for canteens, thousands of women and children taken hostage, a fantastic organisation of Communists dressed as stormtroopers to plunder shops, and, and ...

On the Eve of the Elections

The leader of the Social-Democracy, Wels, applies to the Reich Commissioner von Papen to protest against the ban on the press of his party:

> Social-Democracy has nothing in common with the *Reichstag* arsonist. All its past proves it. Exemplary discipline has always been demonstrated by its supporters. One glance at the Communist press, full right up to now of the harshest attacks against Social-Democracy, shows in the clearest fashion that there exists no united front between the Communist Party and the Social-Democratic Party ...

Such are the words that illustrate the value of the famous 'Non-Aggression Pact'.

A group of the SA arrives in the Bülowplatz. It is the squad that had been commanded by Horst Wessel,[49] the pimp 'poet', the hero venerated by the Nazis. A click of the heels, a half turn, and they are lined up in front of the Karl Liebknecht House. Three men step forward. They are carrying the swastika flag. One order from their leader, and they move towards the headquarters of the Communist Party. They pass through the door where two *schupos* are on guard, and a few minutes later they are seen on the roof. A moment later and the swastika floats on the great flagpole that has so often been decorated with the red flag with the hammer and sickle. The SA men salute with raised arms. The leader makes a small speech: 'The dream of our beloved hero, the most fervent desire of Horst Wessel, has just been realised. The flag he so proudly carried and defended with his blood floats over the Communist fortress.'

During the last days of February the appearance of the streets begins to change. They used to belong to the workers, but they are nobody's now. Abandoned by the workers, they do not yet have a new master. You do not see the Nazis any more, but there are no longer processions of workers, nor of self-defence guards wandering through the streets, returning to their posts.

The elections are coming on. There are few flags in windows. That healthy political feeling that has been apparent until now has disappeared.

Even the Nazi supporters have given up. A strange phenomenon; they have terrorised themselves a little.

On 4 March the magnificent 'Awakening of the Nation' engendered by Goebbels' imagination takes place: there are torchlight parades that same night in all the villages and towns of the Reich, and bonfires lit on all the hills, and in all the mountain villages.

We install ourselves on the corner of the Friedrichstrasse and the Unter den Linden. There are not so many people. There are particularly few Nazi badges: 'I tell you that they are curious, like us.'

All at once there is movement. People are pushing on all sides. Over there, afar off, coming down the Friedrichstrasse on the north side you see a flow of yellow burning points of little flames which tremble and change their positions following the same oscillations: 'They are already coming, they are coming!'

The police are excessively polite: 'Gentlemen, ladies, if you please; move well away. They are going to pass by here.'

A very well dressed little old lady is swept up by the wave while passing; she does not manage to see what is going on:

— But what is it? What is it?
— It is the Nazi torchlight parade ...
— So what?

Her gesture is so dry, so contemptuous, that she must belong to Hugenberg's party, or to the Catholic Centre.[50]

The street corners and the buildings take on a reddish hue. A gleam of fire flickers over them. There they are. All the people without badges about us raise their arms 'in Roman style'. So, they also were Nazis, these cowardly petty-bourgeois, who wouldn't show the swastika flag on their windows nor the Nazi badge on their lapels before the elections! At this period you still didn't have to be a hero not to raise your arm.

They are passing by. One man in twenty is carrying a torch that smokes more than it burns. Goebbels' plan promised better than this. The shouts of the leaders echo: 'Where are the Communists?' And the column replies: 'In the cellars!'[51]

A lorry of *schupos* passes. Smiling, they also openly, once and again, make the Hitler salute. There is great enthusiasm in the crowd.

The stormtroopers call out noisily: 'For a quick one-way journey of the Jews to Palestine.' People are guffawing, laughing heartily: 'Bury Thälmann!' A woman, standing on the footboard of her motor, says: 'Listen to what he is saying: "Bury Thälmann!"' She is laughing hysterically.

One SA man with a nightmarish face is shaking his collecting tin while repeating: 'Give for the repair of Karl Liebknecht House! Go there and look at the swastika. It looks good there!'

We are suffering, we are suffering ...

The meeting to hear Hitler, who will be speaking to all Germany in Königsberg, takes place in Franz Joseph square.

For the first time in Berlin we are seeing stormtroopers exercising the functions of auxiliary police. Each *schupo* is accompanied by two of these men armed with revolvers and truncheons. They are under the orders of the *schupo*, and, very awkward and obsequious at his side, are following him and listening to him like keen apprentices. This chills the spirit.

On the radio a voice is describing, second by second, what is happening in the hall of Königsberg 'where the *Führer* will be speaking'. Soon there comes from the loudspeaker a surging noise that is rising, rising: '*Heil, heil, heil!*' It is the *Führer* coming in.

The wave of cries reaches a culmination. It breaks: '*Völksgenossen, Völksgenossinen!*'[52]

Hitler recites the speech sermon so well known to all. He shouts from the first word. He does not explain, he harangues for an hour, for two if he sees fit, without varying his tone, with an accent that even we foreigners notice. It is said here that he has a Slav accent. He is not as good an orator as Goebbels, who marks his speech forcefully word for word, standing soberly on the platform, with measured, well-prepared and much-rehearsed gestures. Nor does he have the animal energy of face, voice and gesture of Göring, who chews on his words and holds them back in his mouth until they puff out his cheeks, deforming his face, and then releases them like spittle. But he is the man of contempt. Hitler quite simply shouts.

We go home. The Nazi columns we meet are accompanied by lorries of *schupos* who are gazing up at the windows of the houses with rifles at the ready. They are marching towards the triumph of 5 March.

Very close to our lodgings is a bar, in other words, a polling booth. Already early on a *schupo* and a Nazi of the auxiliary police are walking about. We lean out of the window. The representatives of the parties are standing in front of the bar with their placards, a stormtrooper with 'List 1', an old man with 'List 4' (the Centre Party), a member of the Stahlhelm with 'List 5'. Lists '2' and '3', the Social-Democrats and the Communists, are missing. Have they been prevented even this?

We have already witnessed one election day on 6 November, with defeat for the Nazis and triumph for the Communists. We are very soon in the street to see what change there is.

It is a magnificent sunny day. Everybody is on the pavement in Wedding. Is everything as before? No. Nazi guards passing by, with ten or fifteen men armed with revolvers, is new, for example. Likewise are the motors with stormtroopers unceasingly and noisily passing through the streets. So are the façades without flags, which are a new way of showing that you still remain a Communist or a Socialist. We walk on. The blocks of houses are so densely populated that the polling booths succeed each other every fifty metres.

There is a small gathering in front of a billboard on which is fastened a picture of Van der Lubbe, along with an offer of a reward of 20,000 marks for anybody who could supply information on the burning of the *Reichstag*. There is derisive laughter. Someone dares to say out loud as he leaves: 'They maintained nonetheless that they already knew everything; that they were holding the guilty, some Communists. Now here they are offering 20,000 marks for information.'

When we arrive at the corner of the Sparrplatz, in front of the bar, again we read: 'List 1', '4', '5'. But now there is a young worker who is carrying a placard. He is talking with somebody and his back is turned to us. All at once he turns round. From his neck hangs a poster with the well-known inscription: 'Vote for List 3, the Communist Party.'

We almost cry out. It is scant consolation, but at this time it cheers us up considerably to see one of ours! Our surprise is so obvious that the *schupo* and the stormtroopers look at us ironically. We go over to see this friend and shake his hand:

— Hallo, so things are still going on as usual, so it isn't forbidden?
— No, we thought it was. But we came out here all the same and they left us alone. Then we passed the news on.

From the other side of Müller Street we begin to see more frequently lists '2' and '3'. Similarly on the Reinickendorferstrasse these two placards are the only ones to be seen. And at the door of a polling booth we find one sole friend, who has hung a sheet of paper on a string from his chest with 'THREE' written in pencil in block capital letters. Then this also becomes common.

The entrance of Kösliner Street – the street of the barricades – is chock-a-block with people. They are watching a Nazi motorbike that is passing along the Communist fortress from one end to the other. It is no more than a hundred metres long. The stormtrooper seated in the sidecar is carrying an enormous flag with a swastika spread out in the wind, and a revolver in his hand, ready to fire. They come and go. The proles at the windows and on the pavements are looking coldly at this unheard of provocation.

We spend the afternoon in Neuköln. The comrades are able to organise their interventions there. The posters are quietly drawn up. They are handmade but are all alike. People go about quietly. The auxiliary policemen pass by carrying a stretcher. We draw near. It is somebody who is sick being carried to the polling station. There was no lack of these new Lazaruses on 5 March, who heard the call: 'Arise, and go and vote for Hitler.'

At ten o'clock on that same night we are waiting for the results of the elections in a small restaurant in the Westen. What any militant experiencing these months in Berlin could have foreseen is happening. The voice on the radio is repeating and hammering into us the terrible defeat. We note down the numbers for a good while. Then, since no change is taking place, we throw away the pencil.

The question of power is settled. The revolution is defeated. The elections of 5 March have not only been elections, they were a review of the troops.[53]

What we had felt on 30 January has been confirmed and become visible for the broad masses. The battle that has lasted for years has ended with the triumph of Hitler. Our old hope, the hope of millions of workers – *Germany* – has collapsed. The Nazis are parading their victory savagely in the streets:

— The Red Front is smashed!
— The SA is marching, watch out!
— Give up the streets!

The most barbaric rumours are circulating. The boots of the Nazis are setting the rhythm of life. We wake up at night: clomp, clomp, clomp … the Nazis are passing. We are woken up again: yet again the boots of the stormtroopers. Our neighbour on the second floor begins to play the *Horst Wessel Lied*, the Hitlerite hymn, on the piano. Her brother is singing by her side. They are not very gifted, but on the other hand they are persistent. We have the *Horst Wessel Lied* morning, afternoon and night.

The majority of the elections for the factory committees that have taken place reveal disasters for the revolutionary list. They register mass desertions to the Nazis. There are sad, very sad instances. Panic is spreading. All is gloomy.

Now the Social-Democrats are saying: Hitler has come to power legally. So we have to put up with him.

Militants are beaten up at home, in their rooms, in the presence of their wives and children. Workers vanish. Some days later their bodies are found

THE TRAGEDY OF THE GERMAN PROLETARIAT

in the woods. There are cries at night in the streets, and not a window opens. But when the day comes the sun shines as usual. Things look almost normal. Some people manage to deny the terror.

The lorries of the SA armed with rifles, with bloody and triumphal chants on their lips, swarm on the corners of the streets. Nazi headquarters, SA barracks-bars, multiply. Near where we are staying there was only one of them, but now there are three. Every street known for its anti-Fascism and every block of houses is searched from top to bottom, and then infiltrated.

One of the vast colony of maisonettes of wood and metal that you see proliferating on the outskirts of German cities was called 'the New Moscow'. This one, at Reinickendorf, was only lived in by Communists. One morning lorries arrive filled with police and stormtroopers. They surround the colony. For five hours everything is turned upside down. Mattresses and cushions are torn apart. Gardens are devastated. The disarmament is meticulous. Everything that can be used as a weapon is taken away. And this is what they did before they left: the assembly hall, which is right in the middle of the locality, where fifty of the comrades had stood guard every night since Hitler's coming to power, is given over after a ceremony to 'Assault Detachment no. 63'. This will install itself in this hall, and the Communists of 'New Moscow' will have among them enemies they have fought for years, challenging them for control of the locality. There are no words of consolation to end up with here.

Perspectives remain open. For revolutionaries there are no dead ends, there are problems to be resolved. But it is necessary that the truth be told, it is necessary that the world should understand what has to be known, what the German workers know. It must all be told with the heavy bitterness that haunts the factories and the streets of Berlin. And nothing added.

It is necessary that this shame of day after day, when nothing happened and all was lost should lie heavy over everybody as it bore down on them; that it should shatter the confidence of routinism, the vanity that wants to consider nothing again and revise nothing, the interests of those who wish to prevent debate and to go on as if nothing has happened, and the petty courage of those who needed the assurance of an immediate success in order to struggle. Finally, it is necessary that it should bear down with all its weight upon those who are capable of taking up the heavy task of understanding, of correcting, and of starting afresh. Because now it is a matter, in effect, of a new start.

Appendix: Letters to an Argentine Comrade
Letter from Berlin, 31 January 1933

Dear Old Friend

I write in haste. I had just finished a letter – which went by sea – in which I explained our appreciation of the German situation, when matters suddenly came to a head in the way we feared.

Yesterday in the afternoon Hitler took power. He had obtained for himself the Ministry of the Interior for Prussia and that of the Reich. This means that the police (very powerful here) and the state apparatus are in his hands.

You must have read in the Argentine press an account of the triumphal torchlight parade under the Brandenburg Gate (Hitler, like Mussolini, had declared that his men would enter a 'conquered' Berlin through this gate, a sort of triumphal arch). Things were even less 'heroic' and more grotesque than for Italian Fascism, but no less decisive for the working class for all that.

But you don't know what followed: that same evening we were able to learn, with what anxiety you can well imagine, the state of morale of the workers, the members of the Communist Party and of our classmates in the Marxist school whom we questioned about what they had decided to do in the present circumstances, how they envisaged the struggle against Hitler, and what the party's slogans were. We shall never forget the discouragement, the disarray and the total lack of faith in themselves and the party that they displayed in the face of our questions. There they were, overwhelmed, empty, and incapable of giving the slightest response.

Dear old friend, we were forewarned all too well. We knew the ravages caused among the proletariat by the regime and policy of the Communist International. But you have to experience the feeling of isolation, the impotence, and the bitterness expressed in a harsh and raging fashion at this decisive hour which we heard among the best elements of the proletariat in the foremost party of the Communist International, a party that had gained six million votes, to be able to understand the unforgivable crime of those miserable people who have placed their stamp on the Communist International. We were dumbfounded.

And those who show the slightest optimism have ideas so fantastic, so fantastic … For example, that Hitler will not remain in power for more than a month; or, on the other hand, that it will be easier for us to win over the workers whom he has deceived; or that we will pick up trump cards because with him the international situation will become more tense, bringing the revolution closer; that Hitler will not dare ban the party; and also, no, the party cannot call for a general strike, because that would provide a pretext to make it illegal. In a word, we heard the utter emptiness of the inept slogans spread by the Communist Party.

My old friend, we are defeated, and defeated ignominiously. It is the end of our hopes in Germany. There will still be isolated conflicts because here the anti-Fascist workers have weapons, are organised on a district basis, and even keep machine guns whose parts are divided up between the tenants of a block of flats. There will be a bloody terror in the months to come. The best will fall ... Side by side with the devotion and the admirable courage of individuals there is an enormous paralysis and disorientation as far as the class is concerned.

What a ghastly farce! What a pretence is the Communist International after Lenin! What a puffed up windbag!

And the left! At this precise moment Trotsky's faction is split in two, and there only remain fifteen active comrades in the whole of Berlin.[54] The others, who have been leaders for years, have just now joined the party declaring Trotsky's perspectives for Russia and Germany to be false.[55] The other faction, that of Landau, puts out a bimonthly sheet and lags completely behind events. To sum up, the influence of this tiny left is so minimal that it can decide nothing at the present time.

The Social-Democratic Party merits a letter on its own. The mentality of a hardened German Social-Democrat is only comparable to that of another German Social-Democrat. We are acquainted with some of them, and may God forgive us. But we should not forget in passing that along with our movement a social movement that is over sixty years old, the Social-Democratic movement, is also collapsing.

The SAP (a left split from the SPD) is a group of young militants torn apart by permanent internal crises, whose influence is virtually nil.

The Social-Democratic Party and the Communist Party are the two decisive organisations. The reformists have the upper hand in the trade unions and over the majority of those workers who are still holding down their jobs. The Communist Party is isolated from the masses. Now the initiative for extra-parliamentary struggle can only come from the Communist Party. The bourgeoisie fears the general strike as the greatest of evils. But the Communist Party cannot unleash this general strike. You have just seen what it is. *I ought to say: what it was.* For the price the German Communist Party and the present Communist International will have to pay for such falsehood will be the loss of the trust and hearts of the masses. Down with the thousand-times criminal clique of adventurers and bureaucrats who have prepared this fresh and immense defeat! Forward to the new task!

May we take courage so that we may have the strength to put into operation something better than this in the dark days to come!

Rustico

Letter from Paris, 1 June 1933

Dear Old Friend

We are back here after having stayed in Germany for months that burned like molten lead. What terrible days! They preyed on our nerves to such an extent that the least discussion, even with the comrades here, threw us into a state of immeasurable fury.

Day after day we were forced to accompany to the cemetery workers struck down by the Fascists, with no perspective for struggle before us, without ever experiencing a fight that would have allowed us to spit back so much accumulated rage, hatred and bitterness.

At the side of the Spartacists who kept their weapons like holy relics we burned within, devoured by impatience, watching all our positions falling one by one without a struggle; feeling the contempt of an enemy emboldened by the lack of resistance everywhere, becoming more and more insolent: 'Where are the Communists? In the cellars!' Such is the refrain that the Nazis are chanting in all the streets of Germany. And they are forcing militants to wipe the floors of the SA barracks with their red flags with the hammer and sickle ... I cannot go on because I am heartbroken.

The memory which we retain of the German working class under Hitler is this: a few days before leaving, after the Fascist May Day, we went to the Friedrichfelde cemetery where the fighters of 19 January 1919 are buried alongside Karl Liebknecht and Rosa Luxemburg. We went there mainly to place flowers on the grave of dear old Mehring[56] who appeared to us to be clumsily forgotten by the party on the day of the Spartacist anniversary. The cemetery is in a village on the outskirts of Berlin among workers' houses and factory chimneys. There are some lime and chestnut trees in the background, and further on, at the back, the cluster of our graves, to which are added other, more recent ones ...

When we got closer we found out that the Nazis had also passed by here; the huge bronze star with the hammer and sickle which had been upon the red brick monument had been torn off. They had taken the wreaths and flowers from all the graves. There was a notice on the way in: 'Closed', and a lattice of crossed planks to obstruct access. Just bare stones; in the middle, opposite, those of Rosa and Karl. You can imagine the anguish that tightened in our throats.

A few steps further on was a guardian talking with a worker. 'Is it forbidden to put flowers on these graves?', we ask. 'No, no! We have not yet come to that …', reply the men very quickly. And we sense in their voices a hint of recognition and encouragement.

A woman comes up with her basket of provisions. She has obviously come between two shopping errands. When she gets past the barrier she begins to weep. Deeply moved to tears ourselves, we place the flowers that we had brought on old Mehring's grave and go off to look for more, but this time for something for the two Spartacist leaders, the founders of the German Communist Party. At the end of almost half an hour's walk we find some red tulips, very red ones. We return to the cemetery. The woman is still there and she is still weeping.

Whilst arranging the fresh flowers in containers full of water which we placed alongside these two names so dear to us, we are thinking that this gesture will also be good for the woman and the workers who pass by … Fresh flowers, red flowers upon the graves of Rosa and Karl, as they are called here.

You should understand that whilst weeping we were also sharing the unhappy perseverance of this woman worker – the German working class – who stopped in front of each grave earnestly reading the names of *her* fallen heroes. She visited them all while remaining for a long time in front of each stone. Her journey took more than an hour and a half.

A hundred metres from there the first Nazi graves in the workers' cemetery are sinking under the weight of wreaths and ribbons.

On Germany, our conclusions are the following: contrary to the conceptions of official Communism, we think that the situation will develop in the near future towards an intensification of the terror and of the Fascist dictatorship. The contradictions and the difficulties which the Stalinists rightly indicate as causes for the imminent fall of Hitler are those that led to Fascism in the first place: because the crisis of capitalism was very sharp, because to do battle with foreign capitalists the German capitalist class needs a subjugated and docile working class in its own country, because it needs to lower wages and worsen working and living conditions, to conscript the unemployed into 'compulsory labour service' and so do away with unemployment benefit: because it now has to exploit the petty-bourgeoisie even more and create inflation; it is precisely because of all this that Fascism exists in Germany. Because of this the bourgeoisie has been obliged to drop Social-Democracy, and afterwards Brüning, followed by Papen and then a purely military dictatorship: Schleicher.

To think that with the seizure of power this development is going to be cut short immediately and Fascism buried is to understand nothing. On the basis of these same terrible difficulties Hitler will yet triumph over Hugenberg, the German Nationalist Party, the rebellious *Stahlhelm*, and the Centre, and will completely install the exclusive dictatorship of the National Socialists.

This is the perspective for the immediate future, a future that can last for years. The problem of power has been resolved in favour of Fascism. The proletarian revolution has been vanquished.

This is what remains of the revolutionary forces:

1. The greater part, shattered by the demoralisation and the terror, has abandoned the struggle. An important part has passed over to Fascism. There are some very sad cases.

2. A small part of the Communist Party has taken up the struggle after the first months of total collapse, but with the old perspectives and the old concepts: 'Fascism cannot resolve the problems that are posed to it, nor carry out the promises made, and it will collapse after a brief delay.' When they have to admit that these concepts are false, a part of them, worn out, will also give up. The Communist Party will not grow stronger in illegality. *Left to itself*, its progress will not be forward, but, on the contrary, it will disintegrate.

3. The different oppositional groups. This is the essential starting off point for future action: the Left Opposition, the SAP (the German Socialist Workers Party), and the Brandler–Thalheimer Opposition.[57] These groups are carrying on activity.

What are the possibilities for action? Laying aside the illusion of interesting the masses in political action against the government, which nobody takes nor will take seriously in Germany at the moment, it seems obvious to us that the activity of the working class will be exercised here and there on the economic terrain: the defence of living conditions, wages, the length of the working day, etc. The essential task of the present time is to seek to unite the oppositional forces in Germany. That is going on there. Here in France the work is well advanced: the three left groups, apart from the *Ligue Communiste* which is still in disagreement, are on the verge of uniting.[58] We are thinking of a sort of new Zimmerwald,[59] which as a result of the German disaster and the desertion of the Communist International without a struggle, will seek agreement and a common field of action for the oppositional forces. The work of the opposition at the present time in Germany is singularly easy (we are not talking about the enormous difficulties of illegality). Its activity is more and more effectively exercised over the militants of the party. All the party's resources, its apparatus, its press, all its means of influence and coercion are all extraordinarily diminished. The rank and file has a far greater independence, and is often left to its own devices. The factional struggle between the opposition and the bureaucratic centre is much less unequal. And if we add that the oppositional elements were neither surprised nor disorientated by the events you will have a correct picture of the present conditions of work.

But we do not want to be mistaken in our analysis. Hitler took power in 1933 and not in 1922 like Mussolini; at the height of a capitalist crisis, not at the beginning of a relative stabilisation; and in Germany, not in Italy. This means that his tasks are enormously more difficult and his stability much more precarious. We say this to you: the internal conditions that threaten Hitler, left to themselves, will not be decisive for a long time. Hitler is totally dominant. Against him there is no organised force capable of resisting him in the slightest degree. He has defeated them all. Just one detail: in the block of houses where we were living there was only one Nazi headquarters before Hitler's seizure of power; when we left there were three of them, each held by a storm-trooper detachment. This is the case in all the working-class centres, and in the specifically Communist streets. To keep everybody quiet Hitler now possesses all the police and his own militia that he has made the state pay for, the entire apparatus from which he has ousted the Social-Democrats, those of the Centre Party and even his governmental allies, the German Nationalists; he has in his hands the trade-union apparatus which he has torn from the reformists; he has concentration camps for guarding political prisoners in which there are as many stormtroopers as there are prisoners; he has compulsory work camps, and the Nazi cells have just received the order to find a place in the factories for 5000 members of the National Socialist Party (by kicking out the Marxist workers).

With these trump cards Hitler has what he needs to keep hold of those who might dream of abandoning him. Malcontents are isolated and demoralised. The climate in Germany is of suppression and fear; we have spoken with several workers who have been bloodily beaten up. What concerns them, the first thing that they ask you, is that you do not talk about it to anybody, that you say nothing of their plight, for the Nazis have threatened to torture them to death if they tell anything. Terror has silenced hatred and rage for the moment.

Behind the scenes struggles take place between the Fascists and part of the Stahlhelm, and between members of the government, struggles which, even if they do not threaten Hitler, as you can see from the above, on the other hand facilitate revolutionary propaganda.

Things are less easy abroad. Mussolini was able to treat himself handsomely to a noisy foreign policy of pure prestige. His power, in this instance, was conditioned by his weakness as much as by his strength. Italy does not seriously threaten Britain and the United States, etc, as a competitor in the world market ... It barely threatens France, and then only in the military sphere. We thus understand how Mussolini could pronounce his 'terrible' speeches threatening the world with the new Italy, the rejuvenated Italy; how he could make his aeroplanes fly past in combat formation, etc ... Anglo-American imperialism could afford to listen to him while smiling. This foreign policy of nationalist prestige is one of Fascism's main methods of distracting and firing the enthusiasm of its supporters, the petty-bourgeoisie and the university youth, in order to rub out the spirit of the class struggle by the myth of national unity and the fatherland.

Can Hitler afford this luxury? You have seen how the tone of his speech has changed. The immense industrialised power that Germany is cannot allow itself to indulge in jokes. The French have already lost sleep about it, and the British as well. Greedy for markets, each imperialism has fifty per cent of its productive forces unemployed, and at this very moment German capitalism is ready to leave them behind by preparing itself internally to profit from the slightest conjunctural change. All that Hitler can offer to reassure them is this: I will leave you alone in the West, on condition that you leave me a free hand in the East. We need to expand, and this will be at Russia's expense. (I will send you some paragraphs from Hitler's book, in which the programme of a war with Russia is developed in an explicit fashion.) Obviously, this offer is not to be ignored. Rosenberg[60] was sent to London to present it. It has been received with enthusiasm in Deterding's[61] circles – the old dream of Baku oil. But others, supporting France, have shown themselves openly hostile.

I will not expand any more on the above. Hitler's game is very difficult, and his margin of manoeuvre is very narrow at the height of the present terrible crisis of the capitalist world. This does not allow us to anticipate a peaceful development over decades as was the case with Mussolini.

Let us pass on to something else. In order to assess better our position it is necessary to understand and make it clear that what has come to grief in Germany is not only the German Communist Party; it is the policy of the entire Communist International, the same that it is in the process of carrying out in the rest of the world and which will lead us in each country to a repetition of the German disaster.

The Stalinists are now saying:

1. 'There has been no defeat in Germany. The Communist Party retains all its strength and is continuing the struggle.' You will find the reply to that in what has gone before and in the article that we have published in France.

2. 'Social-Democracy is to blame for all this; by holding back the working class and preventing a struggle, it has played the Fascist game.' Yes, this is true. But this argument could only be valid before the formation of the Communist International. For why was it created? Precisely because the betrayal of the Second International in 1914[62] proved to revolutionaries what its role was; to deliver the working class to the bourgeoisie with its hands tied. The Communist parties were founded to avoid this, to pull the masses from their influence, to conquer them and to lead them to victory. What does it imply now, if a Communist now tells us in order to excuse his party that 'Social-Democracy in Germany has betrayed for a second time'? That he still maintained illusions about it? In every case Social-Democracy has been consistent with itself, and we might add that its incompetence and cowardice were such that, thinking that it could adapt itself to Fascism and survive, it has been destroyed by it.

But the fact that it was able 'to hold back the struggle' shows that the decisive masses were with it. And what does this mean other than that after all its betrayals, after a formidable crisis that pushed the masses into action, the Communist Party was bankrupt? For the whole of February we witnessed dark hours in Germany: the revolutionaries were isolated, cut off from the masses, without any real power, in utter impotence, without even the ability to unleash a local strike (!!), waiting, in the tow of the Socialist leaders. During February the Communist Party disappeared from the German scene. Sunk in total demoralisation, you found it neither in the streets, nor anywhere else.

Even the 'manoeuvres' of the united front played into the hands of Social-Democracy. It organised yet another important meeting in the working-class district of Neuköln one day in February, on the eve of the burning of the *Reichstag*. And when we asked a Communist why the Communist Party was incapable of doing the same thing he replied: 'The Social-Democrats keep control of their masses better than we do.' (!) All this is reflected – and we predicted it in advance to our Communist comrades – in the elections of 5 March 1933. At the decisive hour of struggle, 'the party of revolutionary action' was abandoned, that is to say, it lost an enormous mass of votes. Social-Democracy, 'the party of reformism and betrayal', kept nearly all its votes.

3. 'The Communist Party did all it could, the masses did not want to struggle, and the isolated Communist Party could not allow itself to be

massacred. Lenin said: "The vanguard on its own cannot obtain victory." From which follows surrender without a struggle.' This is the most miserable of excuses. To throw the responsibility on to the masses! But hadn't the party been proclaiming the radicalisation of the masses and their will to struggle in every key since 1928? Didn't it even explain the fall of Papen by the offensive of the proletariat? On the other hand, since 6 November 1932 the Communist Party had become the foremost party in Berlin with 800,000 votes, and with nearly six million in the rest of Germany. How did it come about that it could not stop a single factory, nor mobilise its own masses, as it demonstrated on 20 January 1933, when the Nazis dared to march in a demonstration in front of Karl Liebknecht House, the seat of the Communist Party?

'The Communist Party did all it could.' Is launching an appeal for a general strike at the last minute the sole duty of the Communist Party, the revolutionary vanguard? And is this enough to absolve it? For example, on 20 July 1932, when von Papen suppressed the Braun–Severing Socialist government of Prussia by a *coup d'état*, the Communist Party called for a general strike. It did all it could. But let us look closer: when the Nazis organised a plebiscite to overthrow this government, before von Papen's coup, the Communists voted with them against Braun–Severing.[63] When von Papen overthrew that same government, which the Communist Party had described as Fascist, the self-same Communist Party called for a general strike. The masses did not move. Any comment is superfluous.

i) Two years before Hitler's rise to power, the party said through the mouth of Münzenberg: 'After Fascism, us!' And some time later, in the middle of the *Reichstag*, through the mouth of Remmele,[64] the Communist MP: 'A Fascist government does not scare us. It will fall quicker than any other. Then it will be our turn.' For years the Communist Party sowed the spirit of defeat and fatalism among the party and the masses: 'Fascism is an inevitable experience. The masses will turn to us afterwards.'

ii) As Fascism grew and became threatening, the thesis of the Communist Party was: 'Social-Democracy is the main enemy. We must deliver our most decisive blows against it. Without defeating it we cannot fight Fascism.' (Thälmann's thesis)

iii) As far as it was concerned, all parties and all governments were Fascist: Severing, Brüning, Papen, Schleicher ... One of its leaders declared: 'Hitler could not do more than Brüning has done.'

iv) Trade-union policy: it created independent trade unions and abandoned the trade unions to the reformists. Guided by its concept of Fascism it allowed Nazi workers to be elected on to strike committees.

Permanent result: the Nazis unleashed strikes, then broke them, and got the best elements sacked, getting Nazi workers taken on in their places.

v) The Communist Party renounced Marxist theory and copied the programme of the Nazis, thus hoping to emulate their success. During the elections of 6 November 1932 on all the great manifestos stuck on the Berlin billboards, the 'struggle against the Treaty of Versailles' figured as the first point of the programme of the Communist Party in the struggle against crisis and poverty. This was the equivalent of explaining and denouncing as the principal cause of a profound crisis of the capitalist system resulting in twelve million unemployed in North America – a victorious country if ever there was one – the fact that Germany was a vanquished and humiliated victim of the Treaty of Versailles. This was precisely the argument of the Nazis and of the German imperialist bourgeoisie.

vi) The Communist Party adopted the concept of the 'peoples' revolution' and of 'national and social liberation', two bits of baggage belonging to the Nazis, renouncing the concept of the dictatorship of the proletariat and the internationalist theory of the social revolution. These were two enormous crimes which by themselves alone would have been enough to kill off a class party. It was Engels in his *Peasant War in Germany* who said that a revolutionary leader – in our case, the Communist Party – who launches slogans that are not of his class is irremediably lost.[65]

All this is what the German Communist Party did, or rather what the Communist International did. And what did it omit to do?

To say, after a party has worked for years by its policy and its regime to confound, to disorient and to mislead the consciousness of its militants and of the class, to annihilate its will to struggle, to disarm its vigilance, to gnaw at its confidence, to say after all this that 'the party did all it could', means quite simply that it did all it could to prepare the defeat of the working class. And then to accuse the masses of passivity!

The question of the passivity of the masses is almost one and the same thing as the ineptitude and bankruptcy of the Communist and Socialist Parties. For a working class that has expressed its consciousness and political independence for half a century through a working-class party – let us call it such – which is the oldest and most powerful in the world; which is organised in very strong trade unions, and in great formations of anti-Fascist combat: the revolutionaries in the *Rot Front* and the *Antifaschistische Aktion* (Anti-Fascist Action), and the reformists in the *Eiserne Front* (Iron Front) and the *Reichsbanner*; which moreover had the most powerful section of the Communist International; which had habits and a tradition of discipline and self-organisation unlike any other working class; and after all this – the

Social-Democratic Party, trade unions and Communist Party surrendering without a fight and collapsing – to accuse the masses of passivity, and to hope that amidst this enormous breakdown and disorientation, the masses will improvise, will yet again create a resistance outside the limits of their traditional action, is to understand nothing but nothing, and to mock everything.

Now to conclude: if, along with Lenin – as opposed to those who would place their hope in the spontaneity of the masses – we believe that the party is the decisive, essential element for the triumph of the working class, we must now explicitly add that it is a no less decisive element for its defeat. The party prepares as effectively for the one as for the other. It is necessary to understand this very basically after the German disaster, and in the presence of the identical policy and action of the Communist International in other countries.

Rustico

NOTES

All notes were added by Al Richardson.

1. On 3 November 1932 the 20,000 workers of the Berlin Transport Company (BVG), which belonged to the Social-Democratic municipality, struck against a two per cent wage reduction. The strike was led jointly by the Nazis and the Stalinists. The police repression was brutal; there were 1000 arrests, 100 wounded and four killed, and over 2000 employees were sacked.
2. *Reichsbanner*, 'The Flag of the Reich', the Social-Democratic self-defence organisation.
3. On 6 November 1932 the Nazis obtained 11.7 million votes, or 33.1 per cent of the votes as against 37.3 per cent in July 1932. The KPD obtained 5.9 million votes, and the Social-Democrats 7.2 million. The total vote for the KPD and the SPD represented 37.3 per cent of the votes. These results gave rise to an optimism that was to be cruelly disappointed a few months later. The French Socialist leader Léon Blum wrote in *Le Populaire*: 'Hitler has now been excluded from power.'
4. *Vorwärts (Forward)*, the central organ of the SPD.
5. *Die Rote Fahne (The Red Flag)*, the central organ of the KPD.
6. The SA (*Sturmabteilung*), also known as the Brownshirts, was the private army of the Nazi party led by Ernst Röhm.
7. Ernst Thälmann, the KPD's candidate in the Presidential elections of 13 March 1932, received 4,983,300 votes. When, as there was no overall majority, a run-off vote was held on 12 April, Thälmann's vote dropped to 3,706,755 votes, whereas Hitler's vote increased by 1.1 million to 13.5 million, and that of the incumbent President Hindenburg increased by 700,000 to 19.3 million.
8. See note 22, p. 38.
9. See note 23, p. 38.
10. Wilhelm Florin (1894–1944), a metalworker, joined the SPD youth section in 1908.

He joined the USPD, and then the KPD. He became a Central Committee member and *Reichstag* deputy in 1924. In exile from late 1933, he became a full member of the ECCI in December 1933, and a member of the Secretariat of the Communist International in 1935.

11. *Rot Front*: Red Front. It became a ritual exclamation accompanied by the clenched fist salute.
12. On 4 January 1933 Hitler and von Papen met in the house of Schröder, a Cologne banker, to confirm their alliance and obtain the support of big business for their government. Also in their future cabinet was Alfred Hugenburg (1865–1951), the leader of the DNVP.
13. See note 30, p. 39
14. See note 65, p. 112.
15. See note 54, p. 111.
16. *Angriff (Attack)* was a Nazi propaganda paper in Berlin edited by Dr Paul Josef Goebbels (1897–1945), who was also the editor of the *Völkischer Beobachter (People's Observer)*, the main Nazi paper, head of the propaganda apparatus of the Nazi party, and later propaganda minister in Hitler's government.
17. In December 1932 the *Reichsbanner*, trade unions and workers' sports associations were organised into an 'Iron Front'.
18. According to Margarete Büber-Neumann, the leaders of the KPD had received a telegram from Moscow that forbade the Communists from provoking the slightest disturbance during the Nazi demonstration: see Robert Black, *Fascism in Germany*, Volume 2 (London, 1975), p. 905.
19. Hindenburg refused Schleicher permission to dissolve the *Reichstag* and to call another election on 28 January 1933.
20. The *Sozialistische Arbeiterpartei* (SAP – Socialist Workers Party) was a left-wing socialist party founded by nine *Reichstag* deputies who had been expelled from the SPD in September 1931. In 1933 its leadership was assumed by Jakob Walcher, who had split from the KPO (Brandlerites), along with about 1000 militants. One of its prominent figures was Paul Frölich, and it laid claim to the legacy of Rosa Luxemburg.
21. See note 21, p. 38.
22. Heinz Neumann (1902–1938) was a leading member of the KPD. His theory that Brüning's government was Fascist was shared by other KPD leaders. He was used as a scapegoat for the KPD's failures, and was removed from the party leadership in May 1932. He fled to Moscow when Hitler came to power, and perished in Stalin's purges.
23. Julius Leber (1891–1945) was the leader of the Lübeck Social-Democrats and a *Reichstag* deputy; he brought Willi Brandt into politics. He was so well regarded by the workers that they went out on strike when they heard of his arrest, and forced the Nazis to release him. He was later executed for involvement in the resistance against Hitler.
24. Ernst Torgler (1893–1963), the leader of the KPD fraction in the *Reichstag*, gave himself up to the police when the KPD was banned, and subsequently added his voice to Nazi anti-Communist propaganda.
25. See note 76, p. 113.
26. *Freiheit*: Liberty.
27. Franz Künstler (1888–1942) was an SPD MP and head of the Berlin party organisation. His policy during the crisis of 1933 was to hang on to legality at any price.

28. See note 25, p. 39
29. Albert C Grzesinski (1879–1948) was the police prefect of Berlin; he was dismissed by von Papen on 20 July 1932. Refusing to leave his office, he was arrested by soldiers whilst his policemen protested, and he was quickly released.
30. See note 75, p. 113.
31. Galicia, the area with its administrative centre at Cracow, had been part of the Austro-Hungarian Empire before 1919, and was assigned to the new state of Poland at the Treaty of Versailles. As the Polish government became increasingly anti-Semitic, many Jews, who comprised 8.5 per cent of Poland's population, fled abroad.
32. Rudolf Breitscheid (1876–1945) was a member of the SPD fraction in the *Reichstag* who generally stood on the party's left wing. He was handed over to the Nazis by the French Vichy government and perished in Buchenwald.
33. Between 1929 and 1934 the Communist International believed that capitalism was in the third, and final, crisis period of its existence. The whole international apparatus of the Comintern lurched into lunatic ultra-leftism, believing that the only thing that stood between it and revolution was the Social-Democracy, which it defined as the left wing of Fascism, or 'Social Fascism'. Communist parties were directed to concentrate their hostility against Socialists rather than any bourgeois parties. This phase of the Communist International's history is generally labelled 'Third Period Stalinism'. Some commentators consider that Stalin deliberately encouraged the ultra-leftism of the Third Period to ensure that the SPD was kept out of office. The SPD and the liberals favoured a Western orientation, that is to say, they wished Germany to become integrated into Western Europe, whereas the traditional right-wing parties favoured an Eastern, pro-Russian orientation. The importance of German technology for the massive industrialisation drive under the First Five-Year Plan meant that opposition to pro-Western forces in Germany remained a high priority for Stalin. Thus when the KPD leaders denounced the Nazi attempt in 1931 to call a referendum to unseat the Prussian Socialist government, they were instructed by Moscow to support it, leading to the unedifying sight of a joint Communist–Nazi campaign against the last bastion of the SPD, the destruction of which could not benefit the working class.
34. Dmitry Z Manuilsky (1883–1952) was Secretary of the Comintern, and one of the main proponents of the line of 'Social Fascism'.
35. Otto Bauer (1881–1938) was the leader of Austrian Social-Democracy, and the main theoretician of 'Austro-Marxism'.
36. Willi Münzenberg (1889–1940) was one of the founders of the International of Communist Youth. He specialised in appeals to the 'fellow-travellers'. He disappeared in mysterious circumstances when the Germans invaded France during the Second World War, probably assassinated by the GPU.
37. The RGO (Revolutionary Trade-Union Opposition) was set up by the KPD in November 1929 as a rival trade-union centre to the ADGB. Its membership never rose much above 300,000, and stood at 255,000 in January 1933. It was strongest in Berlin and the Ruhr, and about half of its members were miners and metalworkers, although up to 75 per cent of its members were actually unemployed when they were recruited. Overall, it never represented more than a small proportion of the German working class.
38. Dr Kurt Gusko was lecturer in labour law at the ADGB *Bundeschule* in Bernau.
39. Defeat on the Western Front, growing war weariness, and the revolt of the German

working class led to Germany signing the armistice and dropping out of the First World War in November 1918. Almost immediately some sections of the *Reichswehr* began to spread the rumour that Germany had not been defeated by the Entente powers, but had been 'stabbed in the back' by the Weimar politicians, and particularly the Socialists and Communists involved in the German Revolution. They called them 'the November Criminals', and the Nazis took up this myth and added to it that this was part of a Jewish conspiracy against Germany to cause it to lose the war.

40. The *Stahlhelm*, formed in December 1918, was the paramilitary force of extreme right-wing conservatism, generally allied with the traditional party of the German right, the DNVP (German National People's Party), which was led by Alfred Hugenburg. Its second in command was Colonel Theodor Duesterberg (1875–1950), who stood against Hitler in the Presidential elections in March 1932. He was dismissed from the *Stahlhelm* in April 1933 on the grounds that his paternal grandfather had been a Jew.

41. Arthur Crispien (1875–1936) joined the SPD in 1894, and joined the USPD in 1917 and was its Chairman during 1918–22. He rejoined the SPD in 1922, and was its co-Chairman during 1922–33. He was a *Reichstag* deputy during 1920–33. He later moved to Switzerland, joined the Swiss Socialist Party and helped political and Jewish refugees from Nazi Germany.

42. Wilhelm Pieck (1876–1960) was a founder member of the KPD, was the leader of the KPD fraction in the Prussian *landtag*, and as such was responsible for moving a motion of no confidence in the Social-Democratic government of Prussia in alliance with the Nazis on 25 March 1932. A loyal Stalinist, he was subsequently President of East Germany.

43. Anti-Fascist Action, *Antifaschistische Aktion or AntiFa*, was the KPD's self-defence organisation.

44. Paul Thomas Mann (1875–1955) was a prominent German writer most noted for *Buddenbrooks*, a novel depicting the decline of a Hanseatic bourgeois family. He left Germany in 1933, went to the USA in 1939, where he recorded monthly anti-Nazi broadcasts for the BBC. Hounded during the McCarthy period, he returned to Europe in 1952.

45. Karl Höltermann (1894–1956) was the leader of the *Reichsbanner*, the SPD's self-defence organisation in 1932–33.

46. *Genosse* means comrade, in the political sense.

47. Four thousand Communist militants were arrested.

48. Marinus Van der Lubbe (1909–1934) joined the Dutch Communist Party in 1925 and left it in 1931 to work with the Council Communists. He moved to Germany in 1933, and was found by police close to the burning *Reichstag* building. He took responsibility for setting fire to the *Reichstag*, saying that he did it to spur the German working class into action. The actual responsibility for the *Reichstag* fire remains a matter of conjecture: it has long been rumoured that the Nazis themselves started the fire. What is certain is that if the Nazis did not do it, they nonetheless took full advantage of it in order to reinforce their rule.

49. Horst Wessel (1907–1930), a member of the SA, was a pimp who had been mortally wounded in a fight over a prostitute, and was regarded as a hero by the Nazis for refusing to be treated by a Jewish doctor. The *Horst Wessel Lied* was the Nazi marching song.

50. See note 24, p. 39.

51. In a wave of 'Brown terror' over Germany after Hitler had been appointed Chancellor on 30 January 1933, the SA set up its own illegal prisons and torture chambers in the cellars of its local headquarters, where many of those against whom particular SA leaders bore a grudge, in particular Communist and Socialist militants, were murdered.
52. *Volkgenossen, Volksgenossinen*, literally means 'comrades of the people', in the masculine and feminine.
53. The Nazis won 17,277,000 votes, or 44 per cent of the votes cast. They had 288 MPs. The SPD won 7,182,000 votes and still had 120 MPs. The KPD won 4,848,000 votes and 81 MPs. A law forbade them to take their seats.
54. On 31 May 1931 the German group of the Left Opposition split between the supporters of Kurt Landau and those of the Well brothers, Stalinist agents who had penetrated the group in order to paralyse it. Landau's group became the Communist Party of Germany (Bolshevik-Leninist) (KPD(B-L)) publishing *Der Kommunist*, and the other group infiltrated by the Stalinists published *Permanente Revolution*.
55. At the end of 1932, when Hitler was about to assume power, Roman Well moved a resolution on the International Secretariat of the International Left Opposition dissociating it from one of the attacks Trotsky made against Stalin. After issuing a forged copy of *Permanente Revolution* on 20 January 1933 breaking from the Trotskyist movement, he then disappeared. He emerged again in the United States in 1957 under the name of Jack Soblen, where he confessed to having been a Stalinist spy among the German Trotskyists since 1931: G Vereeken, *The GPU in the Trotskyist Movement* (London, 1976), pp. 16–31.
56. Franz Mehring (1846–1919) was an honoured thinker of German Socialism, the author of a well-known life of Marx (English edition, London, 1936). He died shortly after the murder of his friends Karl Liebknecht and Rosa Luxemburg.
57. Heinrich Brandler (1881–1967) was a leading member of the KPD, and was its Chairman during the March Action in 1921 and the abortive 'German October' in 1923. He was later a leader of an oppositional group within the KPD which was expelled in 1929 and became the Communist Party (Opposition) (KPO), which supported Bukharin's 'Right' Opposition in the Soviet Union. August Thalheimer (1884–1948) was a leading member of the KPD, and of the KPO after its expulsion in 1929.
58. In April 1933 the *Ligue Communiste* of Pierre Naville and Gérard Rosenthal united temporarily with the other Left Opposition groups in France, but the group broke up in the October of the same year.
59. The Zimmerwald Conference was a small gathering in Switzerland in 1915 of internationalists and left Socialists who opposed the First World War, among them Lenin and Trotsky, who wrote their manifesto. It is generally regarded by Marxists as a new start after the majority of the Socialist parties had supported their own ruling classes in the First World War, and the nucleus of the future Third (Communist) International. The Trotskyists regarded the behaviour of the Comintern and the KPD in 1933 as the equivalent of the betrayal of Social-Democracy in 1914, and began to agitate for the formation of new parties and a new, Fourth, International from then onwards.
60. Alfred Rosenberg (1893–1946) was born in Estonia, and became a leading Nazi ideologist. An extreme anti-Semite, he also did much to promote anti-Communism within the German National Socialist movement during its early days.
61. Sir Henry Wilhelm August Deterding (1866–1939) was an oil magnate, the head of the firm now known as Anglo-Dutch Shell.

62. The policy of the Second International when war came was to oppose it and call for a general strike. In the event, its largest member party, the SPD, supported the war on 4 August 1914, closely followed by nearly all the other parties.
63. See note 25, p. 39.
64. Hermann Remmele (1880–1937) was one of the leaders of the KPD and a Moscow loyalist, but he was murdered by the NKVD after he fled to the Soviet Union.
65. Friedrich Engels, *The Peasant War in Germany* (Moscow, 1956), pp. 138–39.

Schleicher, Hitler or Revolution?

Daniel Guérin

When you go on a journey, you have two steps to take: one easy, the other tricky. The first involves opening your eyes wide and listening carefully. This is what I have just done over the last five weeks. The second, which begins with these lines, is harder: you have to seek some clarity among a mass of images, facts and contradictory impressions. Will I succeed?

Never have circumstances in Germany been so tangled, with familiar ideas pulled away from their meaning; never have the barriers between parties been so uncertain, or the underlying forces behind events so poorly known, so that there is such great confusion. As for intellectuals with their greater lucidity and with their capacity to foresee the future, and their claim to have the right to lead the masses, these new magicians are, as Louzon[1] says, the first to flounder. So, if grassroots workers fail to understand anything, if they are groping about in the dark, should you be so surprised?

Why should I, a Social-Democratic worker, feel that my main enemy is the Communist in the workshop next door?

Why should I, a Communist worker, exchange blows, often mortal blows, with a Nazi worker, someone like me who is in the queue at the labour exchange?

Yes, why? Nobody knows why any more. They know only that they are suffering, more than words can tell. Eight million unemployed – for one, two or three years' forced idleness, fortnightly waiting at a counter, to get a meagre allowance, just enough to avoid entirely starving to death, with no hope for a better tomorrow, with no signs of things getting better, with no certainty that this regime will not last forever. Such is the state of things that you have to ask: is there any way out?

And everyone is weary – the political parties have promised so much. So many notices have been read, so many leaflets encountered, so many electoral campaigns, so many votes cast, and yet nothing changes. Everything today is much worse than the day before. What little freedom for labour that existed is being eroded, workers' newspapers are being banned, in public meetings an insolent *schupo* can tell any speaker whose words are displeasing to him, to stop. Wages are being cut and whittled away. In certain businesses, pay will soon be less than unemployment benefit.

Everywhere there is bankruptcy. Bankruptcy in that great, proud Social-Democracy, which, from one denial to another, from one compromise to another, was given, without its showing the least resistance, a mighty kick up the backside on 20 July.[2] There's the shifty Communist Party, which over the last ten years (despite its flighty orders and rowdy turns) has failed to win over a majority of the working class. It has failed maybe because it carries on with a policy that is not that of the German workers – and the masses instinctively know it.

Oh! If only the leaders could come to an understanding; if only a united front was possible… but that hope is distant and insubstantial. Why should we not listen to these new saviours – promising bread, work, liberation from our chains? They also tell us that they are a *workers'* party, both anti-capitalist and revolutionary. When you have been for so long in despair, when you cannot hope for salvation through your own efforts, it is enough to have one man, one who utters the words, the necessary words, and you will put your trust in him and forget yourself, and you will follow him. *Heil Hitler!*

This is the drama being played out.

The two parties who claim to represent the working class are *both, equally* responsible for the Fascist groundswell. Given their failure to draw workers behind them, given that they were unable to call a halt to the fratricidal warfare between them, you don't have to look elsewhere for an explanation as to why Nazi-ism is making such ravages in the ranks of German labour.

Bosses Caught in their own Traps

Nevertheless, nothing has been resolved by the appearance of this third party, with its pretension to be a 'workers' party'. Today, German workers are divided three ways, not two, and they have gained nothing from this further division. So great is the doubt and disarray amongst them that you see them shift from one party to another with astonishing ease – Social-Democrats (I know some of them) becoming Nazis; and Nazis becoming Communists – and vice versa. There are Nazis and Communists who move pretty close to one another, out of hatred of Social-Democracy. There are Socialist and Fascists who – in their ideas about workplace organisation, for the nationalisation of the banks, and for state capitalism – are little different from each other. How can even the most sensible heads avoid confusion?

You have to have been present (as I have been) at a Nazi mass meeting to observe with your own eyes how many workers are in that party, and to hear with your own ears the unbelievable anti-capitalist demagogy of its leaders. It was so in Dresden, one evening in an immense sports stadium lit up by lights, when the 'left' leader – Gregor Strasser, the one who forbad Hitler to join a 'bourgeois' government – shouted, 'What is essential today is to recognise that ninety per cent of German labour considers that the capitalist regime has had its day, and want something else… a new economy, a new system…', to hear cries on all sides: 'Hear, Hear!' And he added:

> The plain announcement of 'distress regulations' by the von Papen[3] cabinet has spurred a strong rise on the stock exchange. That indicates that these regulations are directed against the people. You can be sure that when the day comes for popular interests to prevail, that on that day the stock exchange will fall. The masters of international finance will be feeling a fatal blow on that day. (Thunderous applause)

Working-class Nazis believed every word in these sentences. The trickery of Fascism is there in all its entirety.

Despite that apparent confusion there was an underlying secret logic in these events: if the bankruptcy of these two 'Marxist' parties has allowed Hitler to make such ravaging inroads into the ranks of the working class, the unforeseeable accident of his party's working-class composition explains the break in its triumphal rise to power.

The great industrial bourgeoisie financed lovely Adolf in large measure, to have the assurance that they would have a base within the working-class, against the labour élite. When agitation has already incited brother against brother, no one fights better against the working class than the workers themselves. On the Boulevard de Ménilmontant in Paris, there is a no-holds-barred fight when two workers have a difference of opinion; in East Prussia and in Silesia workers massacre workers.

But when the day came for majorities – ever increasing majorities – to take Hitler to the very gates of power, these big donors began to think again. And, suddenly, the leader of the anti-Marxist crusade seemed dangerous. Because the man had made so many promises, he would have to deliver some of them at the very least. And his troops, these anti-capitalist and revolutionary troops, were sticking a knife into the ribs of these bosses. They were shouting, 'All or nothing', at the base. No more make-do substitutes. Oh what a beautiful mess, a 'new system' was wanted, a 'Third Reich'!

The Resurrection of the Bosses' Club

Now the old ruling class – barons, squires, officers and the lovely members of the *Herrenklub*,[4] everyone in 'Old Germany' – all those ousted from power fourteen years ago by Social-Democracy, saw an unanticipated opportunity to recover their status. Finally, after fourteen years, there was an anti-Marxist majority in the *Reichstag*. The gentlemen thought that they had the right to come first, before the Nazis – they had titles as 'von Somethings', and these great members of the bourgeoisie had a better claim to become the government of the Reich than a former painter, or a chemist. These Johnny-come-lately's, with neither education nor experience, might be fobbed off with some minor portfolios, but the levers of command would be reserved for their betters. The big bosses would no longer have to waste the funds they had kept to subsidise the Fascists, they would now have a free hand without having to fork out.

For sure, a violent victory for the Nazis, if things had gone that way, would have meant the complete destruction of labour organisations. But, after all, should the bosses really have an interest in their destruction? Weren't these workplace unions already part of the state apparatus? Wouldn't a strong government be better off taking advantage of them, rather than seeking their destruction? Wouldn't the industrialists deal with these exploited people more easily, if they allowed them to continue organising these mutual associations?

And, on the opposite side of things, wouldn't a collision between Fascism and 'Marxism' expose them to dangerous unknowns? Today the working class was undermined, discouraged and divided by fratricidal conflict, and was therefore powerless. It would be good to keep Hitler in reserve, in case the workers became dangerous again. But today, to let Hitler rush away and throttle them, would that not be the most certain way to revive the dangers, indeed to put a seal on his single revolutionary front? And, if there was a civil war, would the Nazi workers stay on the right side of the barricade? It was a very uncertain adventure!

For Hitler this was the time to make decisions. Should he compromise and take the crumbs in this party? This personality devoid of character, a politician to his very soul, could not have asked for more. But Gregor Strasser and the tumultuous base of the enormous party organisation forbad that choice. '*Everything or Nothing*', they said. And so 'Old Germany', with its base in large-scale industry and in the *Reichswehr*, took over the government on their own.

So, Hitler reined in his forces and for a moment his rise to power was delayed for some time, perhaps for ever ... Once in place the *Herrenklub* team lost no time getting going. But over and above that vague sense of prestige that Hindenburg's senile prestige lent it across the Reich, beyond the apparatus of magnates and the eventual cooperation of 100,000 armed mercenaries with up-to-date arms, so admirably trained over seven years of military service, the Schleicher–Papen[5] government had nobody behind it. They had to work fast to shore up their dominance. So, action followed action. On the occasion of their annual congress there was the assembly of 150,000 members of the *Stahlhelm*, chauvinist petty-bourgeois peasants,[6] forcibly enrolled by their butchers. On that day, the Schleicher–Papen government showed that they too had a clientele. Then a note to France,[7] and a project for strengthening the *Reichswehr*, the praetorian guard, a project clearly directed against the Nazis, who demanded a national army and compulsory military service. Lastly, even more recently, a project to merge all the youth associations into one official organisation – hoping thereby to remove the youngest and most ardent recruits from the Nazis.

So, now there was an unusual phenomenon, which nobody would have foreseen even a few weeks earlier – something of a tacit united front came together from the three parties with a labour base. In the *Reichstag*, 500 voices condemned the gentlemen of the *Herrenklub*.[8] But despite fanfares from the Nazi *Reichstag* Chairman Göring,[9] the gentlemen stayed in place and the *Reichstag* was dissolved. The Nazis were lamentably deflated,[10] they did not dare antagonise the *Reichswehr*.

Two dates: on 20 July the Schleicher–Papen government dismissed Severing from the government of Prussia, without facing the least resistance; and on 12 September Schleicher–Papen dismissed the *Reichstag* and its 230 Nazi members with equal ease. General von Schleicher was in charge. And, since events maintained their logic despite everything, the Nazi leaders, separated from the gentlemen of the *Herrenklub* through simple caste rivalry, found themselves thrown into violent opposition, so much so that the anti-capitalist and revolutionary facet of their movement was accentuated!

So, at this moment, the most significant fact was the outbreak of workplace strikes wherever government distress regulations were implemented, that is to say, brutal pay cuts, on the pretext that unemployed workers would be given jobs. *In these struggles, Nazi workers – the strike-breakers of yesterday – joined in, alongside Socialist and Communist comrades.*[11]

What should we make of these developments? Is the Nazi Party taking huge steps – as some seem to think – towards an internal crisis, perhaps a split? Will the outraged petty-bourgeois and the nationalists continue to cohabit with proletarians who are more and more violently anti-capitalist? And as for some of these Nazi workers, would they not move on rapidly towards the 'Marxist' parties? Or, on the contrary, would this accentuated Nazi demagogy further abuse the masses, and make their conquest even more difficult for the 'Marxists'?

Here an essential factor intervenes: Unity. Whether Fascism falls apart or not depends upon the extent to which the idea of unity makes progress within the ranks of the working class.

Will the Current Crisis Lead to Unity?

Is unity on the way? Apparently not. The few proposals for a united front that saw the light of day in the electoral campaign of last July do not appear to have had any sequels. Everyone has stayed in their place. At the leadership level, not one act and not one speech allows you to have the slightest hope.

But at the grassroots level? Some scenes that presented themselves to me in the streets of Berlin are barely more encouraging. At the exit of a labour exchange, on the pavement a circle was formed – workers in blue helmets; youth, thin, bright-eyed. What was going on? We went closer. Two men were violently engaged in a passionate discussion. They were shouting out loud and seemed not far away from coming to blows. At first, I thought it was a confrontation between a Nazi and a Communist and I readied myself to applaud the latter's arguments and refutations. But I was mistaken. They were two brothers, two enemies. And with the help of the ever-growing number of those listening, they rehearsed every past failing of their respective parties. The majority of spectators appeared to support the Communist. But the Socialist held his own, wouldn't allow himself to be put down and would not renounce his leaders. With great difficulty they were separated.

Yet, when the protagonists from each side were approached individually, and you spoke without passion, when you appealed to their good sense as workers, their discontents soon came up, and their bitterness – and with it their profound and instinctive craving for unity. I met many young Socialist workers who were dismayed by their leaders' disagreements, and I can affirm that in all my journeying I did not find one single Communist who, given a little conversation, would affirm his real agreement with his party's tactics. Like monks seized with doubts, the most orthodox of them would repeat to themselves that their line was correct. Those who were most sincere expressed their discontent very plainly.

The abdication of the Socialist government of Prussia on 20 July had at least the consequence that it set off a crisis within each of the two workers' parties. Amongst the Social-Democrats you can say without exaggeration that things are getting very heated.[12] I took part in a very important section meeting on this matter in Berlin; every speaker, from a *Landtag* deputy to the young 'extremists', violently criticised the pitiable conduct of their leaders; and as for certain big-shots, the current of opinion made itself strongly felt, and they added their own words of mourning to the overall concert.

The same sort of house-cleaning took place on the Communist side. On 20 July the party launched an appeal for a general strike but no one took any notice. Evidently it was difficult to encourage Red workers to leave their factories to protest against the expulsion of a ... Social Fascist;[13] the turn was a bit too abrupt. But on that day the party nevertheless had to take note that despite its electoral successes,[14] its influence among organised workers was zero.[15] Every Communist in Germany today knows that a general strike, and even more so a social revolution, are impossible without the cooperation of the reformist workers.

Given the issues at stake and the times we are in, we must find a way towards these reformist workers. Sometimes some good things come from so much that is bad. From setbacks and repeated humiliations, Germany's working class seems to have been driven into bitter but useful reflection. If unity, if even a single united front, is not yet on the cards for tomorrow, if the abyss which exists between the leaders and in which they are mired is still immense, small steps are nonetheless being made down below – too slowly, certainly – but they give us a small glimpse of hope.

Mass struggles over wages, now beginning or being prepared, demanding a vital minimum pay (without which you would die of hunger), appear to be making for unity between the Socialists and Communists who are involved in the same struggle. Despite divisions, despite privations, despite the demoralisation that follows on from unemployment, despite the fatigue that comes when so many efforts are fruitless, the admirable German proletariat – so educated, so ripe for Socialism – still has immense reserves of strength for revolutionary action and for self-sacrifice. Now least of all is no time for despair.

What Does Schleicher Want?

Now we are on the threshold of winter, the most tragic winter ever encountered by the people of this unhappy land.

Today, every German, whatever their party and whatever their social class, has to ask himself[16] this troublesome question, what will this winter bring? Is the decisive shock, the one expected last spring and not realised then, only delayed? Or will the barons of the *Herrenklub* and their leader General von Schleicher be able to cling on to power, to keep themselves in place, in such a way that neither the forces of labour nor the Nazis will be able to shift them? If the Schleicher–Papen government represents only the backward spirit of 'Old Germany', 'reaction' as the Nazis say, it is doubtful that even with the support of the bosses and the armed forces it will be able to maintain itself against a people impatient for radical change. But there are two unknowns: the economic situation, and the personal project of General von Schleicher.

We should not forget that Chancellor von Papen, in striving to regenerate the German economy by savage interventions, has gambled on an improvement in the economic situation. If that comes about, if vague signs of recovery in world affairs are confirmed – as certain bourgeois assert – if unemployment is partially reduced, it is possible that team Schleicher–Papen will not only survive the winter but might, in the spring, translate its wish to endure by an attempt to restore the monarchy. And if the German working class cannot find the strength to resist, in that case its last remaining liberties will be suppressed, and there will be a retreat to circumstances as they were fifty years before, with pay at misery levels and a jack-boot dictatorship.

But if the conjuncture remains bad, or if it gets worse, if the number of unemployed tops ten million over the course of the winter, if despair incites a groundswell among German workers, then a fatal hour may sound. What outcome can anyone dare to foresee now? The other unknown is the personal policy of General von Schleicher. Deep down, he seems ready to pursue even more risky and ambitious plans than just a policy for 'Old Germany', or a simple restoration of the monarchy. General von Schleicher dreams, no more, no less, of installing in Germany beneath his iron fist a state capitalism, taking men and ideas from the programmes of the Nazi and the Socialists in so far as these might suit his ends. Thus, at this moment, despite overt struggles between his government and the Nazi Party, the General remains in contact with certain Nazi leaders, the most 'leftist' ones (as chance would have it), and so very strange relations are being forged between him and the leaders of the German trade-union movement…[17]

The nationalisation of the banks and certain large industries would give satisfaction to people on both sides. The state bureaucracy would absorb some good fellows among the Nazis, those impatient to try out their talents, such as they are. As for the union and cooperative big-wigs they too might be integrated into the government apparatus and would in any case maintain their existing positions, which is what matters most to them.

Schleicher? Hitler? Or revolution? I write this with complete, albeit unreasoned, confidence. It is for our German comrades to speak.

NOTES

1. Robert Louzon (1882–1976) was a French syndicalist. He became active in the French socialist movement in 1900, joined the SFIO in 1905 and was a founder member of the French Communist Party in 1920. He sided with the Left Opposition and left the PCF in 1924 when his comrades Pierre Monatte and Alfred Rosmer were expelled. He became the editor of the syndicalist journal *La Révolution Prolétarienne* in 1925, fought in the CNT militia during the Spanish Civil War, and revived *La Révolution Prolétarienne* in 1947.
2. This was the date on which the Social-Democratic government in Prussia was dismissed; see above p. 25 and p. 78.
3. See note 22, p. 38.
4. *Herrenklub* – a bosses' club.
5. See note 23, p. 38.
6. Some might say semi-Fascist paramilitaries! See note 34, p. 109.
7. Von Papen made serious suggestions to the French government for a Franco-German customs union and military cooperation.
8. Von Papen and von Schleicher ruled by presidential decree since they had no parliamentary majority in the *Reichstag*.
9. Hermann Göring became Chairman of the *Reichstag* after the July 1932 elections.
10. The Nazis would obtain 11.74 million votes in the elections of 6 November 1932, as compared with 13.75 million in July 1932, a loss of two million votes.
11. For example, the Berlin municipal transport strike; see the following chapter in this volume.
12. Guérin's text reads 'la torchon brûle' – literally, 'rags are burning'.
13. See above, p. 26 and note 28, p. 39.
14. The Communist vote in the July 1932 general election was 5.3 million, up from 4.6 million in September 1930. Its vote increased to almost six million in the November 1932 general election.
15. The Wall Street slump of 1929 had resulted in mass unemployment; Communists were especially hard hit.
16. Guérin uses only masculine terms in this text.
17. General von Schleicher attempted, unsuccessfully, to draw in the ADGB trade unions, associated with the SPD, and Gregor Strasser and the left wing of the Nazi Party to support his regime. A new government was formed in January 1933, with Hitler as Chancellor and with von Papen as Vice-Chancellor. Hitler saw Strasser and Schleicher as traitors, and both were murdered in the 'Night of the Long Knives' in July 1934.

Politicians Put Skids Under Strike of Berlin Transport Workers

Splendid Solidarity of German Strikers Broken by Competing Efforts of Socialists, Communists and Nazis to Win Election

Paul Strehl

The first part of November 1932, the foreign news of the American Brass Check Press made slight mention of a great strike that was taking place in Berlin. The news of the strike was overshadowed by the excitement of the national elections taking place at the time in the two 'great' republics – Germany and the USA. We asked our fellow workers of Germany to report the strike for readers of the *Industrial Worker*. The following was received from them, which I translated from German – Joseph Wagner.

The Strike of the Berlin Transport Workers and Its Lessons for the Working Class

In order to get a fairly objective idea of the great strike of the municipal transport workers in Berlin, it is necessary to have a clear picture of the situation existing immediately prior to the strike, which is as follows:

In order to complete the number of national elections of this year to a full half a dozen, the politicians of all shades had to promise their tired followers to bring down even the blue skies for their benefit. It was generally conceded that the Nazis (Fascists of Germany) would lose heavily of their previous votes[1] because their supreme chief, Adolph Hitler, by passing up his chance of seizing by force the government, got thoroughly discredited. Thereupon, the commical[2] party of Germany decided to fish in the troubled social-democratic pond and the Socialist Party was aware that in that election it would lose even a larger number of votes than it had lost at previous elections.[3]

The Socialist Party sided with the government and it tried to convince it that the capitalist government without the Socialist Party, and without the socialistic trade unions,[4] would be like a man without his dorsal parts. Therefore, as all political parties were wholly taken up with the task of capturing government posts, parliamentary seats and other offices, they thought of everything but the possibility of a strike.

In the midst of this political excitement and turmoil the strike of the municipal transport workers broke out unexpectedly in Berlin. No preparations for it had been made on either side. The trade unions had just consented to a reduction of wages[5] and to a reduction of working forces[6] in order to demonstrate to the Papen government[7] that the trade unions and the SP were with the government through thick and thin. The employees of the Municipal Transport System thus betrayed, got enraged, and the strike broke out spontaneously.[8] The Federation of Trade Unions of Germany promptly outlawed the strike and called on its members to act as strike-breakers. Thereupon the following situation ensued.

Workers belonging to no party, or belonging to the Nazis, or to the Red Trade-Union Opposition[9] organisation and other transport workers with left leanings, went out on strike, and members of the 'regular' trade unions tried their best to break the strike. At first this remained merely an attempt. The strikers had the full sympathy of the people – yes even of the petit-bourgeoisie.

The strike was being carried and fought with all the means at the disposal of the strikers. The tracks were filled in with concrete and soda, and during the night tracks were torn up and removed. Trolley wires were torn down and street cars and auto-buses, with which they tried to carry on some traffic, were demolished, to such an extent that they could not be put to use again. The passengers were considered strike-breakers and manhandled accordingly. The situation was becoming more critical from time to time.[10]

Next, they tried to operate a few cars with police protection. Some few cars thus operated, each having a guard of from two to four policemen. But these cars travelled empty, as no passengers would dare ride in them, for every one of such cars were smashed in with cobblestones. By evening shootings began. There were wounded and dead.[11] The workers of the power plants went out on a sympathetic strike. A General Strike was imminent.

But it came out otherwise. Sunday[12] was election day and it turned out to be the quietest day since the beginning of the strike. Some cars were allowed to operate unhindered.

On the day following the election the meanness of all political parliamentary parties was demonstrated. The Communist Party gained ten seats in parliament and the Nazis, who, thanks to their participation in the strike, had gained considerable sympathy, had not lost as heavily as it was expected. The strikers had carried on election work for their respective parties. Thus, while on every street corner, party workers were standing with collection boxes collecting funds for the Communist Party and for the Fascist Party, there were at no place collection boxes set up for the support of the Municipal Transport Workers' strike. After ten years, finally, the Municipal Transport Workers have once more, gone out on strike. The politicians have once more run a magnificent proletarian struggle into the ground. Two and a half thousand workers were victimised, a large number of honest workers were forced into jails for long terms of imprisonment.

But sadly, as these things ended, yet it was a streak of lightning in the darkness of the most reactionary of all republics. Thousands of workers have been wised up to the SP and the Trade Union Federation of Germany, who have debased themselves to the role of volunteer troops of police and voluntary stool pigeons for the employers.

We hope that the working class has drawn the consequences of this strike, that they have learned that whenever the party politicians get the upper hand of a strike, it is bound to go to the dogs. For it is impossible even with the best of intentions to transform an economic strike into a general strike and at the same time carry on an election campaign for the gaining of seats in a bourgeois parliament, which, at any rate, becomes superfluous by success of the former action.

In addition, it may be stated that a terrible pressure is exercised here over the working class. Our paper, the *Marine Worker*, has again made its appearance after a thirteen-week suppression and, very likely, it will be suppressed again.

NOTES

1. This article was written before the announcement of the results of the general election of 6 November 1932, in which the Nazis polled 11.74 million votes (33.1 per cent); the SPD 7.25 million (20.4 per cent); the KPD 5.98 million (16.9 per cent). In the previous general election, held on 31 July 1932, the Nazis polled 13.75 million votes (37.4 per cent); the SPD 7.96 million (21.6 per cent) and the KPD 5.28 million (14.6 per cent).
2. Presumably a reference to the Communist Party and its absurdities.
3. The SPD had lost some 600,000 votes in the July 1932 general election compared with the general election of September 1930; they had then polled 8.57 million votes (24.5 per cent), as against 4.59 million for the KPD (13.1 per cent) and 6.40 million for the Nazis (18.3 per cent).
4. That is, the ADGB.
5. In negotiations with the employers the unions had obtained a smaller wage reduction than that first demanded.
6. Presumably 'a reduction of the workforce' is meant here.

7. Franz von Papen was Chancellor from 1 June to 17 November 1932. He resigned after failing to secure a parliamentary majority in the November election.
8. On 3 November; it was outlawed the next day
9. See note 37, p. 162.
10. Presumably 'hour to hour' is meant here.
11. Four people were killed by the police, and 100 injured.
12. 5 November.

A Group of Revolutionary Syndicalists To Organised Workers

Workers and comrades, the events in Germany have surprised most of us. Like you, we were amazed to see labour organisations, and especially the unions, failing to put up any resistance to Hitler's sinister coming to power. Worse, we were disgusted to learn that the unions made no attempt to prevent the investment of Hitler's fascism, and that the key leaders of labour organisations submitted themselves to Hitler and his henchmen with the most disheartening casualness, surrendering and integrating the entire union apparatus into the Nazi state.

The absolute betrayal on the part of the German organisations not only demoralised the working class internationally, it has also raised troubles among the leaders of the Swiss labour movement. The bulk of them prevaricate and attempt to explain away the platitudes of the leaders of German Social-Democracy. Some others, sincerely infatuated by democratic and reformist ideas, are disoriented. Revolutionary syndicalist must therefore examine the facts in order to be ready to respond to the fascist danger and to this treachery.

Two Tendencies

Two tendencies have confronted each other in the labour movement for many years – the one called revolutionary, the other reformist. The 'revolutionary' tendency has always evoked the spirit of struggle and commitment to direct action to satisfy day-to-day demands. Its goal is a social revolution, as a means to expropriate the bourgeoisie and end its exploitation. On the other hand, the 'reformist' tendency appeals to the herd instincts of the masses, above all stressing the line of least resistance and appealing to the greatest number of people. Its goal is to develop within capitalist society, while attempting to modify its structure. The very nature of its goals and its methods – its 'reformist' tendencies – give it, naturally, an edge over 'revolutionary' thinking. But today, the consequences are clear: 1914 – unions support the war; 1933 – unions fall in with fascism.

Integration into Capitalism

Given their background and secular education, the masses that have emerged from slavery do not love contemplation, they prefer the least effort. So, they are easy meat for swindlers – they form up in flocks, they wait passively to be sheared, or periodically, pushed into the slaughterhouse. In his day the Kaiser knew all about popular naïveté, just as Mussolini and Hitler do today. Before the war, William II knew how to manoeuvre cleverly, to capture the confidence of German Social-Democracy. The Kaiser's apparent deference helped the unions to line up behind him *en masse*, while sanctioning the union-based welfare schemes which did so much to tie them to that regime. The more the German unions developed their admirable insurance services, the more they needed the state, and the more they integrated themselves into the capitalist system and became entangled with parliamentarianism. So, reformism triumphed. The labour movement became a veritable army, strictly hierarchical, possessing in fact a powerful and omnipotent headquarters. Two calamities – reformism and centralism – complemented each other.

The Reformist Illusion

There were many delegates from German federations within the Labour International.[1] This allowed them a big voice, they were to be heard above those who were subjugated as a result of their numerical 'strength'. Representatives of lands that were best 'organised' spoke of their 'practical' achievements, on behalf of the astronomical memberships of their union federations. No one could gainsay these giants. And their proposals were always accepted, even if occasionally some reservations were uttered in the wings. Everyone was afraid of people who, whenever crossed, threatened to leave, slamming the doors behind them. These old methods – 'tried and tested' by the German reformists – became the dream of their fans in France and Switzerland. As to the former, let us hope that the second resounding defeat of reformism in Germany will have tightened the belts of the big-mouths, former leaders of the *union sacrée*[2] who still take their lead from the ILO.[3] And in Switzerland German methods and directives have been followed to the very letter. Union members are nothing but docile dues-paying sheep. The central committees are all-powerful. An expensive bureaucracy has been installed to administer welfare services.

Reformism Means Submission

We all know the reformist clichés trotted out so frequently in union meetings by nominated union appointees – 'Comrades, in today's society, we have to apply the theory of the "lesser evil", we will attain our freedom through the minimum programme, though the slow and progressive evolution of capitalist society.' This is what continues to be said by those who stand in the tradition of Leipart & Co.[4]

No doubt reformism, notably in Germany, has brought some useful momentary gains for the working class. But it has to be said that these gains were obtained only because of respect earned in earlier struggles, and through the development of class consciousness in those struggles. Also, it was easy to foresee that as unions became bogged down in reformism, resistance and revolt would decline, that the spirit of energetic individual initiative would fall away. The heavy and complex reformist machine, with its centralism and discipline, thought for and acted for the union member.

Centralism – That is the Error

The treachery of German Social-Democracy demonstrates the poisonous nature of its centralised system; betrayal was possible – and took on the dimensions of a catastrophe – because union organisation was concentrated in the hands of a few. Let us repeat, the guilt lay with the centralised system, not with cowardly men.

Today, union members are just dues-payers – paying into funds for sickness and unemployment. Furthermore, local branches have no real responsibilities, they are just cogs in the statist machine, in thrall to all-powerful central committees. To ensure complete subordination centralism appropriates all the dues collected from union members in each locality; everything is for the common fund, and the central committee alone holds the purse-strings. The coffers are not opened as needs arise, but only when thought best by the all-knowing central committee members – people who often are based hundreds of miles away from those needing the funds. Good management depends on the proper administration of collective funds – so it is said. Very well. But how can it be denied that such a system undermines the sense of responsibility among workers who cannot manage their own organisation? Everyone knows that money is a powerful lever in the society in which we have to live. If central committees get away with being so 'bossy', it is only because it is they who control this lever. Strike and unemployment benefits depend on the good-will of the central office, and they can paralyse any local action that lacks their consent. All this obliges unions, before making a move against management, to ask for permission. As workers are forbidden to act for themselves, they are progressively accustomed by such procedures to wait for orders from their leaders. But when events turn towards tragedy – as in Italy and Germany – the great centralisers do not dare issue instructions for action: the working class remains disoriented, it waits, it is defeated.

The crime of the big leaders of reformism and centralism is not so much that they were afraid for themselves at a decisive moment; their big crime is that through their organisational megalomania they have destroyed popular spontaneity and every spirit of revolt.

Workers and Comrades

On so many occasions revolutionary syndicalists have given warnings to the working class. Alas! Always in vain. Nevertheless, they saw things clearly and in the light of their doctrine: that reformism and its methods would inevitably lead workers in every land towards the direst catastrophes. So today take note: against the know-alls of 'scientific' trade unionism, it was the revolutionary syndicalists – long despised, beaten and scorned – who were in the right. The bankruptcy and treason of Social-Democracy and the enormous German unions have opened many eyes. Revolutionary syndicalism should reassert its place in the working class, wherever it is not yet enthralled by dictatorial governments.

Workers must act now, to transform the foundations of the union movement and to prevent it sinking under fascist attacks. The first thing to be done is to replace the current, outrageous centralism by a system of free and supportive union federations. Local sections should be their own masters, the role of central committees should be only that of coordinating the work of the various sections. Collective services (strike-funds and funds for unemployment and health) should cease to be compulsory if they impede the progress of unionism. Comrades, we have had enough of betrayals: roll up your sleeves, fight for the real liberation of workers against fascism.

NOTES

1. That is, the International Federation of Trade Unions.
2. *Union sacrée* – 'sacred union' – an expression from the First World War meaning the support given by the institutions of the working class for the war effort.
3. The International Labour Organisation was set up in 1919 by the League of Nations to bring together governments, employers and workers' organisations of the member states in order to provide reasonable working conditions for workers. Since 1945, it has come under the aegis of the United Nations.
4. See note 65, p. 112. When Hitler became Chancellor, Leipart announced: 'We want to emphasise that we are not in opposition to this government. However, that cannot and will not stop us from also representing the interests of the working class *vis-à-vis* this government.' He added: '"Organisation, not demonstration" is our motto.' He encouraged union members to join the events on the Nazi-organised 'National Day of Labour' on 1 May 1933; on the very next day, Nazi stormtroopers occupied every trade-union office in Germany, arresting or roughing up every union official whom they encountered, and stealing every item of value on which they could lay their hands.

INDEX of NAMES

Alsberg, Max 79, 111 n59

Bauer, Otto 132, 162 n35
Bismarck, Otto Eduard Leopold von 50, 87, 109 n25
Blomberg, Werner von 90–91, 113 n73
Bracht, Clemens 79–80, 111 n54, 122
Braun, Otto 25, 27, 39 n25, 51, 78, 111 n54, 158
Breitscheid, Rudolf 131, 162 n32
Brüning, Heinrich 24–25, 38 n21 and n24, 53, 57, 68, 70–77, 126, 153
Büber-Neumann, Margarete 161 n18

Cavignac, Louis Eugène 48, 108 n20
Chicherin, Georgi 41
Crispien, Arthur 135, 163 n41

Darré, Richard 100, 114 n83
Deterding, Sir Henry Wilhelm August 156, 164 n61
Duesterberg, Theodor 135, 163 n40

Ebert, Friedrich 20, 35 n3 and n4, 48–49, 55
Engels, Friedrich 159

Etchebehere, Hippolyte biographical sketch 31–34
Flick, Friedrich 52–53, 57, 109 n30
Florin, Wilhelm 119, 160–61 n10
Frick, Wilhelm 28, 91, 113 n74

Gessler, Otto Karl 46, 55, 108 n12
Goebbels, Paul Josef 23, 91, 95, 100–101, 111 n58, 135, 145–46, 161 n16

Göring, Hermann 28, 113 n73, 170, 174 n9
Groener, Wilhelm 20, 35 n4, 46, 55
Grzesinsky, Albert 79, 111 n57
Gusko, Kurt 133, 162 n38

Hertz, Paul 92, 113 n77
Hindenburg, Paul 23, 25, 28, 37 n15, 48–49, 70–78, 86–87, 90–91, 125, 160 n7, 161 n19, 170
Hirtsiefer, Heinrich 78, 111 n52
Hitler, Adolf 18–28, 30, 33, 35, 37 n15, 39 n30, 42, 53, 58, 60, 62–63, 68, 74–76, 81, 83–93, 95, 98, 110 n49, 111 n61, 112 n65 and n69, 113 n73 and n76, 117, 120, 126, 130–31, 146, 148–58, 160 n3 and n7, 161 n12, n16, n22 and n23, 163 n40, 164 n55, 168–70, 175, 180
   appointed Chancellor 28, 86–87, 124–25, 130–31, 150, 174 n17, 179, 182 n4
   as Chancellor 88–106, 127–28, 135–40, 146, 164 n51
   social base 23–24, 50, 72–73, 83–84, 86, 91, 99–100, 103–05
Höltermann, Karl 139, 163 n45
Hugenberg, Alfred 86, 107 n3, 112 n69, 120, 125, 135, 145, 154, 161 n12
Hyndman, Henry 29

Kaiser Wilhelm II 19, 36 n9, 43–47, 53–55, 63, 74, 131, 135, 180
Kautsky, Karl 23
Kerrl, Hanns 84, 112 n67
Kreuger, Ivar 99, 114 n82

Künstler, Franz 128, 132, 161 n27

Lahusen, Georg 96, 113 n81
Landau, Kurt 33–34, 40 n37, n38 and n41, 151, 164 n54
Lassalle, Ferdinand 59
Leber, Julius 161 n23
Legien, Carl 21, 36 n9
Leipart, Theodor 84, 112 n65, 120, 133, 181, 182 n4
Lenin, Vladimir 29–30, 60, 151, 158, 160, 164 n59
Ley, Robert 94, 113 n80
Liebknecht, Karl 20, 29, 119, 152, 164 n56
Lossow, Otto von 55, 109 n36
Luxemburg, Rosa 20, 29, 119, 125, 152, 161 n20, 164 n56

Maclean, John 29
Manuilsky, Dmitry 132, 162 n34
Mann, Thomas 139, 163 n44
Marx, Karl 59, 141
Marx, Wilhelm 38 n24
Matteotti, Giacomo 92, 113 n75, 130
Mehring, Franz 152–53, 164 n56
Müller, Hermann 24, 38 n20, 70
Münzenberg, Willi 112 n72, 132, 158, 162 n36
Mussolini, Benito 59, 97, 130, 150, 155–56, 180

Neumann, Heinz 126, 161 n22
Niedner, Alexander 48, 108 n18
Noske, Gustav 20, 35 n5 and n7, 48

Oberfohren, Ernst 90, 112 n72
Oldenburg-Januschau, Elard von 72, 110 n49

Papen, Franz von 24–25, 27–28, 38 n22, 39 n25, 49, 53, 57, 62, 68, 74, 78–79, 81, 83–87, 111 n53, n54 and n61, 118, 120, 125–26, 144, 153, 158, 161 n12, 162 n29, 168, 170–73, 174 n7, n8 and n17, 176, 178 n7

Petroff, Irma biographical sketch 29–30
Petroff, Peter biographical sketch 29–30
Pieck, Wilhelm 135, 140, 163 n42

Radek, Karl 36 n11, 60, 110 n40, n41 and n42
Rathenau, Walther 47, 108 n17
Remmele, Hermann 158, 165 n64
Reventlow, Ernst 60, 110 n41
Rosenberg, Alfred 156, 164 n60

Schlageter, Albert Leo 36 n11, 60, 110 n42
Seeckt, Johannes Friedrich von 46, 108 n13
Seldte, Franz 101, 114 n84
Schleicher, Kurt von 24, 38 n23, 39 n30, 46, 57, 68, 74, 83–87, 100, 103, 112 n66, 118–20, 122, 125–26, 130, 154, 158, 161 n19, 170–73, 174 n8 and n17
Severing, Wilhelm 25, 27, 39 n25, 56, 62, 76, 78–80, 111 n54 and n60, 129, 158, 170
Shaw, Bernard 69
Stalin, Josef 39 n28, 59–60, 161 n22, 162 n33, 164 n55
Stampfer, Friedrich 86, 112 n68
Stinnes, Hugo 44, 52, 96, 107 n5 and n7, 112 n69
Strasser, Gregor 28, 38 n23, 39 n30, 110 n41, 113 n80, 120, 168–69, 174 n17
Stresemann, Gustav 22, 37 n12, 57, 107 n4, 109 n38
Stülpnagel, Otto von 79, 111 n55

Tarnow, Fritz 65, 110 n44
Thalheimer, August 37 n13, 110 n45, 154, 164 n57
Thälmann, Ernst 21, 36 n10, 125, 145–46, 158, 160 n7,
Thyssen, August 44, 52, 107 n6
Thyssen, Friedrich 'Fritz' 107 n6
Torgler, Ernst 36 n10, 127, 132, 143,

161 n24
Trotsky, Leon 21, 32, 151, 164 n55 and n59

Van der Lubbe, Marinus 112 n70, 143, 147, 163 n48
Vögler, Albert 44, 100, 107 n7

Weil, Simone 27
Weiss, Bernhard 79, 111 n58
Weissenberg, Josef 72, 110 n50
Wels, Otto 92, 113 n76, 128, 144
Wessel, Horst 144, 163 n49
Wolff, Otto 52, 109 n28

Zörgiebel, Karl 26, 39 n26 and n27, 55